CELTIC INHERITANCE

CELTIC
INHERITANCE

Peter Berresford Ellis

Illustrations by
Gabriel Sempill

CONSTABLE · LONDON

Published in Great Britain 1992
by Constable and Company Limited
3 The Lanchesters, 162 Fulham Palace Road
London W6 9ER
Reprinted 1992
Text copyright © 1985 Peter Berresford Ellis
Illustrations copyright © 1985 Gabriel Sempill
First published 1985 by Frederick Muller
ISBN 0 09 471370 7
The right of Peter Berresford Ellis to be
identified as the author of this work
has been asserted by him in accordance
with the Copyright, Designs and Patents Act 1988
Printed in Great Britain by
St Edmundsbury Press Limited
Bury St Edmunds, Suffolk

A CIP catalogue record for this book
is available from the British Library

Contents

To Rosemary and David Seton,
'without whom...', this book
is affectionately dedicated.

Perge libelle!
laetus in undis
ibis et austris.

Onward my book!
Thou shalt go in joy
through wind and wave.

Bishop Gille-Pádraig of Dublin
(d. 1084AD).

Introduction

The term 'Celtic Church' is not a strictly accurate one because the early Christian churches among the Celtic peoples, in most essentials, were part of the Roman Catholic Church. Neither was the Celtic Church an identifiable organisation with a central leadership. Nevertheless, for a period of 150 years, during the early Christian era, the insular Celts of the British Isles were cut off from strict Roman influence. While Rome began to reform many of its customs during the 5th Century AD, especially the dating of Easter, the Celts clung to old computations and freely mixed many pre-Christian traditions and social concepts into their Christianity and thus developed as a distinct entity within the wider Christian movement.

The Celtic Church – I shall use that popular term for this entity because any other term would be too cumbersome – could be designated as a singular cultural entity within the greater Christian movement, delineated by its practices, philosophies, social concepts and art forms. These individualistic practices – and its observances and customs in respect of Easter – its asceticism, monastic extremism and, indeed, fanaticism, its attitudes to social order, views on land tenure, contrary philosophies towards feudal and hereditary rights, brought it into early conflict with Rome. Absorption was inevitable; inevitable because of its very individualism, its lack of cohesion and centralism. But that absorption took many centuries. Even as late as the 14th Century AD in Scotland there were still bodies of Celtic monks (Culdees) clinging to the old ways.

In the meantime, while the conflict with Rome continued, Celtic monks and scholars began to take their Christian individualism out of their own lands and to preach to others. The Irish, in particular, were seized by a *peregrinatio pro Christo*. When Augustine's mission from Rome to the pagan English, in 597 AD, was on the point of failure and when, not long after Augustine's death, Mellitus was driven out of London and Paulinus out of York while the English kingdoms returned to pagan worship, it was Irish missionaries who began to proselytise them, even penetrating into the land of the South Saxons (Sussex), the last of the kingdoms to become Christian. Under Dicuil they built a monastery at Bosham, near Chichester. The famous Synod of Whitby in 664AD, when Oswy of

1

Northumbria opted for Roman custom instead of Celtic custom, was not the end of the Celtic Church influence in England. Another full century passed before Celtic missionaries ceased to be welcome among the English. As late as the 9th CenturyAD King Alfred invited the Welsh abbot Asser to attend his court and become his scholastic mentor. And through Asser, Alfred attempted to revive monasticism and start a campaign for literacy among his subjects.

Thousands of Irish missionaries also made their way to the mainland of Europe taking their teachings as far east as Kiev, as far north as Iceland and even into Italy where they established their own monasteries and churches. They took with them a burning desire to teach; they took their great books and a sophisticated degree of literacy; and they took an intellectual curiosity, an enthusiasm for discussion and a desire to learn as well as teach. They also produced great poets and philosophers, perhaps the most famous being Eriugena, the most considerable philosopher in the Western world between Augustine of Hippo and Thomas Aquinas.

European historians tend to pass over this period as 'The Dark Ages' but, for the Celtic peoples it was a Golden Age of learning, of artistic achievement and development – achievements which the Celtic Christian missionaries, in their enthusiasm, took to other lands and in so doing made an exceptional contribution to the culture of those lands at a time when learning was most needed. Their influence has been profound and lasting, although, eventually, they were forced to yield before the new scholars of the Carolingian Renaissance as the Celtic Church finally merged into Roman orthodoxy.

The aim of this book is to present a general history of the phenomenon of the Celtic Church. It is not an academic study. It is a history for the general reader, without footnotes but containing a bibliography for those who would pursue their studies further. In writing such a general history, however, there are certain pitfalls which cannot be avoided and which the reader has to be aware of.

The period is full of scholastic controversy and the cut and thrust of academic argument is difficult to sidestep. For example, we have the controversy of St Patrick. There are three feuding schools of thought. The orthodox school believes that there was one person named Patrick, a British Celt, who was sent on his mission to Ireland in 432AD and died there in 461AD. There are the followers of Professor O'Rahilly who adhere to the idea of 'two Patricks' – Palladius, who was sent to Ireland in 432AD and died there in 461AD – and Patrick the Briton, whom they argue went to Ireland in 462AD and died there in 492AD. Lastly there are the followers of Professor James Carney who argue that there was only one Patrick who arrived in Ireland in 456AD and died there in 493AD.

We also have Arthur Wade-Evans's extremely controversial assertion that the British monk Gildas was not the author of the famous *De Excidio*

Britonum (The Ruin of Britain) but that it was the work of an anonymous monk born in the year of the battle of Badon and so designated 'Auctor Badonicus' (The Badon Author) by him.

Even the simple assertion of dating provides grounds for lively scholastic debate. The accuracy of the majority of dates during the entire period can be opened up to question. Many scholars of the period seem to fix their own chronology and defend it with verbal violence against all comers.

The source material contained in the lives of the 'saints' must be considered sceptically in the context of their time and authorship. They are usually full of apocryphal imagery and gnostic symbolism and few can be accepted as accurate history.

I have attempted to present a readable, general history, and where points are in dispute I have outlined alternatives.

I have refrained from the liberal use of the prefix 'St' (saint) not out of disrespect to the early fathers of the Christian Church but to try to eliminate confusion that might arise. It was the custom of the Celtic Church to designate all its missionaries and teachers as 'saints', a distinction showing that they were men of eminent virtue, holy men preaching the Christian doctrines. It did not necessarily mean that they were canonised.

I have also attempted to eliminate other designations which are confusing to the modern reader – terms such as 'Scot', meaning, at this time, an Irishman. Irish and Scot are used in their modern sense. The term British, however, is used in its original sense to mean a British Celt as opposed to the in-coming English, or rather Anglo-Saxons.

What follows is an attempt to outline one of the most fascinating cultural movements that has ever arisen in the Western world.

1
Pre-Christian Celtic Society and Religion

The broch on Mousa, Shetland Isles. Built circa 1 BC, this Celtic tribal structure was erected for habitation and defence. It still stands to a height of over 15 metres disproving popular notions that the ancient Celts were poor builders.

At the beginning of the Christian epoch the Celtic people were spread across the northern boundaries of the Roman Empire in a geographical arc. At the eastern end of the arc, in Asia Minor, lay Galatia; at the western end of the arc lay Ireland, the only Celtic territory untouched by the imperial armies of Rome. In between lay the partially conquered island of Britain, the annexation of which commenced in 43AD. On the mainland lay Gaul, conquered for Rome in the mid-1st Century BC by Julius Caesar. Isolated Celtic communities also existed on the Iberian peninsula where the Celts had expanded from 900BC to dominate the areas of modern Portugal and Galicia. Other Celtic communities may still have existed in central Europe, in areas around the Danube valley and that of the Vistula from which, according to the Greek chroniclers, the Celts first began their expansion through Europe. More communities may have existed in Illyria, Macedonia and Thrace – all of which had been extensively settled by them in the 3rd Century BC. Thrace had only ceased to be ruled by Celtic leaders in 193BC. Yet more communities may have existed in northern Italy, where they had been pushed during the Celtic invasions and where they certainly remained until imperial Roman times.

By the end of the first thousand years of the Christian epoch the Celtic territories had been greatly reduced. The isolated pockets were quickly swamped. Galatia, while still speaking a recognisable Brythonic Celtic language in the 5th Century AD, had virtually disappeared by the 6th Century. The great mass of Celtic Gaul, which had consisted not only of the territory of modern France but also Belgium and parts of Germany and Switzerland, had succumbed to conquest although the Celtic speech was almost certainly retained there longer than is generally accepted. Sidonius Apollinaris (circa 430-476AD) states that it was only in his day that the leading families of Gaul were attempting to 'throw off the scurf of Celtic speech'. Of the mainland European Celts only the Armoricans, reinforced by migrations from Britain, remained to form the nation of Brittany. In the island of Britain the invasions of the Anglo-Saxons pushed the Celtic inhabitants into the western peninsulas and the north of the island to form the nations of Cornwall, Wales and Scotland. The Celts of the Isle of Man were to remain undisturbed until the Norse conquests. Only the Irish Church was to survive the first thousand years of Christendom relatively intact before the Anglo-Normans began their bid for conquest in 1172AD.

Today, on the north western seaboard of Europe, the descendants of the ancient Celtic civilisation live still; people struggling hard to survive and maintain their individuality in these days of increasing cultural uniformity and deadly sameness of life. The Irish, Manx and Scots constitute the Goidelic branch of the Celtic peoples; and the Welsh, Cornish and Bretons make up the Brythonic-speaking group. Together these six small nationalities (with their latter-day offshoots—the Welsh-speaking area of Patagonia in Argentina and the Scottish Gaelic-speaking area of Nova Scotia in Canada) are the inheritors, through their ancient languages and cultures, of nearly three thousand years of unbroken cultural tradition.

The Celts were the first Transalpine people to emerge into recorded history. It was the ancient Greek chroniclers who first designated them as *Keltoi*. It has been suggested that they were simply called 'the hidden people' for it has been argued that the etymology of the word comes from the Celtic *ceilt*, an act of concealing from which the word *kilt*, the short male skirt of the traditional Celtic dress, also takes its derivation. It has been proposed that they were called 'the hidden people' because of their reluctance to commit their knowledge and scholarship to written records. Julius Caesar commented:

> *The Druids think it unlawful to commit this knowledge of theirs to writing (in secular and in public and private business they use Greek characters). This is a practice which they have, I think, adopted for two reasons. They do not wish their system should become commonly known or that their pupils, trusting in written documents, should less carefully cultivate their memory; and indeed it does generally happen that those who rely on written documents are less industrious in learning by heart and have a weaker memory.*

The Celts were a linguistic group and not a racial one. Professor Eoin Mac Neill has pointed out that there is no such thing as a Celtic race any more than a Latin race, a Teutonic race or a Slavic race. The people of Europe are mixtures of several races – and in fact for the most part the same races. That this admixture of races among the Celts was true in ancient times can be seen from the various descriptions of the 'typical' Celt given by ancient chroniclers – the swarthy, stocky Silurian Celt is equally as 'typical' as the tall, gangling blond Gaulish Celt. Therefore, only language and culture distinguished the Celtic peoples from the rest of Europe.

Reference has already been made to the two branches of Celtic culture – Goidelic and Brythonic. Gaulish and Galatian were actually branches of Brythonic. The main difference between the two branches of Celtic is that the Brythonic languages have simplified themselves in their case-endings and in losing the neuter gender and dual number. The two groups also differ in the matter of initial mutation and aspiration. There is the famous substitution of P for Q in the Brythonic languages. This was the sound which in Indo-European, from which Celtic along with most other European languages descends, gave the *qu(kw)*. This sound in Goidelic later became represented by C while in Brythonic it became P. For example:

English	son	head	worm	feather	everyone
Welsh (P)	map	pen	pryv	pluv	paup
Irish (Q)	mac	cenn	cruiv	cluv	cach

By the 8th Century BC the Celts already possessed great skill in metal work, especially in the use of iron, a metal only then becoming known to the craftsmen of the 'classical' world. By the 6th Century BC their formidable armament of spears, swords and agricultural implements rendered the Celts militarily superior to their neighbours. Their billhooks and axes enabled them to open roadways through the previously impenetrable forests of Europe and to make extensive clearances and till the land with comparative ease. One of the ancient Irish words for road, avenue or pathway, which is still in use, is *slighe*, deriving from the word *sligim*: 'I hew'.

By 900BC they had settled extensively in southern France. They had also crossed into the Iberian peninsula and established themselves in settlements in the areas of modern Portugal and Galicia. And by 600BC they had begun to cross the Alps into the fertile valley of the Po. It is generally thought that the first Celtic migrations to Britain took place during this period but modern scholarship has suggested that the first Celtic peoples may have arrived as early as 2,000BC and definitely not later than 1,000BC. The last series of migrations of Celtic tribes to Britain occurred in the 2nd Century BC when the Belgic tribes arrived in the south from the territory still named after them – Belgium – to escape the pressures of Roman and German expansion.

During the 4th Century BC Celtic tribes dominated northern Europe. The Romans tried to stop their expansion but on July 18, 390BC, the Celtic armies faced the Romans near the River Allia, within a few miles of Rome itself. The Romans were defeated and the city fell. Polybius tells us that the Romans remained under Celtic domination until 349BC when they began to turn the invasion back. By 345BC the Celts had been pushed towards the north again but a large proportion of Celtic settlers remained in northern Italy even in imperial Roman times, leaving evidence of their settlements in such place-names as Trevi, Treviso, Treviglio, Reno, Milan, Bologna, the River Trebia and many others. Their stay in Italy also resulted in some Celtic words being borrowed into Latin – particularly words connected with military weapons and with philosophy. The Celtic scholar Henri Hubert suggested that the Latin writers also benefited from the imagination of the Celtic poets.

> *The story of the Gallic Wars, out of which Livy, a historian of genius gifted with the spirit of divination, has made a very remarkable historical work, is something quite by itself, rather fabulous and very epic. Monsieur Jullian (Camille Jullian,* Histoire de la Gaule, *Paris, 1920) has suggested that the tradition was probably made up of Celtic epics. The well known story of Valerius Corvus, who was rescued in single combat with a Gallic chief by a crow which pecked the Celt's face and hid the Roman with its wings, is an example. The episode is unlike anything else in Roman history or literature. But is is like the famous episode in the great Irish epic of Ulster, the* Táin BóCuailgne, *in which the goddess Morrigu attacks Cuchulainn, who has scorned her love, in the form of a crow. The crow is not a mere flight of fancy, it is the creature which stands for battle and the gods and goddesses of war.*

It might also be added of Valerius Corvus that Corvus is Latin for crow.

The Celts continued to be a threat to Rome for many years and it is ironic, perhaps, that the first time the Germanic peoples (ancestors of the English and French) emerge into recorded history, they are seen fighting for the Celts 'undoubtedly as hired troops or as forces levied on a subject territory', says Professor Eoin Mac Neill. Scholars such as Mac Neill and Carl Marstrander have pointed to the number of words of Celtic origin which are found in the whole group of German languages. 'Some of these words are especially connected with the political side of civilisation and are therefore especially indicative of Celtic political predominance at the time of their adoption into Germanic speech'. The Germanic peoples first emerge into recorded history in the Roman *Acta Triumphalia* for the year 222BC when it is recorded that the Romans, led by their consul Marcellus, won the battle of Clastidium (Casteggio, northern Italy) and defeated the

Celts led by Virdumarus. The Germans are recorded as fighting for the Celts apparently as a vassal group or an ally.

In the 2nd Century BC the Celts inflicted five major defeats on the Romans. Finally, in 104BC, Caius Marius was elected consul and set about the organisation of a new Roman army. It was he who created the ruthless legionary fighting machine which is so well known today. By 101BC Marius was making punitive expeditions into Celtic territory with his army. Forty years later Julius Caesar was to assert Roman domination over the Celts of Gaul.

At the same time as the Celtic expansion towards Rome, other Celtic tribes were pushing further east into the Balkan Peninsula. The Macedonians were unable to impede their progress. The Celtic armies, divided into three columns and began an advance into the Greek interior in 260BC. The eastern army was commanded by Cerethrois and attacked through modern Bulgaria; the western army was led by Bolgios, who defeated the Macedonian army on their own territory and slew their king Ptolemy Cereaunos. The central army advanced successfully against Haemos and Thessaly. This army was commanded by Brennus and Achichorius. Brennus could simply be the Celtic name Bran but it is interesting to note that *brennin* remains the modern Welsh for king and this could simply have been a title. Brennus and Achichorius scattered the Greek armies. They came to Thermopylae where an Athenian army was gathered. It, too, was routed. The Celts turned on Aetolia and Callion; others came through the gorge of Parnassos to Delphi where they sacked the great temple of the oracle. Although the Greeks finally turned back the Celtic invasion, Thrace remained a Celtic kingdom until 193BC. The contact resulted in some Celtic words being adopted into Greek.

During this period, the king of Bithynia, Nicomedes, was quick to see the potential of the Celtic warriors as mercenary troops and he invited certain of the tribes into Asia Minor to serve in his army. These tribes were led by Leonarios and Lutarios and we are told they consisted of 20,000 warriors with their women and children. Having served the king of Bithynia for a while these Celts decided to carve out their own kingdom in what is now modern Turkey. For a time they simply wandered the area sacking cities such as Troy, Ephesos, Miletos and others. Then in 270BC Antiochos Soter of Syria defeated them badly in a battle which was celebrated in verse by Simonides of Magnesia and paraphrased by Lucan. Apparently the Celtic cavalry was destroyed by Syrian elephants. Antiochos Soter was no vengeful monarch for he came to an agreement with the Celts by which he allowed them to settle in the region of the modern Turkish capital, Ankara. Since then the area has been known by its Celtic appellation – Galatia. Henri Hubert says: 'What we know of the Galatian state gives us our first example of the organisation of a Celtic state'. Galatia was governed by an assembly of 300 elected representatives of the clans and sub-clans who met at Drunemeton ('the sacred oakgrove'). The name showed that these Celts carried their druidic religion with them.

Indeed, the 'internationalism' of the druids was used by the Senate of Marseilles during the Roman campaigns in Asia Minor in 197-6BC when they asked the Gauls to persuade the Galatians not to supply Antiochus III or serve as his mercenaries. After the defeat of Antiochus III and his ally Hannibal, Rome took over the government of the area. The Consul Manlius Vulso conducted a campaign against the Galatian Celts which resulted in them being made vassals of the kingdom of Pergamon, held by a 'client king' for Rome. The Celts continually revolted against Pergamon overlordship until Rome finally allowed them to re-establish their independence within the empire. From 25BC Galatia was regarded as a Roman province ruled by a Propraetor. Although the Galatians were surrounded on all sides by Hellenistic cultural influence, they clung tenaciously to their own culture and as late as the 5th Century AD Celtic was their speech. Jerome (Eusebius Hieronymus), born circa 347AD, states that the Celts of Galatia spoke an offshoot of Gaulish and compared their dialect to that of the Belgic tribe called the Treviri.

Language was not the only thing which united the Celts with a common heritage. Religion was the cornerstone of their world. There have been a lot of misconceptions about the pre-Christian Celtic religion; druids have been conjured by writers performing human sacrifices in sacred oakgroves and worshipping the sun as a god. The ancient Greeks and Romans chose to describe the Celtic religion from a rigid Greek or Roman standpoint. Julius Caesar, in particular, merely substituted Latin gods and concepts and succeeded in confusing everyone by a complete misinterpretation.

The Celtic religion was promulgated by the druids who have been – mistakenly – called a 'religious caste'. According to the philologist Thurneysen the word druid came from *dru-vid* meaning 'thorough knowledge'. The druids not only fulfilled religious functions but political ones as well. They were certainly not a caste and anyone in the tribe could undertake the strenuous training required to qualify. According to some ancient writers it took up to twenty years to learn all the druidical canons and laws. This is certainly not to deny that there were some druidic families, in much the same way as some families carry on certain professions today by familiarity rather than by caste. The function of the druid was as minister of the religion, which had a complete doctrine of immortality and a moral system widespread among the Celtic peoples, but they were also philosophers, teachers and natural scientists, who were often called upon to give legal and political and military judgements. Caesar described them in these words:

> *They are concerned with religious matters, perform sacrifices offered by the state and by private individuals, and interpret omens. Many of the youth*

resort to them for education and they are held in high honour by the Gauls. They have the decision in nearly all the disputes that arise between the state and individuals; if any crime has been committed, if any person has been killed, if there is any dispute about an inheritance or a boundary, it is the druids who give judgement; it is they who settle the rewards and punishments. Any private person or any tribe refusing to abide by their decision is excluded from sacrifice. This is the heaviest punishment that can be inflicted; for those so excluded are reckoned to belong to the godless and wicked. All persons leave their company, avoid their presence and speech, lest they should be involved in some of the ill consequences of their situation. They can get no redress from injury and they are ineligible to any post of honour.

The druids were trained in 'international' law as well as tribal law and were arbiters in disputes between territorial groups. The druids had the power to prevent warfare between two Celtic tribes, for whatever their differences the moral and legal authority of a druid was greater than the tribal ruler's authority. Diodorus Siculus (circa 60-21BC) commented: 'And it is not only in the needs of peace but also in war that they (the Celts) carefully obey these men and their song loving poets, and this is true not only of their friends but of their enemies. For oft-times as armies approach each other in line of battle with their swords drawn and their spears raised for the charge, these men come forth between them and stop the conflict as though they had spellbound some kind of wild animals. Thus, even among the most savage barbarians, anger yields to wisdom and Ares does homage to the Muses'.

The Celtic religion was one of the first to evolve a doctrine of immortality. The druids taught that death is only a changing of place and that life goes on with all its forms and goods in another world, a world of the dead which gives up living souls. Therefore, a constant exchange of souls takes place between the two worlds; death in this world brings a soul to the other and death in the other world brings a soul to this world. Thus could Philostratus of Tyana (circa 170-249AD) observe that the Celts celebrated birth with mourning and death with joy. Caesar observed: 'The druids' chief doctrine is that the soul of man does not perish but passes after death from one person to another. They hold that this is the best of all incitements to courage, banishing the fear of death.' Caesar's remark is cynical but to be expected from a military man and the observation, that this religious outlook could account for the reckless bravery of the Celts in battle, was echoed by Pomponius Mela (circa 43AD) who wrote: 'One of their dogmas has come to common knowledge, namely that souls are eternal and that there is another life in the infernal regions, and this has been permitted manifestly because it makes the multitude readier for war. And it is for this reason too that they burn or bury with their dead, things

appropriate to them in life, and that in times past they even used to defer the completion of business and the payment of debts until their arrival in another world. Indeed, there were some of them who flung themselves willingly on the funeral pyres of their relatives in order to share the new life with them.'

Strabo (circa 64BC-21AD) points out that the druids taught the indestructability of the material universe. Lucan, (circa 39-65AD) addressing the Celts, said: 'From you we learn the bourne of man's existence is not the silent halls of Erebus, in another world the spirit animates the members. Death, if your lore be true, is but the centre of a long life.' The Celts looked for their Otherworld towards the West for the West was regarded as the region of perfection because the sun moved westward.

Celtic philosophies were highly regarded in the ancient world. Aristotle, Sotion and Clement of Alexandria all state that early Greek philosophers borrowed much of their philosophy from the Celts. The similarity of druidic ideas on immortality and Pythagorean philosophy has frequently been remarked on. Pythagoras had a slave named Zalmoxis of Thrace, who was a Celt. But while Clement says that Pythagoras and the Greeks acquired the teachings of immortality from the Celts, presumably through Zalmoxis, Hippolytus claims that Zalmoxis took Pythagoras' philosophy to the Celts. 'He, after the death of Pythagoras, having made his way there, became the founder of this philosophy for them'. Hippolytus was wrong because the Celtic belief in immortality was well entrenched long before the time of Pythagoras, who died about 497BC.

The druids remind one of Buddhist monks: of the Zen masters. They dwelt in a firm communion with Nature believing in the consciousness of

Gundestrup Cauldron. This magnificent silver cauldron, 42 cm high and 69 cm across, was discovered in a peat bog in Denmark. It is of Celtic workmanship dated to the 2nd or 1st Centuries BC and displays much of the Celtic religio-mythical symbolism.

11

all things. Trees, fountains, rivers, even the weapons and implements they used were considered to be possessed of an indwelling spirit. Everything was but a fragment of one cosmic whole. Thus, in Celtic mythology, could Manannán Mac Lir's boat know a man's thoughts; or the sword of Conaire Mór sing; or the Liá Fail, the Stone of Destiny, cry out in joy when it felt the touch of a rightful ruler's feet. In *Timaeus*, Plato developed a similar doctrine of a world soul in which all matter was inter-related. This concept is remarkably illustrated in the poem of the druid Amhairghin (Amergin) recorded in the *Leabhar Gabhála* (Book of Invasions). Amhairghin subsumes all things into his own being with a philosophical outlook that is paralleled in the Hindu *Bhagavad-Gita*.

> *I am the wind which breathes upon the sea.*
> *I am a wave of the ocean.*
> *I am the murmur of the billows.*
> *I am a powerful ox.*
> *I am a hawk on a cliff.*
> *I am a beam of the sun,*
> *I am the fairest of plants.*
> *I am a wild boar in valour.*
> *I am a salmon in a pool.*
> *I am a lake in a plain.*
> *I am a word of science.*
> *I am a lance-point in battle.*
> *I create in man the fire of thought.*
> *Who is it that throws light into the meeting on the mountain?*
> *Who tells the ages of men?*
> *Who points to the sun's resting place if not I?*

Caesar says that the Celts regarded themselves as having descended from one central god *Dis-Pater* or universal father, who seems to be equivalent to the Irish god Dagde or Dago-devos, who was also called Eochu Oll-Athair. The Celts, however, believed in the plurality of the gods. Unfortunately it is very hard to recognise all the Celtic gods for what they really are because most of them were forced to wear Greek or Roman masks. Maximus of Tyre, for example, thought the Celtic equivalent of Zeus was a lofty oak tree. True the Celts had a special veneration for the oak as symbolic of the spirit of growth and Nature. Some scholars see a corruption of the Goidelic word for oak *daur* in the Goidelic word for God *Dia*. But attempts to reduce the Celtic gods to particular divinities that approximate to Greek or Latin equivalents is a futile exercise. There are, for example, some sixty names or titles of Celtic war gods which one could say represented the Roman Mars. Of the many Celtic gods only two have remarkably widespread cults – Lugh and Bel.

Lugh, Lleu in Welsh, also appearing as Lud and Lugus, was venerated as the god of arts and crafts. He gave his name to many places: Lyons, Léon, Loudan, Laon in France, Leiden in Holland, Liegnitz in Silesia, to Carlisle (Luguvalum in Roman times) and to London which, like Lyons, had been named 'the fortress of Lugh'. The famous Irish leprechaun comes from a corruption of *Lugh-chromain* 'little stooping Lugh', a fairy craftsman, which is all that survives of the cult of the great god Lugh, potent patron of arts and crafts and father of the hero Cuchulainn.

Bel is a different god. The name is said to mean 'the shining one' and represented the Celtic god of light, the healer, in fact – the sun itself. He was also known as Grannos (the Irish for sun is *grian*) and, as such, he is still remembered in Auvergne in a 'nonsense chant' around a harvest festival bonfire. A sheaf of corn is cut and set fire to while the people dance around chanting: 'Granno, my friend, Granno, my father, Granno, my mother!'

The Celtic gods were basically ancient heroes and the ancestors of the people rather than their creators. Celtic mythology is heroic; for the Celts made their heroes into gods and their gods into heroes. In the lives of these gods and heroes, the lives of the people and the essence of their religious traditions are mirrored. Celtic heroes and heroines were no mere physical beauties with empty heads. The Celtic hero and heroine had to have intellectual attributes equal to their physical capabilities. They were totally human and were subject to all the natural virtues and vices. No sin out of the seven deadly ones was exempt from practice by them. Yet their world was one of rural happiness, a world in which they indulged in all the pleasures of mortal life in an idealised form; love of nature, art, games, feasting and heroic single handed combat. The Irish poet Eochaid O'Flainn (d. 1003AD) wrote a poem in which he examined the ancient gods, debating whether they were demons or devils but suggesting that they were merely human beings without supernatural powers, heroes made into gods by the ancients.

A happy spirit pervaded the majority of gods, although there were a variety of minor evil spirits. The Formorii were lords of darkness and death, dwelling on the edge of the northern oceans. As in the real world, good and evil rubbed shoulders. Some of the Irish gods were said to dwell in the hills and were called the *Aes Sidhe* or 'hill dwellers'; thus, in modern folklore, the *sidhe* have become fairies and we have all heard of the famous banshee or *bean-sidhe*, literally 'woman of the fairies' who shrieks and wails before a death in the family to which she has become attached.

The Celtic year was one of festivals connected to their environment as well as religious outlook. Calendrical record was of importance in Celtic society. Caesar said of the druids: 'They have much to say about the stars and their motions, about the magnitude of the heavens and earth, about the construction of nature, about the power and authority of the immortal gods. And this they communicate to their pupils.'

Cicero pays tribute to the druids as great natural scientists who had a knowledge of physics and astronomy applied in the construction of calendars. The earliest known Celtic calendar, dating from the 1st Century AD, is far more elaborate than the rudimentary Julian one and has a highly sophisticated five-year synchronisation of lunation with the solar year. This is the Calendar of Coligny now in the Palais des Arts, Lyons, in France. It consists of a huge bronze plate on which is engraved a calendar of 62 consecutive lunar months. The language is Gaulish but the lettering and numerals are Latin. Place-names, personal names and inscriptions on the calendar testify to literacy in the Celtic languages. In Celtic fashion, the calendar reckons by nights. Caesar explained: 'They count periods of time not by the number of days, but by the number of nights: and in reckoning birthdays and the new moon and new year their unit of reckoning is the night followed by the day.' The Calendar of Coligny is a masterpiece of calendrical calculation and proves Caesar's statement. The knowledge of astronomy intrigues many scholars today and, if the new theories of earlier time periods for Celtic migrations are accurate, the Celts could have constructed Stonehenge, shown to have been a large astronomical computer, inter-related with the many other stone circles spread across the Celtic lands.

The Celtic year was, in fact, divided into four major religious festivals. The feast of *Samhain*, starting on the evening of the last day of October and continuing through November 1, marked the end of one pastoral year and the beginning of the next. It was also a time when the Celtic Otherworld became visible to mankind and when spiritual forces were let loose on the human world. While the Otherworld was usually described as a pleasant place – 'Land of the Blessed', was one synonym – a mortal obtaining access to it suffered neither age, pain nor decay. But if he tried to return, he withered, aged and died, the moment he touched the real world. During the Christianisation process, the ceremony was taken over. Unable to suppress pagan ceremonies, *Samhain* became a harvest festival and the animals previously offered to Bel were now offered to St Martin, the feast becoming St Martin's Mass (Martinmas). The festival also became known as All Saints' Day or All Hallows' Day. The evening before, Hallowe'en, is still celebrated as the night when spirits and ghosts set out to wreak vengeance on the living and when evil marches across the world. Thus we see the complete corruption of an ancient religious festival.

The next great festival occurred on February 1 which was the feast day of a Celtic goddess known as Brigit in Ireland and Brigantia in Britain. She was the goddess of fertility and her cult was widespread through the Celtic world. The feast was connected with the coming into milk of the ewes and was therefore a pastoral festival. Again, Christianity sought to absorb rather than suppress. Brigit the goddess of fertility was allowed to merge with the image of St Brigid, the founder of the monastery of Kildare in the

6th Century, and February 1 became her feast-day. The cult of St Brigid swiftly replaced the cult of Brigit.

The third festival was the feast of *Beltane* on May 1. The Irish word for the May month is still *Bealtaine* and, until the 19th Century, the Scottish law term in May was called the *Beltane Term*. The name derives from 'The Fires of Bel'. In Scotland, May Day was known as *La Buidhe Bealtuinn* – The Day of the Yellow Fires of Bel. This was the day when the Celts offered praise to Bel, the sun and lifegiver, for having brought victory over the powers of darkness and for bringing the people within sight of another harvest. On that day the fires of every household would be extinguished. Then, at a given time, torches would be rekindled by the druids from the 'sacred Fires of Bel' (i.e. from the rays of the sun) and taken to each household where the fires would be rekindled to symbolically give everyone a fresh start. Numbers of cattle from each herd would be driven in the ancient circles through fires as a symbol of purification. Scholars are at variance as to whether *Beltane* was the start of the Celtic New Year in view of the symbolism of starting life afresh. The consensus of opinion is that *Samhain* was the start of the year. It is interesting to note that in Cornwall, the Federation of Old Cornwall Societies, has managed to preserve this folk tradition of lighting May Day bonfires, a ceremony whose origin is now half forgotten among the Cornish. *Beltane*, too, was claimed for Christianity and was, for a time, merged with the feast-day of St John the Baptist.

The last ceremony of the year was the feast of *Lughnasa* on August 1. It was named after the Celtic god Lugh and was basically an agrarian feast in honour of the harvesting of crops and the celebration usually lasted for fifteen days. August is still called *Lúnasa* in Irish and the festival has become the traditional Christian Harvest Festival.

It was not unusual for the early Christians to seize on pagan festivals and convert them to their cause. Christmas on December 25, which was not celebrated in the Christian calendar until after 200AD, originally derived from the Roman feast of Saturnalia. Easter in England derived from the April festival of Eostre, goddess of dawn, which Augustine and his followers saw as a convenient method of introducing the Latin Paschal celebration, itself derived from the Hebrew Passover. In England's case, the week is made up mainly of pre-Christian English gods' days. The Moon's day (Monday); Tiu's day (Tuesday); Woden's day (Wednesday); Thunor's day (Thursday); Frig's day (Friday); Saturn's day (Saturday); and the Sun's day (Sunday). Thus, the early Christians found it easier to adapt rather than innovate.

One interesting point must be made before passing on. The ancient Celts had a special regard for trinity and the mystical number of three times three permeates Celtic mythology and art. Diogenes Laertius (circa 2/3rd Century BC) specifically mentions that the druids taught in the form of triads – sentences of three phrases and held the number three to be mystical. It is perhaps due to this pre-Christian Celtic tradition of the trinity that the Holy Trinity achieved a prominent position in Celtic symbolism.

Before moving on to the introduction of Christianity among these people, we should also examine what kind of social order existed. Celtic society displayed a primitive communism, or community-ism, which by the 5th Century AD, when the Brehon Laws of Ireland were first being codified, had developed into a highly sophisticated social system. We can assume that the same social system prevailed throughout the entire Celtic world by a comparison of the Brehon Law tracts with those of the Laws of Hywel Dda of Wales and the Breton laws embodied in the Treaty of 1532 which brought Brittany under French suzerainty. Even the laws of the semi-mythical ruler of Cornwall, Dunwallo Molmutine, mentioned by Geoffrey of Monmouth, display an intense regard for democracy and the rights of the individual.

The Celtic law system was a very complex one which finds its closest parallel in the tradition of Hindu law. D. A. Binchey, investigating 'The Linguistic and Historic Value of the Irish Law Tracts' (1943), found that 'Irish law preserves in a semi-fossilised condition many primitive Indo-European institutions of which only faint traces survive in other legal systems'. Basically, dispute could lead only to arbitration and compensation. It was for the injured party to compel the injurer to accept the arbitration and under the system there was a custom of ritual fasting as a method of asserting one's rights. If the injurer ignored the fast and failed to accept the fine imposed by the judges, he lost his honour, a terrible condemnation in a society where honour was highly cherished.

The essence of the Celtic system was that when a tribe, or clan, occupied a territory, it belonged to them as a community. The territory was delimited by natural boundaries and then divided for the benefit of the community. Sections of the land were appropriated for the ruler and his 'civil-service' in return for the work of their position in society. A large section of land was retained for the use of the entire tribe as common land which everyone, no matter his station, was entitled to use. Another section of land was set aside for the maintenance of the poor, the old and incapable members of the tribe. Those who had their own plots were expected to pay taxes for the upkeep of the community, paying for the support of the poor, aged and orphans. If a man died in debt, the surviving relatives were not made to pay those debts. The Celtic law humanely stated 'every dead man kills his liabilities'.

One fascinating aspect of this primitive 'Welfare State' was the Celtic attitude to the sick and feeble. The Germanic tribes used to put their sick and feeble to death. Even in the civilisations of Egypt, Assyria, Babylonia and Greece, there were no provisions made for the ailing poor. And the

Romans regarded disease as a curse inflicted by the supernatural powers and rather sought to propitiate the malevolent deities than organise relief work. There were notable exceptions to the general rule; men like Hippocrates of Greece, for example. It was not until St Fabiola founded her hospice in Rome just before her death in 399AD that it is generally regarded that the first western hospital was founded.

Yet Armagh (Ard Macha) boasted the foundation of a hospital in 300BC by its semi-mythical ruler Macha Mong Ruadh. While admitting the story belongs more to Irish mythology than to provable history what can be proved from the ancient laws is that the Celts, at a very early stage of their civilisation, developed a medical service, a European renowned surgery system and prototype health service whereby sick maintenance, including curative treatment, attendance and nourishing food, had to be made available to all who needed it. Under Celtic law the responsibility of providing for the sick, wounded and mentally handicapped was in the hands of the tribe. The exceptional working of this system was undoubtedly due to the tribal organisation. Celtic tribesmen and women did not have to fear illness; they were assured of treatment, hospitalisation and reinforced by the fact that the society would not let them or their dependents lack food or means of livelihood. The qualifications of physicians were also carefully supervised under law and 'quack' doctors were liable to severe penalties. The Celts recognised that it was rather easy to deceive people who were ill and who, desperately seeking a cure, would grasp at any straw to secure it. Large fines were imposed on people who pretended to be qualified surgeons when they were not. The law was similarly strict about the condition in which the tribal hospital was kept.

Fundamental to the Celtic social attitude was the fact that there was no such concept as absolute ownership of land, and individual ownership was totally foreign to Celtic thought. Each tribesman was able to keep and work his tribal land but he could not sell it, alienate it nor conceal it, nor give it to pay for any crime, contract or debt. Neither was the land worked by the chieftains their own to do with as they willed. Even in the disposal of goods, such as cattle, there were restrictions and permission had to be sought from the clan assembly. Common rules existed in agriculture. Celtic agricultural development was highly praised by Pliny the Elder when he surveyed it in the 1st Century BC. The Celtic plough, he observed, fitted with a mobile coulter, was greatly superior to the Roman swing plough of the same period. The Celts had been able to develop it because they functioned as a co-operative of several interested parties. They had also developed the art of manuring as well as inventing a harvesting machine. According to Pliny, this was 'a big box, the edges armed with teeth and supported by two wheels, moved through the cornfield, pushed by an ox; the ears of corn were uprooted by the teeth and fell into the box'.

The Kingston Brooch. A 7th Century AD piece of Celtic artwork set with garnets and lapis lazuli. It is now in Liverpool Museum.

Celtic society appears to have had six basic social classes but it was possible for a person to rise from the lowest order of society to the highest and likewise fall in the same manner. Position in society was granted according to ability and service to the community. There were, however, few cases of people achieving military distinction who were rewarded by grants of land from the community; unlike feudal society, military service was not a criterion for status.

Starting with the lowest social grading there were the 'non-freemen'. It is impossible to use a more explicit term. Certainly these were not slaves, as many have described them. The idea of one man holding another in servile bondage was alien to Celtic philosophy and the later codified Celtic law systems were uniformly averse to slavery. These non-freemen were generally lawbreakers. A lawbreaker suffered a loss of civil rights, cessation of pensions, prohibition from practising the professions or being employed in any position of trust in the clan. There were no prisons – the lawbreakers simply suffered a loss of civil rights within the community, temporary or permanent unless they could satisfy the fines imposed on them. The offender had to redeem himself. If he could not, the third generation was automatically freed from such restrictions and granted a full citizen's rights again. Although no non-freeman was allowed to leave the tribal territory without permission, he had the freedom to acquire by service his own plot of land to work. As well as lawbreakers, the non-freemen also consisted of cowards who deserted the tribe in time of need, prisoners of war and hostages. Prisoners of war and hostages, of which Patrick the Briton was one, were usually returned to their own tribe on payment of tribute.

The next social grade was that of the tribesman who did not work his own land but hired himself out as a herdsman or worker on other people's land. He took part in the military muster of the tribe as a full citizen but because he was classed as 'itinerant' he had little political say.

The entire basis of society depended on the tribesman who worked his land, paid his taxes for the upkeep of the community, formed the army in time of war and worked out political decisions and ideas by means of an electoral system, electing local assemblies to administer the tribe's affairs.

Above him was the class which the Romans erroneously described as the Celtic nobility. The error came from trying to equate the Celtic system with terms in a totally alien system. The 'nobles' were the elected representatives of the people, more of a 'civil service' class. They were public officers chosen by the tribe to administer the decisions of the assembly. They were assigned land for use while in office for carrying out the duties expected. These duties were to receive taxes, act as executive officer for the welfare of the people, keep the roads and bridges in repair, supervise the running of the tribal hospital, the orphanages, the poor homes and the public hostels; to maintain the public mill and the public fishing nets; to exercise police duties, arrange entertainment for visiting dignitaries; and in times of war organise the army and act as quartermaster general. They also had to make sure that farmers of the tribe were well supplied. If a tribesman had a surplus of stock he had to inform the 'civil servant' so that if another was short a balance could be maintained.

Then came the professional classes: the druids, bards, lawyers and doctors. We have already discussed the position of the druids. Closely associated with them came a professional class of poets, storytellers and minstrels. They were a well trained body of men and women who were highly regarded in society. The Celts were avid in their pursuit of knowledge, of literacy and learning. This group were the repositories of Celtic folklore, legends, history, and poetry. They usually held a salaried position in the retinue of a chieftain. Training a bard was almost as lengthy as training a druid. Diodorus Siculus, Posidonius and Athenaeus have all noted the popularity of music among the Celtic peoples and mention a wide variety of instruments in use including lyres, drums, pipes, trumpets and a harp-like instrument.

Finally, the last social order was that of the chieftains. There was a whole scale of chieftains ranging from the chief of a sub-tribe to the tribal chieftain, to the provincial ruler and so to the High King. Everyone was elected by the various assemblies to which they were answerable. Celtic chieftains, in strong contrast to the Roman leaders and later feudal barons and kings, were not in any sense law-makers but simply officers of the established law. A chieftain was president of the tribal assembly, commander of the forces in war and a judge in the public courts. On the whole, he was very much like the president of a modern democratic republic. As they had to be capable of carrying out the responsibilities involved, they were usually elected from particular families used to the problems a chieftain would encounter but, it must be stressed, there was no such concept as primogeniture. It was difficult for a chief to usurp power, for he was limited and hemmed in by the democratic process of his tribal assembly and dependent on his tribe for support so that it was easier for him to promote their welfare and safer for him to conform to the intention of the law than to become either negligent or despotic in office. When chieftains or kings betrayed their office they were thrown out and a new chieftain or king elected. Thus did MacBeth become High King of Scotland in 1040 in the stead of the despotic Duncan. But in English eyes, viewed by their standards of primogeniture and the philosophy of the divine right of kings, MacBeth was an usurper and it has been the English concept of MacBeth which has made him an immortal character in literature.

One other aspect of Celtic society must be remarked upon. Women could rule as chieftains on their own merits. The status of women in Celtic society and their social prominence has been found remarkable by many scholars. The female had a unique place in the Celtic world compared with other civilisations. She was regarded equally and could be elected as chief; she could, and did, lead her tribe as military commander – as the Icenian Boudicca did in 60AD. Celtic women enjoyed an equality of rights which would have been envied by their Roman sisters. The Roman bride fell, *in manu mariti,* through coemption, and belonged to her husband's family; she could no longer own her property. The Celtic bride remained mistress of all she brought into a marital partnership. The husband had no rights over the property she had. Any personal dowry, such as presents received from relatives, also remained her property which, in the event of the dissolution of the marriage by divorce or death, she took back along with her freedom and any acquisitions she had made during her marriage, or a proportion of them regulated by law. Any land managed by the wife remained her own under the jurisdiction of the tribal assembly and the Celtic laws on the commonality of property.

In parts a sophisticated form of polygamy existed in which man and woman had equal rights. Caesar was shocked when he recorded: 'Ten or twelve men have their wives in common: brother very commonly with brothers and parents with children.' Caesar failed to grasp the essential commonality of Celtic society in which the entire tribe lived as a close knit unit, sharing all the responsibilities of family life and raising children. Therefore, parents were free to follow their work and able to leave their children safely in the care of the tribe. A very strict and detailed series of law tracts on education and fosterage exist under the Brehon Laws.

These then were the people, their society and philosophical outlook, to which the Christian teachings began to spread in the 1st Century AD.

A carved stone artefact from Brugh na Boinne, or New Grange, Co. Meath, Ireland. This is accepted to be a pre-Christian religious sanctuary which is also recognized as a superb megalithic tumulus probably dating from as early as 300 BC. The stone is much later and displays the typical Celtic preoccupation with intricate pattern work.

2
The Spread of Christianity

Glendalough, Co. Wicklow, Ireland. The Christian settlement here at 'The Valley of the Two Lakes' is attributed to St Kevin in the 7th Century. The church, dating to that time, is St Kevin's while the Round Tower, one of the most famous of such constructions, is a remarkable and characteristic feature of Irish building of the early Christian period. It is thought the towers were intended as watch towers and places of refuge against Viking raids.

The first Celtic community to emerge in recorded history as accepting Christianity was Galatia in modern Turkey. Christianity arrived in Galatia in the person of Paul of Tarsus who visited Pessinus, on the Galatian frontier, which was the tribal capital of the Tolistobogii, sometime between 40 and 50AD. Paul was apparently sick when he arrived but was surprised by the warmhearted Celtic hospitality he received and, on his recovery, succeeded in converting many to the new faith. The Galatians received a permanent place in Christian history when, about 50-55AD, Paul wrote his famous 'Letter to the Galatians' which is now part of the New Testament. Paul admonished them:

I am astonished to find you turning so quickly away from him who called you by grace, and following a different gospel. Not that it is in fact another gospel; only there are persons who unsettle your minds by trying to distort the gospel of Christ.

Paul is so heated that at one point he exclaims: 'You stupid Galatians! You must have been bewitched!'

The document is reflective of the first great schism within the early Christian movement; the break between the teachings and ideas of Paul and those of the original Christian movement led by Jesus' brother Jacob

(James) in Jerusalem. Paul, who had Latinised his name from Saul, was a native of Tarsus in Cilicia; a Jew born a Roman citizen and brought up within a Hellenistic cultural environment but also with a strict Judaic orthodoxy. He was sent to Jerusalem to study under the celebrated Pharisee Rabbi Gamaliel and also learnt the trade of a tent-maker. But Paul was a Sadducee, an aristocratic traditionalist sect. He became an agent for the Sadducee High Priest and began a persecution of the Christian sect. This sect, then called the Nazarenes, still saw themselves as part of the Judaic faith, believing in Jesus as the last of the Jewish Messiahs. Jesus was not regarded as divine by them nor did they consider themselves to be outside Judaic law. This was the movement led by the original disciples of Jesus.

Paul had witnessed the execution for blasphemy of Stephen in Jerusalem in 35AD, acknowledged as the first Christian martyr. It was about the following year that he converted to the Nazarene sect and soon established himself as one of its teachers. However, his views of Jesus' life and philosophical teachings were at variance with the leaders of the movement. It was Paul who gave Jesus a divine status, declared that he had abrogated Judaic law and introduced the 'salvation doctrine' and gnosticism. Many ideas seemed to spring from his Greek background. Paul's important innovation was that he did not see his religious interpretation as being confined as part of Judaic religion and he went out of his way to convert non-Jews. Initially those non-Jews who converted to Christianity were seen as converts to Judaism and had to be circumcised. But soon Paul was teaching that this was not necessary. The bulk of his followers came from a pagan Hellenistic background which enabled them to respond to the gnostic aspects of his teachings.

Paul's innovations brought him into bitter conflict with the Nazarene leaders such as Jacob (James), John and Simon Bar-Jonah who was nicknamed 'The Rock' – *Kephas* in Greek and *Petra* in Latin and it is by the Latin, Peter, that he is known to Christendom. Paul freely admits his quarrel with them and speaks of a face to face confrontation with Peter. To the compilers of the New Testament it seemed unseemly that Paul should quarrel with Peter; after all, according to the Gospel writers Peter was the man designated by Jesus to lead his movement. To get round this, they left the Greek 'Cephas' in the contentious passages while translating the name to the Latin Peter in others. Thus, in places, Cephas and Peter appear two different people instead of the same man – Simon Bar-Jonah.

Paul himself, claiming authority for his 'breakaway' group, wrote to the Galatians (Chapter 2, verses 7-9) that Jacob, John and Peter had given him their wholehearted approval. They

> . . . *acknowledged that I had been entrusted with the Gospel for the Gentiles as surely as Peter had been entrusted with the Gospel for the Jews.*

> *For God whose action made Peter an apostle to the Jews, also made me an apostle to the Gentiles.*
>
> *Recognizing, then, the favour thus bestowed on me, those reputed pillars of our society, James (Jacob), Peter and John, accepted Barnabus and myself as partners and shook hands upon it, agreeing that we should go to the Gentiles while they went to the Jews.*

On the evidence of the later conflict it was obvious that the Nazarenes were appalled that Paul was surrendering their teaching to pagan idolatory, as they saw it. Within a short time there had been a deep split between the Nazarenes, who claimed they were the authentic transmitters of Jesus' teachings, and Paul's new movement. In this conflict the Nazarenes held their own for a little while and sent out missions to counteract Paul's teachings, spreading their version of Jesus' message. The Celtic Galatians were among the first to take notice of the Nazarenes and it was this that brought forth Paul's famous letter which was an attempt to bring them back to his movement. 'You were running well,' he told them. 'Who was it hindered you from following the truth? Whatever persuasian he used, it did not come from God!'

For one breathtaking decade, during the 60s AD, the struggle between the original Nazarene Christians and Paul's breakaway 'Gentile Christians' continued with neither side pre-eminent. Then in 67AD the Roman emperor Nero, angered by the continuing Jewish revolts against Roman rule, decided to move against the Jewish insurgents. The veteran general Vespasian was sent to bring them to heel. In the spring of that year he over-ran the flat regions of Galilee and attacked the stronghold of Jotapata, defended by Flavius Josephus (born in Jerusalem about 37-38AD). Josephus surrendered and, thankfully for posterity, was allowed his freedom. As a historian Josephus provides an invaluable source of information on the period.

After Nero's death in July 69AD, Vespasian was elevated to emperor and the campaign against the Jews continued under the general Titus. Jerusalem was besieged that summer. After its fall the Nazarenes, who had been in the forefront of the fight against Rome, suffered greatly. Josephus tells us that Annas, the High Priest, saw a chance to destroy this irritating movement completely. 'He assembled the Sanhedrin of judges and brought before them Jacob (James) the brother of Jesus who was called Christ, and some other men whom he accused of breaking the law and delivered them to be stoned.'

This single event was a considerable blow to the Nazarenes although they continued to exist and, indeed, existed as late as the 5th Century AD. The 'Gentile Christians' now constituted the bulk of the Christian movement and saw their opportunity to declare the Nazarenes as heretical. In 90AD the Nazarenes were also expelled from the Judaic fold for the same reasons. Their Gospels were suppressed although fragments have been found. To the end they taught that Jesus was the last Jewish Messiah but not a divinity and that Paul was the heretic who had perverted the teachings and merged them with pagan Hellenistic philosophy.

For the first two centuries of Paul's 'Gentile Christian' movement, both Peter and Paul were treated as equal apostles. But the early tradition was that Jesus had personally nominated Peter to found his church. According to the Gospel of Matthew, written about 80AD, Chapter 16, verse 17:

And Jesus answered and said unto him, Blessed art thou Simon Bar-Jonah
for flesh and blood hath not revealed it unto thee but my Father which is
in heaven. And I say also unto thee, that thou art Peter, and upon this rock
I will build my church; and the gates of hell shall not prevail against it.
And I will give unto thee the keys of the kingdom of heaven...

It was at the beginning of the 3rd Century AD that Pope Callistus, quoting this passage as his authority, declared Rome as the centre of the Christian Church; a claim hotly disputed by the Eastern and African Churches. Tradition then had it that Peter had journeyed to Rome, worked with his old antagonist Paul, and was executed there about the same time as Paul during the repression of Nero. There is no evidence of this, however, and, in view of the schism between the Nazarenes, of whom Peter was a leader, and Paul's 'Gentile Christians', it does not seem credible. An interesting point about Matthew's Gospel is that its author was not a Jew and that scholars claim that he was probably a Galatian.

It was from Rome that the Christianity of Paul of Tarsus began to spread through the Roman world, into Celtic Gaul and into the newly acquired territory of Britain. The new religion came to the Celts of the west not by deliberate or planned missions but through the normal intercourse between the Roman provinces. By the end of the 2nd Century AD Christianity had taken a strong hold among the Gaulish Celts. In Lugudunum (Lyons) we hear of a community presided over by its bishop Pothinus and a priest Irenaeus. In 177AD a persecution of incredible severity descended on this community. Pothinus was put to death with some companions, after being tortured, while other members of the community fled. The story of this persecution is the first written account of the Gaulish Celtic Church and is contained as a quotation in a letter written by Eusebius, bishop of Caesarea (circa 260-340AD). Eusebius was apparently quoting a contemporary letter which this Gaulish community sent to Eleutherius, bishop of Rome. 'We charge Irenaeus, our brother and our companion, to deliver this letter to you and we beg you to hold him in esteem as a zealot of Christ's testament', wrote the Gauls. Irenaeus managed to escape the persecution and reach Rome, according to Jerome.

Irenaeus apparently wrote a considerable amount. According to Gregory of Tours (circa 540-94AD) Irenaeus (circa 130-202AD) was a boy in Smyrna and was a disciple of Polycarp (circa 69-155AD) who, before his martyrdom there, sent Irenaeus to Lyons. Irenaeus eventually returned to Lyons to become bishop in place of the martyred Pothinus. His principal surviving work was *Adversus Omnes Haereses*, a treatise attacking gnosticism. Originally written, and partly preserved, in Greek, the principal language of the Christians at this time, it survived as a whole in an early Latin translation. In it Irenaeus apologises for his deficiencies in Greek because, he explains, he is a resident among the Celts (*Keltae*) and uses 'a barbarous dialect'. Irenaeus' *Presentation of Apostolic Preaching* has been preserved through an Armenian translation of the Greek text. Irenaeus was regarded as the most important theologian of the 2nd Century AD.

When Pope Victor, in 189AD, made an attempt to assert Rome's authority over Christendom during the first major Easter controversy, Irenaeus intervened. The Asian Church had argued against the date and manner of celebrating Easter. Victor declared he would excommunicate the entire church if they did not follow Rome's ruling on the matter. Irenaeus wrote to Victor urging him to take a more conciliatory attitude and Victor had the good sense to accept this advice.

By the 4th Century AD, the Gaulish Church was well established and a powerful organisation. In 392AD Ambrose makes a reference to the numerous councils which the Gaulish bishops were holding and in 404AD Pope Innocent I, in a letter to Victricius, bishop of Rouen, forbade the Gauls to write about their theological differences to other Christian provinces. The correct place to discuss such matters was at Rome.

The Celts of Gaul were certainly among the first to accept Christianity from Rome and it seems logical that their fellow Celts in Britain learnt the new religion from them. Legends of the arrival of Christianity among the British Celts are legion. A Welsh legend has it that Bran the Blessed brought the faith to the island in the middle of the 1st Century AD. More popular was the tale recorded by William of Malmesbury that Joseph of Arimathea came to Glastonbury bearing the Holy Grail and planting a Holy Thorn tree there. The British monk Gildas claimed that the faith reached Britain some six years after the crucifixion while Freculphus, bishop of Lisieux, says Christians arrived in Britain in 37AD and were given refuge by Caradoc (Caractacus) who, during the Roman invasion of 43AD, was chosen as the High King to turn back the legions of Aulus Plautius. Another tradition has it that when Caradoc, finally defeated after nine years of warfare, was taken in chains to Rome, with his family, his son Linus was converted by Paul of Tarsus and this Linus is the same person as the Linus who sends his greetings to Timothy via Paul in his second epistle. Linus is also acknowledged by the Catholic Church to have taken over the leadership of the Christian movement after the death of Paul about 67AD.

There is yet another story linking Caradoc's family with the early Christian leadership. It is a tradition that he had a daughter named Claudia who married a Roman called Pudens, both of whom are mentioned in Paul's second letter to Timothy. The poet Martial in his *Epigram* (xi, 53) speaks of Claudia as being 'from Briton' and a 'stranger' newly wedded to Pudens (iv, 13). Tradition also has it that Claudia and Linus were connected with the Regni tribe whose capital was at Chichester in Sussex.

Yet another account is given by Bede, the Northumbrian monk (673-735AD), who says that a British ruler named Lucius sent to Eleutherius, bishop of Rome, in 167AD, asking to be baptised in the faith. This Lucius, adds the British monk Nennius in the 9th Century AD, was known as Lleuer Mawr ('Great Light') on account of his acceptance of the faith. Still another story claims that when Pothinus' community in Lyons was suppressed, some of its scattered members sought refuge in Britain and began the conversion of their fellow Celts.

All these stories and legends aside, what we can be assured of is that Christianity reached the Celts of Britain at a very early stage. Tertullian, writing about 200AD, counting the countries which were Christian, mentions 'places in Britain, which though inaccessible to the Romans, have yielded to Christ'. Hippolytus (writing about 217-235AD) mentions the existence of a Christian movement in Britain while his contemporary, Origen (circa 230AD) speaks of Christianity in Britain as being 'vague and wordy but sufficient to confirm us in thinking that it is really there'. Finally, Jerome, writing at the end of the 4th Century AD, expressed a belief that Britain was Christian at an extremely early date.

There is also archaeological support from a Roman villa at Chedworth, Gloucester, built around 180AD. This was found with its walls covered in Christian monograms. In a well of a contemporary villa at Appleshaw, Andover, a pewter dish was found with the Chi-Ro symbol – an X and P, usually placed over the top of each other, being the first two letters of the name Christ in Greek. Another villa at Lullingstone Park, near Eynsford, Kent, dating to the 4th Century AD, has a room which has been set aside for Christian worship and decorated with Chi-Ro monograms on its south wall and Alpha and Omega enclosed in a wreath. There are also six praying figures on the west wall. The house was apparently abandoned in 380AD.

Gildas says that under the reign of Diocletian (284-305AD) the British suffered three martyrdoms for their faith. He mentions that of Alban at Verulam, Aaron and Julius at Caerleon-on-Usk. There was a general persecution of Christians at this time, wrongly ascribed to Diocletian. The son of an Illyrian slave, Diocletian established his capital at Nicomedia and devoted himself to the affairs of the eastern empire, leaving a colleague to look after the affairs of the west from Milan. Later, he appointed two more 'junior emperors' to govern from Trèves on the Moselle and Sirmium on the Danube, near Belgrade. The persecutions seem to begin with Diocletian's colleague, Galerius, and they extended to 311AD after Diocletian had resigned as emperor.

Nothing is known about these three British martyrs except that Alban was supposed to have been executed for sheltering fleeing Christians. The first reference is given in the 5th Century AD *Life of Germanus of Auxerre* according to which, when he visited Britain in 429AD, the relics of Alban were contained in a church at Verulam which, in later years became known as St Albans. Germanus, according to his biographer, took a handful of dust from the grave to place in his new church at Auxerre which he dedicated to Alban.

The persecution of the Christians within the Roman Empire ended when Constantine issued his Edict of Milan in 313AD allowing toleration of the religion. The following year the first great open council of the Christian Church was held at Arles and attended by Gaulish and British Celts. We are told that Eborius, bishop of York (although the name is suspect for Eboracum was the Latin name for York); Restitutus of London and Adelphius, probably from Lincoln, were there. Sylvester, the Pope, was not present during the great debates on the state of the Church. Constantine, who had allowed Christian toleration, was baptised into the faith on his deathbed in 337AD becoming the first Christian emperor of Rome.

With the Christians now free to debate and spread their doctrine in public a new problem arose which threatened to split the movement. Arius of Alexandria (d. 336AD) propounded the philosophy of monotheism, ascribing divinity only to God the Father and thus, as the original Nazarenes did, denying divinity to Jesus. Opposing Arius was Hilary, the Gaulish Celtic bishop of Poitiers (circa 315-373AD) and Athanasius, bishop of Alexandria (circa 296-367AD). It was at the Council of Nicaea in 325AD that Arius was banished from Alexandria and the Nicene Creed was adopted which is the basis for the Apostles' Creed. However, at this time Arius' followers (Arians) equalled the followers of Hilary and Athanasius, and Constantine II was an Arian supporter. It was some years before Arianism was ousted from the Christian movement. Indeed, Constantine became an antagonist of Athanasius and tried to have him arrested several times. The Council of Sardica had to formally acquit Athanasius of heresy in 347AD.

Hilary is regarded as the first native Celt to become an outstanding force in the Christian movement. His writings, with those of Athanasius, are said to have laid the foundation of Catholicism and western Christianity. He had become bishop of Poitiers about 350AD but, because of his opposition to Arianism, he was exiled to Phrygia about 356-360AD. This allowed him the leisure to write his greatest work *De Trinitate*, defining his

St Patrick's Bell. Also
known as *Clogan an-
udhachta* or 'The Bell of the
Will'. It is dated to the 6th
Century although it is
popularly believed to have
belonged to St Patrick
himself. A fine and
intricate piece of early
Celtic Christian art, now in
the National Museum,
Dublin.

belief in the Holy Trinity. Hilary's ideas about the Trinity have become the accepted Christian attitude. As a Celt, Hilary must have been imbued with the Celtic mystic traditions concerning trinity; it is fascinating to wonder how much the Christian belief in the trinity owes to the pre-Christian Celtic cultural concepts passed on by Hilary. During his exile Hilary also learnt a great deal about the Eastern Church and its ascetic hermit monasticism. On his return to Gaul, his fellow churchmen sent him a letter praising him and reiterating their stand against Arianism. Sulpicius Severus says that Hilary was acknowledged as the man who won the battle against the Arian creed. No British Celts attended the Council of Nicaea, when Arianism was condemned, but they did attend the Council at Ariminium (Rimini) in July, 359AD and affirmed their acceptance of the teachings of Athanasius and Hilary and the Nicene Creed. In 363AD Athanasius was able to observe with satisfaction that the British were among the most loyal to this belief.

It was during this period that Martin became bishop of Tours and established himself as 'Father of Celtic Monasticism', shaping the structure of the Celtic Church for the next 700 years. Martin was born in Sabaria in Pannonia about 315AD. He was the son of a veteran of the Roman army. Both his parents were pagan. Educated in Pavia, in Lombardy, he became a Christian, although his conversion did not stop him enlisting in the Imperial Cavalry of Constantine II. He became an officer. He left the army and settled in Gaul, entering the Christian movement and taking instruction from Hilary of Poitiers. From him Martin seems to have imbued himself with the asceticism of eastern monasticism. Christian monasticism began when Anthony (b. circa 250AD) took up residence in a deserted fort in Pispir on the Nile in 285AD. Pachomius (b. circa 290AD) converted to Christianity in 310AD and followed Anthony's example at Tabenissi, near Dendrah, five years later. Martin, like Hilary, was apparently influenced by the lives of these two men. He built his own hermitage near Amiens and lived there for nearly twenty years.

About 370AD Martin was asked to become bishop at Tours. He did not consent to dwell in the town but formed a monastic settlement outside which attracted many followers. The Celts called it the 'place of the big family' – *mor-munntir* or, as it is known today, Marmoutier. His biographer, Sulpicius Severus, visited Martin at Marmoutier and recalled:

> *The bishop (Martin) occupied a cell of wood. Many of the brethren live in similar cells, but the greater number dig out caves in the overhanging rock in which to instal themselves. There were here about eighty disciples and all following the example of their blessed master. No one possessed personal property, everything was in common.*

Although, by all accounts, Martin was a man of great personal charisma and courage, his method of converting the Gauls to Christianity was to go around the countryside at the head of a fanatical mob of followers burning and destroying sacred druidical sanctuaries. It has been suggested that Martin may have had positive instructions from the Emperor Gratian to do this as the druids had long been a political thorn in the side of the Roman administration.

One of Martin's ardent disciples was a Gaul named Victricius, who became bishop of Rouen and apostle to the Morini and Nervii Celts who occupied the coastal area between the Seine and Meuse. Victricius wrote at least one treatise – *De Laude Sanctorum*, On the Testimony of Sanctity – and, about 395AD, crossed to Britain where he was asked to mediate in a dispute between the British clergy. Martin was to have an important influence on two other people who were to leave their mark on Celtic Christianity. They were a British priest named Ninian and a woman called Elen, the British born wife of Magnus Maximus, who was to be declared emperor by his legions in 383AD.

Magnus Maximus was a Roman from Spain who had arrived in Britain about 368AD. He was said to have held high office in western Britain and is known in Welsh tradition as Maxen Wledig (*gwledig* meaning ruler). His wife Elen (*Elen Lwddog* – Elen of the Hosts), sometimes known as Helen, was reputed to have had connections with Segontium near Caernarfon. She was a Celt and the kings of Cornwall at one time claimed descent from her father Eudaf. Soon after the western Emperor Gratian was assassinated in 383AD, Maximus was declared emperor by his legions and crossed to Gaul to establish his court in Trèves. Theodosius, the eastern emperor, acknowledged him as co-emperor and he was approved of by the leaders of the Church. Martin of Tours became a frequent visitor at his court and Sulpicius Severus, in his *Dialogues*, mentions the effect he had on the emperor's wife, Elen.

Maximus was an ambitious man and was not content with being simply 'western emperor'. In 387AD he marched his legions into Italy and in January, 388AD, Rome was within his grasp. The Roman emperor, Valentinian II, fled from the city. Theodosius decided that Maximus constituted a threat and rallied the eastern empire against him, defeating him in several battles. At Aquileia, Maximus was betrayed, captured and put to death on July 28, 388AD. According to some Welsh scholars, the red dragon standard of Wales has its origin with Maximus because Ammianus Marcellinus, the historian, describes how the emperor was recognised in battle by his imperial standard showing a dragon on a purple flag.

After her husband's death, Elen, is said to have taken her considerable family back to Britain where, in the area of modern Wales, she began to work on behalf of the Christian movement leaving her name in such places as Llanelen, Monmouth; in Llanelen in Llanrihidion in West Gower; in Capel Elen in Penrhosllugwy, Anglesey, and in several other

31

church foundations. Her son Publicius (Plebig), a disciple of Ninian, is said to have founded the first monastic settlement in Wales called Llanbeblig after him. He is also said to have founded a settlement at Llanfeugan. Another son Leo was acknowledged to have founded a dynasty of Kentish kings. Constantine (Cystennin ap Maxen) has his tomb at Segontium; another son Eugenius (Owain ap Maxen) is claimed as the ancestor of the kings of Glywsing in South Wales, while Demetus, another son, is seen as the founder of a dynasty who ruled Dyfed. Another son Antonius is claimed as the ancestor of the Celtic kings of the Isle of Man. Lastly, a daughter Severa, is recorded as marrying the ruler Vortigern, said to have invited the Anglo-Saxons into Britain as mercenaries in his service. Severa's son Brydw was blessed by Germanus of Auxerre during his visit to Britain.

The other person influenced by Martin and his teaching was Ninian, the son of a British Celtic chieftain born near Carlisle, close by Hadrian's wall. It seems that as a young man Ninian went to Rome where, according to Bede, he was ordained by the Pope—probably Siricius (384-399AD). This was a fascinating period for Rome; it was the swansong of the old Roman order. Gratian, who had been assassinated in 383AD, had been much dominated by Ambrose, the bishop of Milan, and through his influence had revoked the toleration of every religion except Christianity. Ninian was in Rome about the same time as Augustine of Hippo.

Augustine had been born in 354AD in modern day Souk-Ahras. He died on August 28, 430AD in Hippo (modern Annata). He has become generally recognised as the greatest Christian theologian of this early period, fusing the religion of the early Christians with the Platonic tradition of Greek philosophy. He studied at Carthage and then, at the age of twenty-eight, went to Rome. Becoming fascinated by Christianity he went to Milan to meet Ambrose and was converted to the faith and baptised there in 387AD. *City of God* was the work in which he most clearly advanced his religious philosophy of pre-destination which the British theologian Pelagius found so destructive for man's advancement.

In fact, at this time, not only theological questions were splitting the Christian movement but the power struggle for leadership. Ammianus Marcellinus, the last prominent Roman historian, a non-Christian but a man of utmost religious tolerance, could observe: 'No wild beasts are so cruel as the Christians in their dealings with each other'. Marcellinus, born in Antioch in 330AD, and who died in Rome in 395AD, came of a Greek family but had served in the Roman army. His *Rerum Gestorum Libri* was a history of the empire of which only the sections covering the period 353-378AD survive.

Marcellinus was referring to a particular power struggle in the Christian Church at this time. Pope Liberius (353-366AD) had been exiled to Beroea, Thrace, by the pro-Arian emperor Constantine II. He had an

Arian named Felix proclaimed Pope in place of Liberius. In November, 365AD, Felix had to flee when Liberius returned to popular acclaim. When, on October 1, 366BC, Damasus I became pontiff, many supported Felix and a follower of Felix named Ursinus was declared Pope in rivalry to Damasus. The prefect of Rome exiled him but Ursinus tried to organise a *coup* in September, 367AD. He was exiled to Gaul. However, he was still active against Damasus from Milan during the years 370-72AD. Damasus occupied the papal throne until 384AD to be succeeded by Siricius.

Having spent time in Rome during this turbulent period, Ninian the Briton began to make his way back home but he stopped his journey at Tours, at the monastery of Marmoutier which had now become widely known as *Magnum Monasterium* and 'The Pure House' or 'White House'. Ninian was extremely impressed at Martin's monasticism. He determined, on his return to Britain, to establish a monastery on similiar lines.

During the same time as Ninian was in Rome there was another Briton there named Pelagius. He is generally accepted to be a British Celt although there is one reference to him as being 'full of Irish porridge' and thus a tenuous claim has been made that he was Irish. He was born about 354AD and went to Rome about 380AD. He was distressed at what he saw as the laxity of moral standards among Christians there. He was to later blame moral laxity on the doctrine of divine grace as expounded by the writings of Augustine of Hippo. Pelagius believed that men and women could take the initial and fundamental steps towards their salvation, using their own efforts and not relying on divine grace. He argued that Augustine's theories imperilled the entire moral law. If a man were not responsible for his good and evil deeds there was nothing to restrain him from indulgence in sin. Pelagius' view is more simply stated by the poet W. E. Henley:

I am the master of my fate,
I am the captain of my soul.

Such a philosophy would have certainly been part of the Celtic ethos and it is interesting that those who condemned Pelagius accused him of trying to revive the druidic philosophy on Nature and Free Will. This might well have explained why Pelagianism was so popular among the Celts. It could be that Pelagius was simply a man of his own culture and that instead of the Celts being subverted by Pelagianism, as Rome maintained, they were just following their ancient cultural traditions.

About the time of the fall of Rome to Alaric's Visigoths in 410AD, Pelagius and his friend, a lawyer named Celestius, went to Africa. It was at this time that Pelagius encountered the hostility of Augustine of Hippo who published several denunciatory letters against him. In 412AD Pelagius passed on to Palestine. In the absence of Pelagius, Celestius was accused of heresy by Paulinus of Milan, the biographer of Ambrose. A Council at

Papil Stone from Shetland, dating to the 8th Century, typifies the Celtic obsession for portraying myth and religious concepts.

Carthage in 411AD, condemned him and he moved to Ephesus. Having been successful in condemning Pelagius' follower, Orosius of Spain became Augustine's representative to Jerome at Bethlehem, accusing Pelagius himself of heresy. Pelagius succeeded in clearing himself at a Council in Jerusalem and at another Council at Diospolis (Lydda). In response to continued attacks from both Augustine and now Jerome, he wrote a treatise entitled *De Libero Arbitrio* – On Free Will. Augustine finally convinced the African bishops to condemn both Pelagius and Celestius at two councils at Carthage and Milevius in 416AD and persuaded Pope Innocent I (410-17AD) to excommunicate them.

When the Greek Zosimus succeeded Innocent on March 18, 417AD, Celestius hastened to Rome to have the case reconsidered. Zosimus pronounced Pelagius innocent of heresy after reading his work *Libellus Fidei* – Statement of Faith. The African bishops refused to ratify the Pope's decision and at a Council in Carthage on May 1, 418AD, they issued a series of nine canons affirming, in uncompromising terms, the Augustinian doctrine on the Fall of Man and Original Sin. Meanwhile, on April 30 that same year, the Emperor Honorius (395-423AD) had issued an imperial decree denouncing Pelagius and Celestius. The Pope now had no choice but to revoke his pronouncement and, by his *Epistola Tractoria* of that year, affirm the judgement of Innocent I. Pelagius seems to have disappeared at this date and tradition has it that he died in Palestine.

Pelagius' extensive writings were largely lost, destroyed or transmitted by other names. His most considerable surviving work is his *Commentary of St Paul's Epistles* which has come down in a work ascribed to Jerome, the *Libellus Fidei* and an address to a Roman lady who became a nun. His beliefs were still defended by Julian of Eclanum who conducted a literary debate of great bitterness with Augustine which only ended with Augustine's death in 430AD, caused by hardship during the siege of Hippo by the Visigoths. In 429AD Celestius asked a colleague, Nestorius, to intercede with Pope Celestine I to alter the decrees of Innocent I and Zosimus but in 431AD Celestine I decided that the denunciations of his predecessors should stand. Pelagianism, however, continued to be a strong force among the Celts, especially in Britain during the 5th Century AD while in Gaul a movement called the Semi-Pelagians was identified which was condemned at the 2nd Council of Orange in 529AD.

The issues on Free Will were to raise themselves again during the Reformation with Pelagius still being regarded as a heretic by the Catholic Church. The pattern of the official attitude towards him was set by Prosper of Acquitaine in a verse repeated by Bede containing more than a touch of racialism against the British Celts.

Against the great Augustine see him crawl,
This wretched scribbler with his pen of gall!

In what black cavern was the serpent bred,
That from the dirt presumed to rear its head?
Either the coast of Britain saw his birth,
Or else his heart pours its own venom forth.

One of the most savage attacks on Pelagius has come in the 19th Century. This was not, strangely enough, on his philosophy of Free Will, which is now generally accepted; it was an attack on his social teachings. A contemporary Pelagian writer known as the 'Sicilian Briton', a British Celt writing in Sicily in the early 5th Century AD, and tenuously identified by R. S. T. Haslehurst as a man called Fastidius, was very explicit on Pelagius' teachings on egalitarianism. According to *Tractatus de Divitiis* – a Tract on Wealth – Pelagians saw mankind as divided between *'Diuitiae, paupertas, sufficientia...'* 'wealth, poverty and sufficiency.' The solution to the problems of poverty was simple. *'Tolle diuitem et pauperum non inuenies ... Pauci enim diuites pauperum sunct causa multorum ...'* 'Overthrow the rich man and you will not find a poor man ... for the few rich are the cause of the many poor.' Heady, revolutionary stuff, claim recent scholars such as John Morris who attacks Pelagius as a proto-socialist and points to this as a greater heresy than Free Will. Yet in this Pelagius was not out of step with the other theologians of Christendom.

In the *Didache* we have this statement: 'Share everything with your brother. Do not say "it is private property". If you share what is everlasting you should be that much more willing to share things which do not last'. The *Didache*, or teachings of the Twelve Apostles, is the oldest surviving Christian Church Order written in Egypt or Syria in the 2nd Century AD. It contains sixteen short chapters on morals and ethics. This principle was echoed by Tertullian who said: 'We, who share one mind and soul, obviously have no misgivings about comity in property.' Quintus Septimus Florens Tertullianus, born circa 155/160AD in Carthage, was one of the first important Christian theologians and moralists, an initiator of Latin theological words and phrases. He became a leader of the African Church.

Basil, born circa 329AD, died January 1, 379AD, coined the phrase 'Property is theft'. It was not, as is generally thought, an original phrase of Pierre-Joseph Proudhon in his book *What is Property?*, published in 1840, which was freely quoted by Karl Marx and which gave Marxists a popular catch-phrase. Basil, who studied to be a lawyer in Constantinople, converted to Christianity and became bishop of Cappadocia. 'The rich take what belongs to everyone,' he wrote, 'and claim they have a right to own it, to monopolise it!'

Ambrose (339-397AD), the second son of the commander of the emperor's Gallic bodyguard, who was unexpectedly acclaimed bishop of Milan in 374AD, was very severe on social abuses, especially in his tract *De Nabuthe* (On Naboth). 'Nature furnishes its wealth to all men in common,' he wrote. 'God beneficently has created all things that their enjoyment be common to all living things and that earth become the common property of all . . . only unjust usurpation has created the right of private property.' He went on: 'The bread which the rich eat belongs to others more than to them. They live on stolen goods. What they pay comes from what they have seized . . . You have gold dug up from the mines, only to rebury it. And how many lives are buried with it? And this wealth is kept for whom? For your heirs who wait idly by to receive it . . . It is not the poor who are cursed but the rich. Scripture says of the rich, not of the poor, that the man who increases the price of corn will be cursed.'

Another contemporary of Pelagius propounding the same egalitarian views was John Chrysostum (born circa 347AD, died September 14, 407AD). Born in Antioch, the son of a high ranking military officer, he trained in law but then became a Christian priest in his native city, eventually becoming archbishop of Constantinople. He was also unequivocal. 'The rich man is a thief . . . You have a thousand excuses for robbing your brother but excuses will not prevail against God and Man.'

Even in the 6th Century AD this philosophy was still strongly held and Isidore of Seville (560-636AD), regarded as the last of the Western Church Fathers, echoed it. He warned 'those who oppress the poor must know that their sentence is heavier because of those they try to hurt. The more they press their power over these wretched lives, the more terrible their future condemnation and punishment will be.'

Pelagius was very much a part of this school of thought; but he was, as we have seen, a man of his culture. His point of dispute was not social teachings but his ideas on Free Will conflicting with Augustinian predestination.

Illumination from the Book of Kells. This most famous of Irish illuminated manuscripts is a fine example of early Celtic Christian Art. It is dated to the 8th Century and thought to have had its origins at Iona before being brought to the monastery of Kells in Ireland to safeguard it from Viking raids. It is now in Trinity College, Dublin.

3

The Separation of the Celtic Church

The 5th Century AD was to be a time of tremendous change for the Celtic world; a time when the map of Europe was completely redrawn. Alaric and his Visigoths, once mercenaries of the Roman emperors, turned on their former masters and captured Rome in 410AD. Alaric died soon afterwards and his brother Athaulf demanded that the emperor Honorius allow him to move his Visigoths into Gaul and recognise him as ruler of the territory. He also married Honorius' sister. The Celts were pushed out of the area settled by him. Towards the end of the century, the Franks, pushing across the Rhine as part of the Germanic expansion, began displacing the Celts in that area.

The Roman world was further disrupted by the Vandals, led by Genseric, who crossed to Roman Africa in 429AD and sacked Hippo (Augustine died during the siege) and Carthage. From this base they raided Roman supply lines and finally, in 455AD, landed in Italy and sacked Rome more ruthlessly than the Visigoths. Then came Atilla and his Huns sweeping through the eastern empire, ravaging Constantinople and moving into Gaul where, in 451AD, he defeated the combined forces of the disintegrating empire before returning eastwards. For a few years puppet emperors ruled for short periods in Rome under the jurisdiction of the conquerors. Then in 476AD Odovakar declared himself emperor and ruled until Theodoric the Ostrogoth came out of the Balkan peninsula and defeated him, declaring himself 'king of the Goths and Latins' with his capital at Ravenna, a hundred miles south of Venice. Theodoric ruled from 493 to 526AD and proved an able ruler. At this time Clovis, king of the Franks, moved his people south, from a territory near the mouth of

Little Skellig, Ireland. Na Sceallaga, the rocks, are three small islands eight miles from the Kerry coast out in the Atlantic. Little Skellig, Skellig Michael and the Great Skellig comprise the group.

the Rhine, displacing the Celts and seizing most of Gaul. Clovis was baptised in 496AD in the Roman faith while Theodoric's Goths were Arian Christians.

The conquest of Clovis and his Franks marked the end of Celtic Gaul and soon only the peninsula of Armorica remained to the Celts. Armorica was soon to be known as Brittany while the Franks gave their name to the rest of Gaul – France. It has generally been assumed that Latin had displaced the Celtic speech of Gaul in the 3rd Century AD. This was not so. Latin had become the *lingua franca* of the province, as with most provinces of the old Roman Empire, but Gaulish was still being spoken even by the ruling families into the 5th Century. Writing to Ecdicius, son of the emperor Avitus, Sidonius, his brother-in-law and bishop of the Averni (died 479AD) says 'at one time it was due to you personally that the leading families, in their efforts to throw off the scurf of Celtic speech, were initiated now into oratorical style and now again into the measure of the Muses'. More Celtic words than French scholars care to admit passed into the French language via the vulgar Latin which merged with the Germanic speech of the Franks.

At the same time, too, the face of Celtic Britain was also being changed by the incursions of the Angles, Saxons, Jutes and other Germanic peoples. Early sources have it that Vortigern, described as the ruler of Kent, invited the Jutes of Hengist and Horsa into Britain to act as mercenaries against the raids of the Saxons. No sooner had Hengist and Horsa arrived than they decided to take over Vortigern's kingdom. They fought the Celtic ruler at Aylesford on the Medway, four miles below Maidstone. Horsa was slain but the ancestors of the English were now in Britain to stay and began the process of pushing the Celts westward. It was a long, slow, process and the Celts contended every mile of land with dogged determination. Nearly fifty years after their victory at Aylesford, the Germanic invaders were still trying to gain a hold in Sussex. It was not until 490AD that the Saxon chiefs Ella and Cissa finally pushed the Celts out and established the South Saxon kingdom.

The Germanic invaders of Britain seemed to have been more ruthless than their cousins, the Franks. In their conquest of what was to become England there was no allowing the indigenous inhabitants to remain nor was there intermarriage on a wide scale. Some scholars do believe that intermarriage took place but as Mario Pei points out in his *Story of the English Language* (1968): 'One might imagine that the Celtic of the original Britons would have supplied a fertile field for loan words to the Anglo-Saxon. Such is emphatically not the case ... The reason for this seems to lie in the scantiness of social relations between the two races, the English considering the Celts as inferior and their own race and tongue superior.' Enforced migration or massacre seems a more accurate picture.

It was during these Germanic expansions that the Celts of Britain and

Ireland became cut off from the mainstream of Roman Christianity and thus the Celtic Church began to develop as a unique institution. By 'cut off' I do not mean that the insular Celts lost all contact with Rome but that Rome ceased to have an immediate influence. And during this time the basis of Celtic monasticism was laid in the north of Britain.

At the end of the 4th Century AD the British priest Ninian, having spent some time with Martin at Marmoutier, returned to his homeland. So impressed was he with Martin and his monastic concept that he decided to make his own monastic foundation and, with a number of followers, he chose a site called Rosnut – the little promontory – at modern Whithorn in Wigtown, Galloway. Tradition has it that the monastery was just being completed when Ninian learnt that his mentor, Martin, had died – the date being November 11, 397AD. He therefore called the place *Teach Martin* or Martin's House. However, the monastery became known as Candida Casa or The Pure House, often translated as White House or Whithorn (from the English *hwit aern*). It is interesting to find that near Whithorn is a place called Physgyll Cave whose interior contains a number of grave markers dating from the 7th Century AD. An 8th Century AD poem about Ninian refers to the fact that he used to withdraw to some *horrendum antrum* – awesome cavern – to meditate. Although Bede speaks of Ninian we do not have a complete Life until Ailred, the abbot of the Cistercian monastery of Rievaux in Yorkshire, wrote one in the 12th Century AD.

Ninian's Candida Casa became the great centre of Celtic Christianity in Britain. We are told that the songs of Hilary of Poitiers were popular there and the first few words of one such song have been found incised on a stone there. Ninian, having consolidated his position, decided to take a mission north towards the pagan Picts. He moved north of the Forth establishing churches as he went and reaching the west bank of Loch Ness. He returned to Candida Casa and then sailed for Ireland, the first record of a Christian mission to Ireland. One Irish source says he founded a church in Leinster before returning to Candida Casa where he died in 432AD.

Ninian's monastery was the first big monastic foundation of the insular Celts based on the model of Marmoutier and its pupils were to become some of the famous names of the Celtic Church. Plebig son of Maximus is said to have studied here and so did David of Wales. On the death of Ninian Caranoc became abbot. According to the Books of Ballymote and Lecan, Caranoc went on a mission to Ireland in 412AD and met a British hostage there named Patrick whom he baptised in the faith. It is a highly doubtful tale. Caranoc's successor was a Pict named Ternon and this fact must show the success of Ninian's proselytising efforts in the Pictish kingdoms.

As the 5th Century AD commenced, the Celtic theologians were still expressing support for Pelagian concepts. A British bishop named Fastidius is mentioned as the author of a series of pro-Pelagian texts circa 420-430AD. Grennadius of Marseilles (circa 490-500AD), in his continuation of Jerome's *De Viris Illustribus*, mentions 'Fastidius, a bishop of the Britons wrote to a certain Fatalis a book on *De Vita Christiana* – The Christian Life – and another on *De Viduitate Sevanda* – The Preserving of Widowhood – sound in doctrine and worthy of God.' This same Fastidius has been equated with the anonymous 'Sicilian Briton' author by R. S. T. Haslehurst.

Another British Celt, Faustus, became a leading churchman in Gaul. He was born about 405-410AD and entered the monastery of Lérins, becoming its abbot in 433AD. He was consecrated bishop of Reii (Riez) about 460AD and is on record as attending the Council of Rome in 462AD. He opposed the Arians and this caused his banishment when Euric, the pro-Arian king of the Visigoths annexed the territory of Reii in 476-477AD. He was allowed to return and his writings are known to have included various letters and tracts *De Gratia*, On Grace, and *De Spiritu Sancto*, On the Holy Spirit. After his death his writings were condemned as heretical because they were apparently Pelagian.

Faustus was well known to the writer Sidonius who was born at Lugudunum (Lyons) about 430AD. Sidonius' grandfather had been Praetorian Prefect of Gaul and was the first of his family to accept Christianity. Sidonius was educated in Lyons and Arles; married Papianilla, the daughter of the future emperor Avitus, and had a son and three daughters. Sidonius followed Avitus to Rome, delivered a panegyric in his honour, but fell into disfavour after the overthrow of his father-in-law. Pardoned by Marjorian, the new emperor, Sidonius concentrated on his writing. Later he was appointed prefect of Rome, president of the Senate, head of the judicature and police in Rome and one hundred miles around it and also controller of food supplies. After his term of office ended, he returned to Gaul and in 469-70AD was elected as bishop of the Averni in modern Clermont. Like Ambrose, who passed from baptism to the episcopate within a week, Sidonius made a rapid transition from layman to bishop. He took his new status seriously and wrote no more worldly verses. He died in 479AD.

Sidonius wrote a long poem to Faustus, showing a lack of knowledge of the scriptures, and some letters. In one letter he says: 'I have read those works of yours which Riochatus, the priest and monk, and so twice over a pilgrim and stranger in this world, is duly carrying to your dear Britons on behalf of you . . .' It is thought that this Riochatus, one of the first pure Celtic names we meet among the early Christian leaders, was the 'St Riochatus' of Welsh tradition.

Prosper of Acquitaine says that Pelagianism was flourishing in Britain at this time. He says that Agricola, son of a Pelagian bishop named

Severianius, 'corrupted the churches of Britain with the subtle wiles of his doctrine.' It seems that Palladius, the same Palladius who was shortly to undertake a mission to Ireland, sought the support of Pope Celestine to send a mission to Britain to counter Pelagianism. Prosper records: 'Pope Celestine sent Germanus, bishop of Auxerre, in his stead, routed the heretics and restored Britain to the Catholic fold.' The mission of Germanus was not that simple.

Germanus, according to the life written by Constantine of Lyons about 450AD, was a native of Auxerre and the son of wealthy and influential parents. He had married Eustochia, a lady of influence, and in May, 418AD, he was appointed bishop of his native town. As a companion on this mission to Britain, Germanus chose Lupus, bishop of Troyes, brother-in-law of the bishop of Arles, another Hilary, and a friend of Prosper of Acquitaine from whom we know the details. Being Gauls, even at this time, it is obvious that both men were chosen because of their knowledge of the Celtic language.

Germanus went to Verulam to see Alban's tomb, where he picked some earth from the grave to take back to Auxerre for the dedication of his new church. Instead of simply taking part in theological debates, we find that Germanus was mixing freely in British politics. He was to visit Britain again, this time with Severus, bishop of Trèves, in 443AD, and the numerous details of both visits have been confused. However, it must have been during his first visit in 429AD, that he came into conflict with Vortigern.

As we have seen, tradition has it that it was Vortigern who allowed the ancestors of the English to establish themselves in Britain by inviting them into the country as mercenaries. Vortigern is an enigmatic figure; much more than a local British ruler as the very name implies for it is Celtic for Over-lord. Vortigern's son Brydw or Cadell Ddyrnllug had quarrelled with his father and was supported by Germanus in becoming ruler of modern Powys. Germanus helped the British defeat an attack of Saxons and Picts at Maes Gorman, identified as Mold, in Flint, and then turned his wrath on Vortigern, pursuing him until he was tracked down to Dyfed where he perished on the banks of the Teify. Church historians, supporting Germanus, claimed that Vortigern had committed incest by marrying his daughter and having a son by her.

If Vortigern, as the name implies, was actually High King of Britain and the only person to unite the British Celts against the invading Germanic tribes, then his death was a tragic blow for the British. Three years after his death a letter was sent to the Roman ruler Aetius in Gaul appealing for military aid against the invaders. It became known as *Gemitus Britannorum* – 'The Groans of the British.'

As the 5th Century AD drew to a close Britain became lost in a mist of continual warfare between the Celts and Anglo-Saxons. It became an age of legends, of shadows caught intriguingly through a swirling fog; the age of Arthur, of Tristan and Iseult, of the wandering 'saints', of the struggle for supremacy between two opposing civilisations. When the mists begin to clear towards the end of the 6th Century AD, Britain is no longer a Celtic island. The Anglo-Saxons are in firm control of the lowlands, dividing up their territories into small kingdoms – Kent, the South Saxons, the West Saxons, the East Saxons, the East Angles, and Mercia, Deira and Bernicia to the north. The Celts had been pushed to the west and north, and a great many had fled the country. There had been large migrations to Armorica and to northern Spain.

For a brief time the Celts had managed to check the Anglo-Saxons by a victory at a place called Badon, linked inseparably with the name of Arthur, which seems to have been fought in 516AD. According to the *Annales Cambriae* it was Arthur who succeeded in uniting the Celts against the invaders. But Arthur was killed at Camlann, supposedly fought about 537AD. By 577AD Caewlin and Cutha forced a Saxon wedge between the Celts of the area which is today called Wales and the Celts of the south western peninsula Dumnonia – Devon and Cornwall. The northern Celts of Cumbria were also isolated. To the invaders the Celts were merely foreigners – *weahlas* or *welisc* – hence the name Wales and *Kern-welisc* for Cornwall.

Before the clouds of war enveloped the insular Celts, making it difficult for intercourse between them and Rome, Rome turned a thoughtful eye on the island of Ireland and decided to send an official Christian mission to the country. Palladius was chosen. According to Prosper of Acquitaine, Palladius was ordained by Pope Celestine as the 'first bishop to the Irish believing in Christ' thus implying that there were already Irish Christian communities at that date. It is now that we come up against the problems of scholastic arguments.

Orthodox tradition has it that Palladius died in Britain on his journey to Ireland in 431AD and therefore a British Celt named Patrick was sent as a replacement bishop. Professor Thomas O'Rahilly believes that Palladius actually reached Ireland and did not die until 461AD after which Patrick the Briton was sent there during the following year. Confusion arises, he says, because Palladius was also known as Patrick. Professor James Carney refutes both the orthodox school and Professor O'Rahilly. He says that Palladius did spend some time in Ireland but that Patrick was sent in 456AD.

Without getting too deeply involved in the arguments, Professor Carney's sources and deductions make a great deal of sense. Patrick was certainly a British Celt and probably born at Bannarem Taberniae (sometimes spelt Bannavean), identified as Dumbarton on the Clyde. He was originally named Sucat or Sucatus, and was the son of a Christian deacon. During a raid made by the Irish when he was sixteen years old, he was taken as a hostage by a chieftain named Milch. Obviously Patrick's family were unable to meet the hostage fee and for some years the young Briton herded sheep on the slopes of Slemish, near Ballymena, Co. Antrim. Then he escaped on a ship to Gaul. He joined a Christian settlement there, traditionally said to be Lérins, where the Briton Faustus was abbot. From there he went to Auxerre, arriving during the episcopacy of Germanus.

If we accept Professor Carney's chronology, giving the year of Patrick's birth as 418AD, we must also accept that Palladius was working in Ireland for some years and that three other bishops had been sent there in 439AD–Secondinus, Auxilius and Iserninus. Carney attributes the foundation of Armagh as a bishopric to Secondinus in 444AD. Secondinus' father was Restitutus from Lombardy. According to Carney he remained bishop of Armagh until 457AD and his *Hymnus Patricii*, the earliest version dating to the 8th Century, is not his work at all. Carney points out that it is similar to the hymn of Camulacus in the *Antiphonary of Bangor*.

As for Iserninus, who was certainly in Auxerre when Patrick was there, we find him in Leinster long before Patrick. He was apparently imprisoned by the ruler Ende Censelach and when Patrick converted Ende Censelach's grandsons, he managed to have Iserninus released. Iserninus seems to have been in Ireland between 440 to 468AD.

At the time Patrick went to Ireland the Ui Neill, descendants of Niall Noigiallach (Niall of the Nine Hostages) had established themselves as the family from which the High Kings at Tara were elected and thereby claimed sovereignty over the entire island. In reality the Eoghanachta, descendants of Eoghan, another High King, were ruling the southern half of the country from Cashel, in Co. Tipperary. During that time the Ui Neill of Tara were also engaged in conflict with the Lagin, the people of Leinster, who also challenged their right to rule the midland plains. Under the High Kingship were five provincial kingships (the Irish word for province is *cúige* – a fifth) although in reality there were seven provinces with Ulaid (Ulster) being divided into three.

Tradition has it that Patrick landed at Strandford Lough, with a follower named Seginis. His first convert was a chieftain named Dichu. He then set off to see his old master Milchu. We are told that Patrick's intention was to pay the man his hostage fee. Milchu, hearing he was coming, shut himself into his fortress and burnt himself to death. One wonders what manner of man would put such fear into a person to make him immolate himself? Ironically, we are told, Mochaoi, the grandson of Milchu, became a Christian and was abbot of the monastery of Nendrum on Strangford Lough. Patrick was said to have lit the druid's sacred bonfires on the Hill of Slane and converted the practice into a Christian custom. We are told he worked many years in Ireland but it is highly doubtful that he accomplished all that is ascribed to him. There survive copies of his *Confession*, recounting his life, and a letter addressed to a British ruler named Coroticus, who has been identified as Coirthech of Strathclyde, whom Patrick criticises for a raid on an Irish coastal settlement in which the British carried off newly baptised Irish Christians and confirmed neophytes.

It is extremely interesting that, although he is now the patron saint of Ireland and acclaimed as the man who converted the Irish to Christianity, his name, as a leading churchman, does not occur in records until the 7th Century when he is first mentioned in a letter from Cummian, abbot of Durrow, to Seghine, abbot of Iona, about 623AD. Cummian says the Dionysian Easter computation was introduced to Ireland by Patrick and adds that there was now a considerable body of Irish clergy in the southeast who were in favour of conforming to the Roman computation. It is also remarkable that during the Synod of Whitby the Irish make reference to Colmcille as the founder of their church and fail to refer to Patrick. The oldest sources for Patrick's life are those written by Muirchu Maccu Machtheni, who wrote at the desire of Bishop Aed of Slebte (Sletty) who died in 698AD, and some notes on his life by Tirechan, a pupil of Ultan of Ardbreccan who died in 656AD. Both these records are included in the *Book of Armagh*, compiled between 807-846AD. The controversy of Patrick continues but, as Professor Carney says: 'The sources are not yet exhausted – the position is rather that no Patrician scholar has yet succeeded in digesting them.'

Detail of the chancel arch of the Norman church at Tuam, Co. Galway, Ireland. Tuaim da ghualann (Tuam) was one of the leading Irish monastic schools dating from the 6th Century. Little remains of the original buildings, however.

An 8th Century AD *Catalogue of the Saints of Ireland* says that during Patrick's time there were about 350 'saints' or rather missionaries working in Ireland with one mass, one liturgy and one tonsure from ear to ear. 'They did not reject the service and society of women because, founded on the rock, Christ, they feared not the blast of temptation.'

The comparative ease with which Christianity was assimilated into Celtic life has frequently been remarked upon. There is hardly any evidence of fierce opposition, or harm done to the missionaries. It has frequently been remarked that the Celtic Church is unique in its lack of martyrs. Alban the Briton was martyred by Romans not by the British. Only in Gaul is Martin of Tours 'blood and fire' policy of conversion a black stain on the record but, of course, Martin was not a Celt. Rather than a clash of beliefs the druids and bards, already with a doctrine of immortality, of a world soul, of the mysticism of the trinity, simply absorbed the new philosophy and created a new brand of Christianity which was the basis of the Celtic Church. In a short space of time it was the druids who became the Christian priests, the bards who became the scribal monks. There was no social upheaval as happened in other cultures but a gentle change of the labels by which things were known.

When Rome began to take a particular interest in the Celtic Church towards the end of the 6th Century AD there were several differences between them. Rome looked to Peter as its founder while the Celtic Church cited the authority of John. The Celtic sabbath was celebrated on a Saturday and had more in common with the Greek service than the Latin. More often than not, until the 7th and 8th Centuries AD, the service was conducted in Greek. The Eucharist, the bread and wine, was given by the celebrant who stood facing the altar and not behind it. The wine was given by a deacon. When the blessing was given, the Celtic priest held up the first, third and fourth finger to represent the Trinity. The Roman priest held up the thumb, first and second finger. The blessing in the Celtic Church was given before communion and the breaking of bread was at the end of the service.

The Celtic Church emphasised active participation by the people, sharing in the worship while the deacon led the congregation in prayers and the people would make responses with psalms and hymns. The deacon fulfilled an important role as a link between the priest and the people. Choral services were established early. The Celtic bishops celebrated in crowns and not mitres; and the mass, called such by Rome from the Latin word *missa* meaning dismissal, was called the 'Offering' as in the Eastern Church. Celtic bishops were under the authority of abbots. While monks were usually unmarried, being ascetics, the clergy, including bishops, were married. This was not unique, however, as marriage was common in the Roman Church and the married priesthood continued until the 12th Century AD.

Confession was not obligatory but voluntary and made either in public or to a chosen 'soul friend'. Nor did absolution follow immediately, only after a penance sometimes lasting years. The strict asceticism of Celtic monks was different to the Roman rules. The Roman monks adopted what they called the tonsure of St Peter, shaving the head on the crown as symbolic of the crown of thorns. The Celts claimed they used the tonsure of St John, shaving a line from ear to ear. The evidence is, however, that this was a druidic relic. It was regarded as 'barbaric' by the Roman orthodoxy.

The most famous diference between the Celtic Church and Rome was the dating of Easter. The rules governing the Roman Christian calendar were fixed at Nicaea in 325AD with the years reckoned from the birth of Christ. Under Pope Leo I (440-461AD) Rome altered the computation of Easter; this was known as the Alexandrian computation adopted in 444AD. Pope Hilary (461-468AD) adopted that of Victorius of Acquitaine and finally, in 527AD, Felix III (IV) adopted amendments made by Dionysius Exiguus.

The Celtic Church's computation seems to have been one inherited from the Council of Arles in 314AD. They claimed John as the authority for this. The computation was based upon the Jewish lunar calendar which allowed Easter to fall, as did the Passover, in the month of Nisan (March/April). The first Easter had been on the 14th Nisan. Using this calculation the Celts celebrated Easter on the Sunday falling between the 14th and 20th days after the first full moon following the Spring Equinox. They would do this even if Easter so calculated fell on the same day as the Passover, and used an 84 year cycle. The Council of Nicaea in 325AD had declared it unlawful to celebrate a Christian festival on the same day as a Jewish one.

There were many other customs and rites that differed, baptismal rites and the rite of episcopal confirmation. The Celtic monasteries, while differing from locality to locality, were more like the Zen monasteries of the east. The Zen quality of the philosophy of the Celtic monks, an inheritance from the older druidic philosophy, comes through very clearly in an anonymous Irish verse of the 9th Century AD which Frank O'Connor translated thus:

To go to Rome—
Is little profit, endless pain;
The Master that you seek in Rome
You find at home, or seek in vain.

There was another major difference between the Celtic and Roman Churches—their attitude to land ownership. We have seen (in chapter one) that the native Celtic attitudes to property were akin to a 'community-ism' which did not recognise the right of absolute ownership.

The teachings of the early Church Fathers (Tertullian, Basil, Ambrose, John Chrysostum, Isidore and others) were forgotten as the Roman church developed, gaining temporal power as well as spiritual power. Property became an important concept to Rome. The Pope and his cardinals developed as temporal princes and eventually as feudal barons. Tribute in all forms of property was demanded and given to the Roman Church. The Celtic Church remained based on the Celtic social concepts.

According to William E. Montgomery (*Land Tenure in Ireland*, 1889):

Each clan had its own bishop, and its own priests, the diocese was merely the district occupied by the clan. There was naturally a great number of bishops . . . and it was not until the 12th Century that the present system of definite diocese grouped in provinces was introduced. The clan allotted to its clergy, for their support, certain lands . . . looked after by an officer who was generally a layman. The clergy of a clan mostly lived in communities under their bishop, so that the church was both tribal and monastic.

This meant that the Church had exactly the same restrictions on its land and property as any other person in society; they could not sell or buy land, nor try and use it in any way contrary to the tribal assembly. The Celtic monks and clergy had to contribute towards the welfare of the society in which they were living. They could not, as the Roman Church was now doing, demand tithes and tributes for the upkeep of their clergy without reciprocal contribution. These social attitudes were also an important cause of the subsequent conflict between Rome and the Celts.

At this historical point I propose to follow the fortunes of the Celtic Church in those territories in which it flourished under their modern designations for the sake of clarity. Although it is not technically correct to speak of Wales, Cornwall, Scotland, etc., during the 5th Century AD, by this time we can no longer speak meaningfully about a British Church, although the term 'British' as a description of the Welsh, Cornish, Cumbrians and Strathclyde British continued for many centuries afterwards. By dividing the history of the Celtic Church up into those areas now recognised as Celtic, it will make for an easier understanding.

Angel from a bronze at Clonmacnoise, Co. Offaly, Ireland. Clonmacnoise is the site of one of Ireland's most famous monasteries founded by St Kieran in 545. The remains here are the most extensive of their kind to be found in the country. It was finally destroyed by the English who removed everything of value in 1552. *The Book of the Dun Cow*, the most ancient of Irish manuscripts extant, and one of the greatest sources of Irish legends and myth, was compiled at Clonmacnoise.

4
Wales

St Govan's Chapel, spectacularly situated halfway down a cleft in cliffs at St Govan's Head, Bosherton, Dyfed. The building is 4 metres by 6½ metres and has been dated to the 11th Century, although it may be much older. Its origins are obscure. St Govan was an Irish saint who died in 586.

By the end of the 5th Century AD the British Church no longer existed for, as we have seen, the British had been pushed back to new geographical boundaries. One of these areas was a squat mountainous peninsula, thus affording some geographical protection from the incursions of the Anglo-Saxons which they were to call 'the land of foreigners' or Wales while the Welsh called it 'the land of comrades' – Cymru. The name Cymru was also the designation of the land of the Celts of the north west and has survived in the name Cumbria or Cumberland. After the establishment of the first monastic settlement in the Snowdonia region at Llanbeblig by Peblig ap Maxen in the early 5th Century AD, the country rapidly became Christianised by wandering monks who left a permanent impression on the countryside by their zeal and enthusiasm.

There are many traditions of this 'Age of Saints'. We hear of Brychan, who gave his name to Brycheiniog (Brecknock), who was said to have arrived in Wales from the Strathclyde British kingdom with thirteen sons and twenty-five daughters, all of whom became 'saints' in their stead. Their cults also appeared in Cornwall and Brittany. Also, at the beginning of the 5th Century AD, there is a tradition that a chieftain named Cunedda arrived in Wales. He had originally come from Manaw, just west of modern Edinburgh, and with him he brought eight sons all of whom perpetuated their names in church foundations and place names in Wales. Cunedda is also recorded as driving off Irish raiders. He 'expelled the Irish with immense slaughter from those regions who never returned again to inhabit them'.

Of the countless 'saints' who move as shadowy figures across the canvas of history at this time, a few stand out clearly – an indication of their importance. Dyfrig (Dubricius) was regarded as a major church leader during the second half of the 5th Century AD. Tradition has him born at Madly, a mile south of the Wye, and six miles west of Hereford, about the year 450AD. His mother was one of the many Celtic women involved in the early monastic movement – Efrddyl, daughter of Peiblio, ruler of Erging. Dyfrig is said to have founded monastic colleges at Henllon and Mochros, both on the Wye, where over 1,000 monks studied. He encouraged a monastic settlement on Caldey Island and, in his last years, he lived on Bardsey Island – known as Enlli, the holy island of the saints – where he is recorded as dying on November 14, 612AD. His name is found in many place-names. Saint Devereux in Hereford is but a corruption of his name. Medieval legends claim him as the archbishop who crowned Arthur while, in the 12th Century AD, the Normans used his name, claiming him as one of the founders of Llandaff, to establish it as a Norman bishopric. His relics were removed from Bardsey Island and placed in Llandaff in 1120AD.

Illtyd is another prominent name that occurs. According to the early *Life of St Samson* he was a Breton. There were, during this period, a number of Armoricans or Bretons working as monks in Wales, Cadfan, for example, who founded the monastic settlement on Bardsey. There were also numbers of Irish missionaries and their influence is shown in the numerous Ogham (early Irish) inscriptions and Irish-style crosses such as those at Nevern and Carew in South Wales. Illtyd, however, was said to have been born about 425AD and trained as a warrior. He seems to have been a soldier of fortune and entered the military service of Poulentius, the ruler of Glamorgan. He was dissatisfied with his life and a monk named Cadoc urged him to become a religious. He left his wife, who apparently became a nun, and threw himself enthusiastically into the work, establishing the great monastic school of Llanilltyd Fawr (Llantwit Major in Glamorgan). He also gave his name to Llaniltud near Coatbridge. According to the author of the *Life of St Samson* he was 'the most learned of all the Britons in the Old and New Testament, and in every kind of philosophy, that is, geometry and rhetoric, grammar and arithmetic and in all the arts of philosophy'. He was also 'by descent a most wise Magus Druid and a fore-knower of future events in whose magnificent monastery I was, whose wondrous deeds, if we took them one by one from the beginning we should be led to excess'. Illtyd died in 505AD.

Among the pupils who studied at Llanilltyd Fawr were David, Samson, Paul Aurelian and Gildas the historian.

Samson was a great influence not only in Wales but also in Cornwall and Brittany. What we know of him comes from the oldest of the extant complete *Lives* of the Celtic saints, one written about 610AD by an anonymous Breton who was urged to undertake the task by Bishop Tigernomalus, abbot of Dol in Brittany. Samson appears to have been born in 480AD and educated from an early age at Illtyd's monastic college. He was ordained by Dyfrig in 504AD and went to Caldey Island, *Ynys Byr*, opposite Tenby. Soon after he arrived there the abbot, Piro, died and Samson became abbot. After some time Samson returned to Llanilltyd. Illtyd was now dead. On February 2, 521AD, Samson was ordained bishop there. However, he was a restless man, and he soon left on a pilgrimage into Dumnonia, travelling through the still Celtic territories of Gloucester, Somerset, Devon and into Cornwall. He stayed there a short while before moving on to Brittany (chapters five and six). He became a significant founding father of the Breton Church and is on record as attending the Council of Paris in 557AD. He died in 560AD.

Paul Aurelian, or Pol, was a fellow pupil at Llanilltyd. He was the son of a local chieftain in South Wales and the first surviving account of his life was written by a monk Wrmonoc at Landévennec in Brittany. It is obvious that Wrmonoc was working from an early source. Pol eventually quit Wales and took a group of monks to Brittany via Cornwall where his sister, Sitofolla, was living as head of a religious community. Her name is connected with St Sativola of Laneast, near Launceston, and with Sidwell in Exeter. Pol stayed with her for a time at a monastic settlement near Gwavas Lake, Newlyn, and gave his name to the small parish of Paul there.

One of the famous pupils at Llanilltyd was Gildas, the author of *De Excidio Britonum* – The Ruin of Britain. He was born in the year of the battle of Mount Badon (516AD) in Strathclyde at Alcluyd (Dumbarton). His father was a chieftain named Caw. Gildas married and had two sons, Gwynnog and Noethon, who are accounted 'saints' in Denbigh. It was about 540AD that he wrote his history, although it is not so much a history as a fierce denunciation of the rulers and churchmen of his day. Maelgwyn Gwynedd, son of Cadwallon Lawhir, ruler of north-west Wales, is one of those singled out for attack. Although the work is the only surviving narrative of 5th Century AD Britain, unfortunately, for the historian, it does not add greatly to our knowledge.

Gildas' reputation stood high among his contemporary churchmen but he is less well thought of by later historians. Arthur J. Wade-Evans does not even believe that he wrote *De Excidio Britonum* arguing that there are stylistic differences with that work and *Epistularum Gildae Deperditarum Fragmenta* (Fragments of a Lost Letter of Gildas) and *De Poenitentia* (Gildas' Preface on Penance). It is not a popular theory.

Gildas is said to have worked among the Strathclyde British for a while with his 'soul friend', Cadoc, and stayed at the famous Candida Casa at Whithorn. One chronicler records a visit to Ireland in 560AD after which he is said to have migrated to Brittany and founded the monastery of St

Gildas de Rhuys in Morbihan where, in later years, the famous Abelard was abbot. The *Annales Cambriae* record his death there in 570AD.

Gildas' 'soul friend' Cadoc or Cadog emerges with great confusion. The earliest surviving *Life* is a 12th Century document written by Lifricus, son of Bishop Herwald (d. 1104AD), which places his birth at the impossible early date of 400AD. We are told that Cadoc went to study at Lismore in Ireland under Tatheus Mochuta. When he returned to Wales he brought with him three disciples; Finnian, who was to found Clonard monastery, Mac Moil and Gnawan. He is the traditional founder of Llancarfan, west of Cardiff. Tradition also has it that he visited Cornwall and Brittany, where he went to live as a hermit on an island off the coast near Vannes. The incursion of Frankish raiders forced him to leave and return to Wales. The *Life* is full of wild flights of fantasy.

The most famous of all the pupils at Llanilltyd, especially from the viewpoint of the Welsh, was their patron saint – Dewi or David. He was born in modern Pembroke. His mother was 'St Non' remembered there in St Non's Bay with its nearby St Non's Well and the scanty ruins of St Non's Chapel beyond which stands the 'Creed Cross Stone,' a rough stone engraved with a cross dating to the 5th Century AD. David's father was a chieftain named Sant, son of Ceredig, after whom Cardigan is named. After leaving Llanilltyd, David went to Candida Casa where he met many famous missionary workers such as Finbar of Moville, Co. Antrim. He worked in Somerset, Lincoln, Derby, Hereford and in his native Wales, founding twelve monasteries and many churches. His most famous foundation was on the land of Mynyw or Menevia (St David's).

What now remains there is Norman although David's Celtic monastery and church flourished, despite occasional Norse raids, attracting a significant reputation in Europe. Two pilgrimages to St David's became the equivalent of one to Rome. It was under the third Norman bishop, Peter de Leia, that the main reconstruction of the cathedral took place and the work continued to the 15th Century AD. St David's shrine was actually built in 1275AD close to a smaller and similar shrine to St Caradoc, a pious monk who died there in 1124AD. The south transept contains, on the east wall, the Abraham Stone, bearing a knotwork of a Celtic Cross, a Maltese Cross and a Latin Cross and an inscription to Hed and Isaac, the sons of Bishop Abraham, who were killed there with their father during a Norse raid. Tradition has it that the stone was a portable altar brought by David from Jerusalem during his pilgrimage to the Holy Land.

Little is really known about David. It is recorded that he became a bishop in 540AD, went on a pilgrimage to Jerusalem, with a friend Teilo, who hailed from Penally, near Tenby, and was a fellow pupil at Llanilltyd. Teilo founded Llandeilo Fawr in Carmarthen, and it is said that on his return from Jerusalem he stayed with Samson in Brittany during the period of the 'Yellow Plague'. David is also on record as taking part in two councils at Llandewi Brefi and at Caerleon. He went to Llandewi Brefi to preach against Pelagianism. As the crowds could not see him he mounted an earth mound on which the church now stands, Llandewi taking its name from him. The village is now small but at that time it was an important religious centre and in 1287AD Bishop Bec of St David's built a college there. It was at Llandewi Brefi that David was elected bishop of Caerleon and recognised as one of the most important churchmen in Wales. After a while David moved his bishopric to Menevia. Some chroniclers record his death there in 589AD.

These 'saints' were many and their *Lives* numerous. It was from the work of these shadowy men and women that the Christian Church was built among the Celts of Wales. Most of the prominent 'saints' of the period appear in South Wales while the only name of any importance in the north is that of Beuno whose cult was widespread.

Little remains of the monasteries and churches that these early missionaries built. The oldest remains are generally of Norman construction. Of these the most interesting is that of Strata Florida while Caldey Island still has a Cistercian monastery built on the site of a medieval priory. St Dogmael's ruined abbey still exists but this was rebuilt in 1115AD by the Norman Robert Fitz Martin. At Mwnt, Cardigan (from *Traeth y Mwynt* – Strand of the Mount) stands a little whitewashed church which dates to the 14th Century or slightly earlier which was built on the site of a Celtic chapel that was a station for pilgrims during the Dark Ages. One chapel that still seems to retain its early Celtic outlook is St Govan's Chapel at Bosherton which is spectacularly situated half-way down a cleft in the cliffs, access to which is made by a steep flight of stairs. Legend has it that Govan was Arthur's Sir Gawaine who turned hermit but there is also an Irish saint Govan who is recorded as dying in 586AD. The building is tiny, about 12 feet by 20 feet and most of it was rebuilt in the 11th Century.

At the great teaching monastery of Llanilltyd little remains from the period. In the grounds of the church which stands there now is a tall pillar on which is carved the words: *In nomine di sunmi incipit crux salvatoris quae preparavit Samsoni apati pro anima sua et pro anima Iuthelo Rex et Artmali tecani.* In the name of God Most High begins the cross of the Saviour which Abbot Samson prepared for his soul and for the soul of King Iuthael and Arthmael the Dead. The stone has been dated to the 9th Century AD and certainly there was a king of Gwent named Iuthael who, according to the *Annales Cambriae* and *Brut y Tywysogion* (Chronicle of the Welsh Princes) was killed in 848AD. Another stone is inscribed: *In nomine di patris et spiritus sancti anc crucem Houlet properabit pro anima Res patres eus.* Again, according to the *Brut y Tywysogion* Howel was king of Glamorgan and died in 855AD.

The monks in these early monastic foundations, with their literacy in Latin and Greek, also become repositories for the bardic learning that had once been a sophisticated oral tradition. They also recorded, in their native language, the vast collection of myth and poetry. According to the 9th Century AD Welsh historian, Nennius, during the 5th Century AD the works of the bards were written in Celtic. 'At that time Talhaern, father of the inspired song, was famed in poetry, at the same time also Aneirin and Taliesin and Bluchbard and Cian called Gwenith Gwawd were also alike famed in British poetry.' The earliest forms of collections of Welsh literature, however, dated from the 9th Century AD, and the works referred to as 'The Four Ancient Books' (White Book of Rhydderch, Red Book of Hergest, Book of Taliesin and Book of Aneirin) date from the 13th Century AD. Compared to the poetry inscribed by Christianity in Ireland, Welsh Christianity seems rather joyless. The vigour of the early Irish poets, the expressive joy of nature, the wonder at all living things, is not there. Instead of joy, sadness is the feeling which comes to one anonymous Welsh monk in the 12th Century as he reflects:

Month of May, loveliest season,
The birds loud, the growth green,
Plough in furrow, ox in yoke,
Green sea, land cut dapple.

In the fine treetops when cuckoos sing
My sadness is greater:
Smoke smart, manifest sleep lack,
For my kinsfolk gone to rest.

In hill, in dale, in isles of the sea,
Wheresoever one may go,
From Blest Christ there's no escaping.

In the secular poetry recorded, however, there is still a firm Celtic vibrancy and a tenderness that is the equal of the early Irish verses. A 7th Century AD 'Song to a Child' written by an anonymous scribe is an example of this.

Dinogad's cloak is pied, pied—
Made it out of marten hide.
Whit, whit, whistle along,
Eight slaves with you sing the song.

When your dad went to hunt,
Spear on shoulder, cudgel in hand,
He called his quick dogs, 'Giff you wretch,
Gaff, catch her, catch her, fetch, fetch!'

The Great Cross of St Brynach. This Celtic cross, 4 metres high, dates from the 10th Century. It stands by St Brynach's Church in Nevern, Dyfed, which was said to have been founded by Brynach in the 6th Century. The church is much restored although there are traces of the original stones and there is a 6th Century Ogham inscription nearby.

From a coracle he'd spear
Fish as a lion strikes a deer.
When your dad went to the crag
He brought down roebuck, boar and stag,
Speckled grouse from the mountain tall,
Fish from Derwent Waterfall.

Whatever your dad found with his spear,
Boar or wild cat, fox or deer,
Unless it flew, would never get clear.

It is fascinating that the 'classical period' of Welsh poetry did not begin until the Celtic Church was in decline. This period is regarded as being that between 1120 to 1250AD and represented by poets such as Cynddelw y Prydydd Mawr, Llywarch ap Llywelyn, Einion ap Gwgon and Dafydd Benfras. It was Dafydd Benfras who exclaimed in 1245AD:

I have never known a word of English...
I do not know a word of lively French...
May the Son of God
Give flowing Welsh to the land of Dafydd.

Benfras was not, of course, referring to St David–Dewi rather than Dafydd–but to Dafydd ap Llywelyn who was ruler of Wales 1240-46AD.

The monasteries of the 5th to 9th Centuries AD produced great religious books, copies of the Gospels, tracts and commentaries and theological works. One of the surviving and most famous of these books is the *Book of St Chad* now in Lichfield, which is known to have been produced in Wales sometime before the end of the 8th Century AD. Its Celtic artwork shows close affinities with early Irish manuscripts.

The church in Wales, as in other Celtic areas, based itself on the clan system and was monastic. These monasteries were organised on a *clas* or family basis. Members of the monastic community were often related, wives lived with husbands and children with parents as a religious family. Even after the Norman Conquest, when the *clas* system was prevalent in the chapters of cathedrals, members refused celibacy and the laity also refused to observe the long list of proscribed marriages announced at Rome. In all other respects the Welsh conformed with Celtic Church institutions. Certainly, from a very early stage, a lively intercourse between Wales and Ireland was established.

During the 8th Century AD important political changes took place which affected the country. A 'final' border between the Welsh and English was fixed by the powerful king of Mercia, Offa (757-796AD), who, following a victory over the Welsh at Hereford in 760AD, built a dyke which ran from the Severn to the Dee and effectively cut off the Welsh peninsula. The dyke, incidentally, cut off a large portion of the old kingdom of Powys – the richest agricultural portion, in fact. From a poem attributed to Llywarch Hen we hear of the desolation which was caused as the Anglo-Saxons annexed the area around Shrewsbury, formerly the city of Pengwern where Cynddylan once ruled.

> *The court of Pengwern is a raging fire...*
> *The hall of Cynddylan is dark tonight,*
> *Without a fire, without a bed,*
> *I weep a while, then fall silent.*

There is a pillar cross in the vale of Llangollen, set up in the first half of the 9th Century AD, by Cyngen, the last king of Powys. Cyngen commemorates the defeat of his great-grandfather Elis or Elise. 'It is Elise who annexed the heritage of Powys ... from the power of the English, which he made into a sword land by fire.' Cyngen died on a pilgrimage to Rome in 854AD. His sister's son Rhodri became king of Powys.

Rhodri was the ruler who finally united Wales into a centralised kingdom. It was during the period when the kingdoms of Britain were assuming the shapes by which we recognise them today. In 828AD Egbert of Wessex was recognised as overlord of all the English kingdoms and can therefore be said to be the first 'King of England'. In 843AD Kenneth Mac Alpin united the Dal Riadan kingdom with that of the Picts. Within a few centuries the Strathclyde British kingdom, the Cumbria British kingdom and parts of Bernicia would join to make Scotland, although Cumbria would soon be annexed to England. In Wales, too, the kingdoms of the Cymry began to unite. In 844AD Rhodri Fawr (Rhodri the Great) had succeeded his father Merfyn to the throne of Gwynedd. Rhodri's mother Nest was sister of Cyngen of Powys and when Cyngen died Rhodri claimed this kingdom. Later, on the death of Gwgon of Seisyllwg, in South Wales, he extended his rule to that kingdom and thus Rhodri was acknowledged ruler of all Wales.

It was Rhodri who discouraged the Norse raids into Wales for a time. Anglesey had been sacked in 853AD and thereafter attacks on the monasteries and churches were frequent. Rhodri won the praise of many western seaboard rulers, including the Franks, when he slew Gorm, the powerful Norse leader. But the Norse returned sporadically and in 984AD St David's, Llanilltyd and Llancarfan as well as Llanydoch went up in flames. St David's was attacked several times: its bishop Morgenau was killed in 999AD and bishop Abraham and his sons were killed in 1078AD. Rhodri himself was slain in 878AD by the English.

It was at this time that the anarchistic monasticism of the Welsh Celts also began to alter. The *Annales Cambriae* record that Bishop Elbddug of Bangor introduced the Roman calculation of Easter in 768AD in the kingdom of Gwynedd. *Brut y Tywysogion* maintains that it was introduced in 755AD. The South Wales kingdoms followed in 777AD. Elbddug, or

Elfoddw, we are told, put forward a claim to be metropolitan of all the Welsh territory. He seemed intent on Romanising the Celtic Church in Wales. When he died in 809AD 'a great dispute arose among the clerics because of Easter, the bishops of Llandaff and Menevia refusing to submit to the bishop of Gwynedd, themselves claiming to be bishops of older standing'. The 9th Century AD Welsh historian Nennius, whose *Historia Britonum* – History of Britain – dates from 829AD, was a disciple of Elfoddw. Nennius' history seems to be a series of 'excerpts' drawn from older sources.

The Celtic social order was still in existence when Hywel Dda (Hywel the Good), grandson of Rhodri, became ruler of Wales in 916AD. His reign, which lasted until 950AD, is of particular significance as the time when the codification of the Welsh law system was made. There are some seventy manuscript lawbooks which survive, most written in Welsh and a few in Latin. About half of these are late copies made during the 16th, 17th and 18th Centuries AD. The other half are older written between 1200 and 1500AD. One of these books was compiled by Iorwerth ap Madog who says he compiled it 'from the best books which he found in Gwynedd, Powys and Deheubarth'. Tradition has it that Hywel summoned a council of the chief ecclesiastics, together with six chieftains from the sub-divisions of the country. This assembly then examined and discussed the laws of Wales for a period of forty days and, as a result of their deliberations, they made improvements and changes and the revised laws were then recorded in one authorative book. Early texts say that the compilation was carried out under the supervision of one Blegywryd, archdeacon of Llandaff. Some references make him Blegywryd ab Einon of Gwent, 'a man learned in law' although some scholars are doubtful about his existence.

This was the period, too, when there came a despairing lament of the displaced Celts. A poem entitled *Armes Prydein* – The Prophecy of Britain – appeared calling on the Celtic world, the peoples of Wales, Cornwall, Cumbria, Strathclyde, Brittany, Ireland, Man and Scotland, to join together and throw the English out of Britain. St David would assist them from the heavenly sphere while the reincarnations of Cadwaladr and Cynan would be their leaders. The poem appeared about the same time that Athelstan of Wessex had just conquered Cornwall, and in 937AD, had also crushed a Celtic confederation of Scotland, Strathclyde and Ireland. It is probable that *Armes Prydein* was written in support of this struggle.

Following the Norman Conquest of England in 1066AD, individual Norman warlords, with their private armies, began to move across the Welsh border. Petty internal squabbling among the Welsh chieftains allowed many Normans to establish themselves in the country. The Normans found a church which was still markedly Celtic in character, in spite of the reforms of Elfoddw. Its institutions and customs differed widely from those with which the Normans were familiar. Such a state of affairs could not be tolerated and the Normans used their power and influence to bring the Celtic Church into line. In 1107AD Urban became the first Norman bishop in Wales, taking over the bishopric of Llandaff. Significantly, he made a full profession of obedience to Canterbury as the primacy.

Records exist, although they have not been accepted as authentic, that as early as the late 9th Century AD, Bishop Cyfeiliawe of Llandaff (d. 927AD) had accepted the primacy of Canterbury and been consecrated in office by its archbishop. After the Norman Conquest both Lanfranc and Anselm of Canterbury interfered constantly with Welsh ecclesiastical matters in spite of the claims of independence put forward by the bishops of St David's from 1070AD.

The Normans' policy was to replace the Welsh bishops with their own nominees. Rhygyfarch, the biographer of St David, had succeeded his father as bishop of St David's in 1089AD. After his death Daniel, the third son of Bishop Sulvin, was nominated by the Welsh clergy. The Normans set aside their decision in favour of Bernard, one of their number who became the first Norman bishop of the cathedral. He died in 1148AD and in the following years the struggle between the Welsh and Normans hardened. Eventually the struggle centred around the figure of Giraldus Cambrensis or Gerald of Barry. Gerald had been born in 1146AD, was educated partly in Paris and became archdeacon of Brecknock in 1175AD. His histories vigorously opposed Anglo-Saxon and Norman authority in Wales. Among his books were 'History of the Conquest of Ireland,' 1189AD; 'Itinerary of Wales,' 1191AD; and 'Description of Wales,' 1194AD. He was nominated bishop of St David's by the Welsh clergy in 1176AD. Henry II, knowing Gerald's attitudes, forced an ecclesiastical meeting at Winchester to appoint his favourite Peter de Leia, the prior of Wenloch Abbey. Gerald decided to fight the appointment all the way to Rome. During this period he rejected four Irish and two Welsh bishoprics to devote his time to demanding Welsh ecclesiastical independence from England. After two trips to Rome, he retired from the struggle in 1204AD and decided to write his biography. He visited Ireland for a second time in 1205-06AD and made another pilgrimage to Rome in 1207AD. He died about 1223AD.

The struggle was over but as late as 1284AD a bishop of St David's raised a formal protest against the visit and authority of Archbishop Pekham of Canterbury.

The Normans, now controlling the bishoprics, began to change the Celtic organisation moving against the *clas* system. The *clasau* were suppressed and their endowments transferred to Norman monasteries in England and in Normandy. Dedications to Celtic saints were replaced by dedications to more orthodox saints recognised by Rome. The great teaching monastery of Llanilltyd was shut down and its possessions passed to the abbey of Tewkesbury. Celtic monasteries were replaced by Benedictine Houses. To the end of their existence in Wales the Benedictines, or 'Black Monks', were recruited from the non-Welsh population and failed to make an impression on the people. When the Cistercians began to form their communities they were not associated with the conquerors in the Welsh minds. They lived a life similar to the old Celtic monks, seeking out the solitude of mountains and moorland and in their austere discipline there were also similarities. It was the Cistercians that established cradles of learning, became patrons of literature and pioneers in agriculture. Strata Florida, Conway, Valle Crucis, Margam and Tintern were among their most hallowed foundations in medieval Wales. Dominicans and Franciscans followed them.

Under Norman supervision the old Celtic order was broken. Bishops, with Wales divided into four bishoprics of St David's, Llandaff, St Asaph and Bangor, now drew emoluments from tithes and offerings of the parish. Sometimes a Norman feudal lord would give away a church and its parish to some English or Norman Abbey in return for ecclesiastical favours. One thing the Normans failed to make an impact on was the celibacy of the clergy. Right down to the eve of the Reformation the Welsh priests continued to marry.

But there were some sympathetic people among the settlers who had arrived in Wales with the Normans. A Breton family had accompanied the Normans and settled in Monmouth. The son of this family was named Geoffrey. He spent some years as a secular canon at Oxford before being ordained and eventually becoming the bishop of St Asaph in 1152AD. Geoffrey's fame rests with his work *Historia Regum Britanniae* – The History of the Kings of Britain – which purports to be an account of the history of the British Celts from 1100BC to the time of Cadwaladr of the 7th Century AD. Geoffrey disclaimed that he was the author of this history, saying he was just a translator. In his opening remarks he says:

> *Walter, Archdeacon of Oxford, a man skilled in the art of public speaking and well informed about the history of foreign countries, presented me with a certain very ancient book written in the British language. The book, attractively composed to form a consecutive and orderly narrative, set out all the deeds of these men, from Brutus, the first king of the Britons down to Cadwallader the son of Cadwallo. At Walter's request I have taken the trouble to translate the book into Latin . . .*

It has been the fashion among scholars to dismiss this statement as a piece of 'dressing' and place the work as a result of Geoffrey's fertile imagination. Sir John Lloyd has written: 'No Welsh composition exists which can be reasonably looked upon as the original or even the groundwork of the

History of the Kings of Britain.' Even if we ignore the quite reasonable prospect of a Welsh manuscript being lost, why must the 'British language' be Welsh? There were two other languages at this time that were regarded as being 'British' too. As Geoffrey came from a Breton family he might have been more specific if he were dealing with a Breton manuscript. My contention is that the book had its provenance in Cornwall.

In the 12th Century AD John of Cornwall wrote a poem in Latin hexameters dedicated to Bishop Warewast entitled 'The Prophecy of Merlin'. John claimed that he was simply translating this from an early Cornish manuscript. The only copy of John's work that survives is one in the Vatican Library dated October 8, 1474AD, but this work, thankfully, contains glosses and notes in the original Cornish. Geoffrey's work also contains a section entitled 'The Prophecies of Merlin' and the content of the two pieces can be compared.

Geoffrey's *Historia* was written about 1136AD and in 1155AD Geoffrey popularised his work by using the material to write an epic poem in Norman French entitled *Roman de Brut*. This 15,000 line poem was apparently completed by Wace, a native of Jersey. Geoffrey's only other known work was *Vita Merlini* – Life of Merlin – written about 1148AD, a fanciful poem of over 1,500 lines.

Anglo-Saxon England had fallen to the Normans at a blow but in Wales the struggle took two centuries with violent swings of the pendulum before the last native Welsh ruler, Llywelyn ap Gruffydd ap Llywelyn was slain in December, 1282AD. Even then the struggle continued for another six months under the leadership of his brother David who was eventually captured and put to death at Shrewsbury in June, 1283AD. The poet Gruffydd ab yr Ynad Coch summed up the despair:

Oh God! that the sea might engulf the land!
Why are we left to long drawn weariness?

Yet the Welsh were a tenacious people. There followed rising upon uprising against the English. Rhys ap Meredith in 1287AD: that of Madog in 1294AD; of Llywellyn Bren in 1301AD and finally the most famous Owain Glyn Dŵr who declared Welsh independence in 1401, summoning a Welsh parliament in 1404AD and managing to retain independence until 1415AD when he was slain in battle. In 1535AD Wales was annexed to England and the Act of Annexation (re-named the Act of Union in the 19th Century as a sop to Welsh national feeling) set out its intentions to 'utterly extirp' the Welsh language and culture. It was an intention that failed and it was the pen of Gerald of Barry who put the Welsh attitude in the mouth of an unnamed Welshman speaking to Henry II at Pencader in 1163AD.

This nation, O king, as it deserves, may be oppressed and very largely destroyed and weakened through thy might and that of others, now as in days gone by and many times to come. Completely exterminated, however, it will not be through the wrath of man, unless it be the wrath of God accompanies it. And no nation, so I deem, other than this of the Welsh, and no other language, upon the stern Day of Judgement before the Most High Judge, will answer—whatever may happen to the greater remainder of it—for this little corner of the earth.

The Reformation met with little resistance in Wales. The repression after Owain Glyn Dŵr of the monks and lower clergy who had supported him made religion in Wales seem merely part of the foreign domination. All Welsh bishops were appointed from England and few members of the clergy were actually natives. The people were scarcely aware of religion as a body of doctrine, but simply accepted the practices of the church as a system which was permanent and immutable, governed by bishops (most of whom never even visited their dioceses but preferred to live in England) and clergy appointed by a foreign nation. In no sense did the Reformation come as a liberation of the human spirit. It was simply another political change ordered by an alien government.

What the Reformation did bring to Wales was a flurry of activity in the native language. In 1567AD a Welsh version of the Book of Common Prayer and then a New Testament were published. In 1588AD the first complete Bible in Welsh appeared to be followed by a new translation in 1620AD while *Y Beibl Bach* (The Little Bible) was issued for general distribution in 1630AD. A group of Welsh Catholics tried to counter this and Morris Clynnog, who became rector of the English College in Rome (ironically founded by another Welshman Owen Lewis in 1578AD) produced a book entitled *Athravaeth Gristnogawl* (Christian Doctrine) in 1567. Another Catholic Griffith Roberts, who published a Welsh Grammar entitled *Gramadeg Cynmraeg* also in 1567AD, wrote and published a work called *Y Drych Cristianogawl* (The Christian Mirror) in 1585AD. While the title page claims it was published in Rouen it seems to have been printed on an 'underground' press in a cave in North Wales.

Both Anglican Church and Catholic Church vied with each other to claim the allegiance of the Welsh. Wales rejected them both and turned to Puritanism, to the Nonconformity of Presbyterianism which took strong root in Wales towards the middle of the 17th Century AD. Presbyterian and Baptist chapels began to appear everywhere and then, in the 18th Century, the Wesley brothers found Wales a fertile ground for their new teachings of Methodism. The ancient traditions of the Celtic Church were no more.

Capital from the doorway of the 12th Century Round Tower at Timahoe, Leix, Ireland.

5
Cornwall

For centuries Cornwall had been left in peaceful obscurity. There is scarcely any sign of Roman penetration and settlement and it was not until the Saxon expansions that the Celts of the peninsula began to feel threatened. As the Saxons established their kingdom of Wessex, so the Celtic population were constrained westward to form a kingdom called Dumnonia (from where Devon takes its name) which became separate from the Celts of Wales when the Saxons Caewlin and Cutha forced a Saxon wedge as far as the Severn river in 577AD. It was not until the 8th Century AD that Dumnonia crumbled and the land of the 'Cornish foreigners'—*Kern-welisc* (Cornwall) stood by itself.

Because of the lack of Roman penetration it is assumed that Christianity made little impact on the extreme west of Dumnonia until the 'Age of Saints' (450-600AD). Then came a period of legends:— the legends of Arthur are the strongest in Cornwall, reinforced with place name evidence; legends of King Mark of Cornwall and his nephew Tristan and Iseult; legends of tribes of 'saints' from Ireland and Wales and even Brittany. Many stayed in Cornwall, others moved on; most left their names in remembrance; names attached to holy wells, churches, towns and villages. There is evidence that these 'saints' also wandered and settled in other parts of Dumnonia but that the early Saxon conquest of the eastern part—Dorset and Devon—quickly dispersed any growth of Celtic tradition.

Most of the *Lives* of the Cornish 'saints' were preserved in the monasteries there but then destroyed during the Reformation. John Leland was just in time to see a few of them and make notes from them in his *Itinerary* which he wrote during a series of journeys through the country between 1535-1543.

St Michael's Mount, which legend suggests is the east side of the drowned kingdom of Lyonesse. The Cornish name is *Cara luz en cuz* (the hoar rock in the wood) and there are remains of an underwater forest around it. A Celtic monastery was founded there as early as the 5th Century. In 1044 it became a Benedictine house in the wake of the English conquest of Cornwall. In 1425 it was given to the Brigettines of Syon who remained there until the Dissolution. It became a National Trust property in 1954.

One interesting group of Irish missionaries were said to have landed in Cornwall at this time (6th Century, AD led by Gwinear, thought to be synonymous with the Irish Fingar and who appears as Guigner in Brittany. Among his group was his sister, Piala (remembered in Phillack), Ia (St Ives) Uny and Erc and many others. This group of missionaries landed at the Hayle Estuary and then proceeded to a town called Conetconia (Lelant) where they encountered Tewdrig (Tudor) who put many of them to death, including Gwinear. This is the only traditional martyrdom of Celtic Christians. The medieval *Life* of Gwinear says that Tudor had the missionaries executed 'fearing lest they might convert his people to the faith of Christ'. The same source makes Tudor, ridiculously, a Muslim. Some scholars have suggested that he was a Christian who simply resented the Irish intrusion. He is an intriguing person – the origin of the name Tudor means 'king of the tribe' – and he appears again in *Bewnans Meriasek*, the medieval life of Meriasek or Meriadoc, the Breton who became the patron saint of Camborne. Meriasek only just managed to escape a martyr's fate at the Cornish ruler's hands.

At Phillack, named after Gwinear's sister Piala, the medieval church has a stone set over the door of the south porch which bears a 6th Century AD *Chi—Rho* symbol. Of Gwinear's group, Ia (St Ives) is said to have been the daughter of an Irish chieftain who arrived in Cornwall floating on a large leaf. Anyone who has seen an Irish curragh will know what visual imagery the writer had in mind. St Ives, in Cornish, was known as Porth Ia. The legend is that she escaped from Tudor and, under the protection of the chieftain named Dinan, built her church at St Ives. Ia's brother Uny, one of those slain, is remembered in many place names and the ancient church which existed in Wendron was dedicated to Merther Uny (The Martyred Uny). Ia's other brother Erc is remembered in St Erth.

Perhaps the most famous of these early 'saints' was Petroc, the son of a Welsh chieftain, whose name is remembered not only in Cornwall but in Somerset, Devon, Wales and Brittany. He is recorded as being an uncle to Cadoc of Llancarfan. After studying at an Irish monastery he went on a mission to Cornwall, landing in the Camel estuary. About this time a wandering monk named Gorran had built a hermitage on the south west side of Bodmin moor. When Gorran moved to a new site near Mevagissey Petroc decided to found a monastery at the former hermitage from which the town took its name of *Bod-minachau*, the place of the monks. Petroc is said to have journeyed widely through Dumnonia and also to have founded what was to become Buckfast Abbey. His chief monastic centre was to be at Padstow (Petroc's town). It was here that Petroc is said to have given hospitality to Samson who journeyed through Dumnonia to Cornwall in 521AD. Samson also stayed at the monastery of Docco, St Kew, founded by Dochau, a cousin of Illtyd. Today St Kew is known for a 6th Century AD Ogham stone with the name 'Iusti' – Justus. This might be a fascinating reference to St Just, claimed to be an Irishman who once coveted and pocketed a piece of plate belonging to his friend Keverne. Petroc died at his monastery of Padstow in 543AD and his monks took his remains for burial at Bodmin. In 1177AD a malcontent canon at Bodmin, Martin, stole the relics and took them to St Meén's monastery in Brittany. After some protest, the remains were returned.

Of the mainly Irish saints who arrived in Cornwall during this period none became more popular that Piran, now regarded as the patron saint of Cornwall. His name is widely also celebrated in Wales (where there is a medieval chapel dedicated to him in Cardiff) and in Brittany. The name, sometimes recorded as Perran, is thought to be synonymous with Ciaran of Saighair who died circa 480AD. Exeter Cathedral once claimed to have preserved one of his arms while an inventory of 1281AD mentions that St Piran's Church had his head which was placed in a specially made case in 1433AD when Sir John Arundell donated forty shillings for this purpose. On the shifting sands at Perranzabuloe (Perran-in-the-Sands) lies a half buried oratory dated to the 6th Century AD, built in the manner of the Celtic chapels of Ireland. This is said to be the oldest church in the south-west and claimed as the centre of Piran's monastery, thought to be in occupation until the 11th Century AD. Today, St Piran's Day, March 5, is regarded as Cornwall's national day and the Cornish flag, bearing the cross of St Piran, can be seen everywhere in the duchy.

Cuby (known as Kebi in Wales) was rare among the 'saints' as being a native Cornishman. His father was said to be Selevan, a Celtic form of Solomon, which has been corrupted in the place-name St Levan. Cuby is said to have been born in Tregony, went to Wales where he became a friend of David and founded a monastery on Anglesey, now known as Holyhead. Cuby, in Cornwall, is a parish without a village. The church is interesting in that it has a 6th Century AD stone inscribed 'Nonnita, Ercilinus, Rigatus, the three sons of Ercilinus'.

St Mawgan is claimed to be a disciple of Patrick who built an oratory at St Mawgan in Pydar; Mawes was another Irishman who settled down at a Holy well to meditate on the setting sun and gave his name to that spot; Buryan is said to be the daughter of an Irish chieftain who arrived in Cornwall in the 5th Century AD. Her tomb at St Buryan was visited by Athelstan, the conqueror of Cornwall, about 931AD who promised that if he conquered the Scillies he would return and build a church in her honour, which he did.

One of the most mysterious 'saints' was Neot, dated to the 5th or 6th Century AD and said to be a monk from Glastonbury who moved to Cornwall in search of greater solitude. At the place now given his name there is said to be an older shrine to Gueryr, another missionary. There is also a claim that his name forms part of Menheniot – the sanctuary of Neot, though it is St Lalluwy (Ladislas) to whom the church is dedicated.

In a *Life* of Neot we are also told that he was a half brother of Alfred and that he founded a school at Hamstoke. The same *Life* gives us the popular tale of Alfred burning the cakes! However, as Alfred lived in the 9th Century AD, and the traditions of Neot are mainly four centuries earlier, Neot becomes a confusing figure.

The *Lives* of the 'saints' cannot be judged as trustworthy historical documents or evidence as to certain individuals. Taken as a whole they do show that this corner of the Celtic world was very much a hive of Christian activity at this period. There is also much archaeological evidence which supports the activity of evangelisers from Ireland, especially in the area of the Camel river. Five of Cornwall's six Ogham inscriptions come from the region. There are several further stones, not Ogham, bearing Irish names. Of the Ogham inscriptions, one at St Endelion, near Roscarrock, records: 'Brocagnus lies here, the son of Nadottus.' Some scholars are prepared to accept that Brocagnus was the semi-mythical Welsh Brychan and point to the fact that the names of his 'saintly' children are to be found across Cornwall – St Endelion, St Teath, St Minver, St Mabyn, St Kew, St Issy and St Ive (not to be confused with St Ives).

It has been estimated that there were some 98 monastic foundations in Cornwall during this period. One of the most intriguing was at Tintagel (alas, not Arthur's Camelot). The people who go to see the castle there, believing they are looking on Arthur's famous fortress, are, in fact, gazing upon a Norman 11th Century AD construction. They tend to miss the remains of the Celtic monastery on the island that lies behind the castle. The remains of a 4th Century AD farmstead were found there. Tradition has it that about 500AD a wandering nun named Juliot, also claimed as a daughter of Brychan, built a cell here which swiftly grew into the monastic community. Archaeologists have found various extensions to the site made up to the 9th Century AD when the monastery was deserted, presumably during the Saxon conquest. Certainly by the time of the Domesday survey in 1086AD, the monks no longer inhabited the crumbling ruins.

More famous, St Michael's Mount sprung out of another Celtic monastic foundation. Legend has it that the island was all that remained of the lost Arthurian kingdom of Lyonesse and that the bells of scores of drowned churches may be heard tolling beneath the sea around the island. The Cornish originally named it *Cara luz en cuz* – the hoar rock in the wood. There are traces of submerged forest around it and tradition has it that it was once surrounded by dense woodland. One tradition says that in 495AD a vision of St Michael appeared to a group of local fishermen and they built the first chapel on the island. Certainly, during the 'Age of Saints' a monastic settlement was established. In 1044AD the monastery was given to the Benedictines and it became a daughter house of St

Michael's Mount in Brittany. In 1425AD the Benedictines were turned out and it was given to an order known as the Brigettines of Syon with whom it remained until the Dissolution. The refectory is now the oldest building on the Mount, its walls surviving from the 12th Century AD.

One of the most important monastic foundations in Cornwall was Glasney Priory. Although we have no hard evidence that it was founded before the Saxon Conquest, it became the most important centre of early medieval Cornish learning. Glasneth, Old Cornish losing the final *th* sound, means 'green vegetation' and stood on a heavily wooded area of Penryn, bordering a river. Walter Brandscombe, the bishop of Exeter, laid a foundation stone brought from Caen for the monastic college in 1265AD. The priory became renowned as a seat of learning not only for Cornwall but all the south-west and many of its provosts were drawn from prominent scholars of Oxford. Had it not been suppressed in 1535AD it might well have become the foundation of a university of Cornwall. However, after lingering on into the 1540's, it became a borough gaol and was pulled down in the 19th Century.

Glasney is important because it was where the Middle Cornish 'miracle plays' appear to have been written, the centre of Cornish literary activity and bulwark against the increasing pressure from the English language.

It seems that the Celtic Church in Cornwall first submitted to the jurisdiction of Canterbury in the mid-9th Century AD. A century before, Dumnonia was still fairly intact as a kingdom and its ruler was Geraint. In 705AD Aldhelm, the first English scholar of distinction, who, in that year, had been appointed by King Ine as the first bishop of Sherborne, wrote to Geraint rebuking him for adhering to the Celtic Church and asking him to turn to Roman orthodoxy. Within a few years of this date the West Saxons were once more extending their frontiers and by 710AD they had reached as far as Exeter, Geraint had been slain in a battle at Langpert and the Dumnonia kingdom had ceased to exist. Geraint makes an appearance in legendary form in the Welsh Mabinogion. There is also 'A Lament to Geraint' supposedly written by Llywarch Hen, but Sir Ifor Williams has shown that the poems attributed to Llywarch Hen were written about him at a later date. The death of Geraint was a bitter blow for the Celts of the south west.

In 721/2AD they managed to rally and defeat the Saxons on the banks of the Camel. This battle is traditionally called Slaughter Bridge, near Camelford, and has become entwined in the Arthurian legend. The defeat of the Saxons gave the Celts a further century of freedom. In 814AD Egbert of Wessex resumed the attack. In 825AD we hear of another major defeat for the Celts. It is then that Bishop Kentsec emerges as bishop of the south west Celts or Cornish. He is on record as writing to Ceolnoth, archbishop of Canterbury (833-70AD) acknowledging his jurisdiction. Yet in 838AD the Cornish made an alliance with the Norse to expel the

Carved 9th Century figure of a saint, in the wall of the 12th Century church on White Isle, Co. Fermanagh, Ireland.

Saxons from their lands. That year a combined Cornish and Norse army met Egbert at Hingston and were defeated.

By a stroke of luck Egbert died the following year and was unable to follow up his advantage. His successor ignored Cornwall which still flourished under its native rulers. One ruler we know about was Dumgarth, or Doniert, who was said to have drowned accidentally in 878AD. In St Cleer, north of Liskeard, stands a stone monument dated to this period which states: *Doniert Rogavit pro Anima* – Doniert set this up for the good of his soul. We also have an intriguing monument which stands outside Penlee House, Penzance, commemorating a Cornish king of the 10th Century, who surely must have been the last of the native Cornish rulers. *Regis Ricati Crux* – the cross of King Ricat(us).

During this period we find interesting evidence of the fear of the Saxon incursions. In 1774AD, at Trewhiddle near St Austell, a hoard of silver artifacts was discovered – mounts for drinking horns, rings, a brooch, a large pin with an engraved head, a small box, a scourge of silver wire, a silver chalice and a collection of Saxon coins, many of them silver. The date of the coins, from Wessex and Mercia, points to the treasure being buried around 878AD, probably by a nervous Cornish monk in anticipation of the next raid.

It was not until 930AD that Athelstan, the grandson of Alfred, finally conquered and brought the Cornish remnants of the Dumnonia kingdom under English control. Here we have an intriguing piece of historic interpretation for Athelstan is on record as having driven the Celts out of Exeter and established the Tamar as the boundary between England and the *West Welisc*. It has been argued that this means that the Celts were still living east of the Tamar as far as the environs of Exeter until the 10th Century AD, and that in 930AD Athelstan simply drove them to the Tamar, settled the dispossessed areas and asserted his suzerein authority over the land beyond the Tamar. Orthodox scholarship dismisses the idea entirely, believing that the Tamar was a boundary between the Celts and the English long before this date. Yet, at the time of the Norman Conquest, we still find that Cornwall is ruled by a native Cornishman, Cador (sometimes written as Condor) who was recognised as the *eorl* of Cornwall. He was deposed by William of Normandy but his son Cadoc was reinstated. In 1104AD the daughter of Cadoc, Avice or Beatrix, married Reginald Fitz Henry, son of Henry I, who inherited the earldom through his wife. It was clear that Athelstan and his immediate successors did not absorb Cornwall as they had the rest of Dumnonia. Edmund (939-46AD) had a charter drawn up in 944AD in which he styled himself 'King of the English and this British Province' while the phrase 'in Anglia et Cornubia' occurs in several medieval documents.

However, with Athelstan's overlordship of Cornwall beyond dispute, the Celtic Church began to be reorganised on the Saxon model. In 931AD

Athelstan created a diocese of Cornwall appointing (again significantly) a native Cornishman named Conan as its first bishop with the seat of the primacy at St Germans. It was an astute political move because this placed the ecclesiastical capital on the eastern border with England. Padstow, Cornwall's principal monastic foundation, would have been an obvious choice but it was here that Celtic monasticism was at its strongest. It was at Padstow that the only surviving Celtic gospel book from the period was written. This is the famous *Bodmin Gospels*, originally known as *St Petroc's Gospels*, written sometime during the 9th and 10th Centuries AD. The book was kept in Petroc's monastery until its sack in 981AD. On the spare leaves and margins of the book is a record of the ceremonies of manumissions, the freeing of slaves, covering the period from 940 to 1040AD. Of the 122 slaves listed as being freed the overwhelming number of names are Cornish, the majority of slave owners being Saxon.

With the death of Athelstan, it seems that all subsequent bishops of Cornwall were appointed from Englishmen and the Celtic monasticism was on the defensive. The Celtic form of service was abandoned and Roman orthodoxy was in force. The Celtic community at St Michael's Mount was dissolved and it was reconstituted as a collegiate church in 1050AD. At the same time another Celtic monastery at St Buryan was dissolved and reformed as a collegiate church. In the reform of the Celtic monastic centres it is more than a probability that a wealth of manuscripts not only in Latin but in Cornish were destroyed, accounting for our sad remains in early Cornish manuscripts. That such manuscripts did exist at some stage can be demonstrated by John of Cornwall's 12th Century reference to such a work which he translated into Latin (see under *Wales*). Unfortunately the destruction of the Celtic monasteries of Cornwall saw much of worth destroyed.

When in 1040AD the English bishop of Cornwall, Burghold, died, the diocese was abolished and Cornwall was brought under the bishopric of Crediton in Devon. In 1050AD this see was moved to Exeter where it remained until a new Cornish diocese was created in Truro in 1876. Now the slow decline of the Celtic way of life in Cornwall began. Although it is not in the Celtic Church period, it is fascinating to note the popularity of medieval religious plays in the Cornish language. The Cornish 'Miracle Plays' constitute the bulk of early Cornish literature. The biggest of these works is the *Ordinalia*, a cycle of three religious dramas, said to have originated from Glasney during the period 1275AD to 1450AD. These plays include 'The Creation of the World', 'The Passion of Christ' and 'The Resurrection of Our Lord'. The most interesting play surviving from this period is *Bewnans Meriasek*, the Life of Meriasek, mentioned earlier. In the earliest manuscript of this play we find the signature of cominus Rad Ton and the date 1504AD. He has been identified as Dominus Ricardus Ton who, in 1537, was parish priest of Crowan, near Camborne. There were other plays which are now lost, a fragment of one containing 41 lines was found on the back of an old charter dated 1340AD. Another work from the period is *Pascon agan Arluth* – The Passion Poem, a versified narrative of the Passion of Christ.

Religion, even in the Roman form, therefore kept the Cornish language and consciousness alive during this period. In 1497AD the Cornish rose up against Tudor centralism and were defeated. When, during the Reformation, English was introduced into religious services in 1540 and in January, 1549, Parliament passed its first Act of Uniformity introducing the English language in all religious matters in England, Wales and Cornwall, the Cornish rose up once again. The leaders of their insurgent army drew up articles of supplication to the king. Their demands were entirely conservative, concerned wholly with religious demands such as retention of usage. Perhaps the most important item was that of Article Eight in which they pointed out: 'we, the Cornish men, whereof certain of us understand no English, utterly refuse this new English' (service). After initial military successes the Cornish were defeated at Exeter. The new service was ruthlessly enforced.

For some time the Cornish clung to Catholicism, sending their priests abroad to be educated and ordained. We find that in 1600AD a Cornish priest named Richard Pentrey, then a student at Valladolid, actually gave an oration to Philip III and his wife Queen Margaret in the Cornish language. An account of this was given by Don Antonio Ortes in his book entitled 'Relation of the visit of the Catholic Kings' published that year. Through the 17th Century both language and religion in Cornwall fell into a decline. One of those fascinating historical 'ifs' presents itself. If the Bible and Prayer Book had been available to the Cornish and the native language used in the new Reformation services, as it was in Wales, then perhaps Cornish might have survived longer than it did. As a community language, it did survive into the 18th Century, while in religious matters the Cornish seemed in a limbo. Then, at the end of the 18th Century the Wesley brothers arrived and found a receptive audience for their work. Within a few short years Cornwall had turned to the Nonconformity of Methodism.

A border from the Book of Durrow, a 7th Century Irish illuminated manuscript now in Trinity College, Dublin. It is a volume of the Gospels which were recorded as having been in the possession of the monastery of Durrow, near Tullamore, Co. Offaly.

6
Brittany

Brittany was first called Armorica – the country beside the sea – by its Celtic inhabitants. During the Roman Conquest of Gaul it had been a centre of strong resistance and Julius Caesar was eloquent about the seafaring power of the Veneti, who gave their name to Vannes and who sent a powerful fleet of 220 ships to oppose the Romans. After the conquest Armorica still proved troublesome but was eventually incorporated into the administration of Roman Gaul. During the Germanic incursions into Gaul, a defensive military system was drawn up by the Emperor Honorious (395-423AD) seeking to protect the peninsula. Neither the Franks nor the Saxons succeeded in getting established there. But now there came wave after wave of Celtic emigrants from Britain and soon Armorica had become Brittany – 'Little Britain.' According to Nora Chadwick, the orthodox view that the British Celts were escaping from the Anglo-Saxon invasions in Britain is not true. She maintains, with conviction, that the migration to Brittany began earlier and was, because of place-name evidence, from the south-west of Britain, an area not then feeling the attacks of the Anglo-Saxons. She also maintains that the bulk of the leaders of this migration came from Wales, an area where no Saxon threat was then felt. Her contention is that the British Celts left to escape Irish raids in Britain. However, Gildas, our earliest authority for the migration, speaks of the *ferocissimi Saxones* and regards them as responsible for the movement.

Mont St Michel (Britanny's St Michael's Mount). The first buildings on this granite outcrop 80 metres high are recorded as being established by St Aubert in the 8th Century, although legend has it that there had been an earlier Celtic settlement. The earliest remains, however, date to the Carolingian Abbey in the 10th Century and most of the prominent remains are from the Gothic erections of the 13th to 16th Centuries.

Nora Chadwick's place-name evidence is, however, sound. The kingdom of Dumnonia could also be found in Brittany as Damnonia and Cornwall (Kernow) could be found as Cornouaille (Kernev) thus creating confusion among historians as, in some documents, one is unsure whether the references are to Britain or Brittany. Whatever the causes of the migrations, by the 6th Century AD Armorica no longer existed but Brittany had emerged speaking the British Celtic language. Again we enter into scholastic dispute. Abbé Francois Falc'hun suggests that at first the indigenous Armoricans retained their Gaulish speech while the immigrants spoke British and that British was then absorbed into Gaulish to create Breton. This is disputed by Professor Kenneth Jackson who says that British pre-dominated and that Breton is not a survival of Gaulish. However, it is not a significant point of contention because both Gaulish and British were dialects of the same Brythonic branch of Celtic.

What is clear is that the British Celts did not invade Armorica as military conquerors. All the evidence suggests they settled peacefully and that the leaders of the migrations were churchmen. Place-names and traditions incorporated in the many 9th Century AD Breton *Lives* of the 'saints' back up the idea that the settlers were families of priests and monks and their followers. The original inhabitants were already Christian, part of the early Gaulish Church. One of the earliest records of Christianity in Brittany occurs with the record of the martyrdom of two young brothers Donatianus and Rogatianus of Nantes in 288AD. The Armoricans, at the time of the British migrations, had been brought under the jurisdiction of Rome and governed from Tours. Peretus of Tours presided over a Council at Vannes in 465AD. But the settlers brought with them the traditions of the insular Celtic Church and a strong determination for independence. They had seen their own country falling before the Anglo-Saxons and were determined that their new country would not fall before the Franks. Gregory, bishop of Tours, such a vital source for gossip on church affairs, is strangely silent on the Celtic Church under his titular jurisdiction. However, we do find the Council of Tours having to pass resolutions which sought to bring the Celts of Brittany into conformity with the Roman Order. The Bretons simply tended to ignore Tours and in 866AD the Council of Tours meeting at Soissons complained to Pope Nicholas I that the Bretons never attended their council meetings.

The Bretons clung determinedly to their traditions. Between 515AD and 520AD three bishops of the province of Tours wrote to two Breton priests, Lovocat and Catihrin, accusing them of abuses by allowing women to administer the Eucharist. In Celtic society, as we have seen, women enjoyed equal status and the Celtic Church gives us nearly as many traditions of women 'saints' as male 'saints'. Breton independence in religious matters was certainly a sore point with Tours and in 567AD the Council of Tours warned the Bretons.

Let no pontiff presume to give episcopal consecration in Armorica either to a Briton or a Roman without the sanction of the Metropolitan or the bishops of the province on pain of excommunication.

The British immigrants changed the face of Brittany and by the 6th Century AD three important kingdoms had emerged; that of Domnonia or Dumnonia covering the north and, after 530AD, including Léon in the north west; that of Cornouaille (Kernev) to the south west from Mont d'Arrée and east to the River Ellé; and last the land known as Bro Erech or Bro Weroc, the land of Weroch, which is believed to have been named after the Breton ruler Weroch II (circa 577-94), covering the south. Weroch established himself in this area and hotly disputed the territorial advances of the Franks.

The foundation of these kingdoms was due in no small part to the 'saints'. It seems highly significant that, reading the 9th Century AD Breton *Lives* we find that most of the 'saints' came from the ruling families of British tribes and kingdoms. It is reasonable to suppose that many of these 'saints' were also tribal chieftains who had moved their entire tribes to the new homeland.

Like Cornwall the 'saints' are legion and still live in the place-names throughout the peninsula. Among them was the famous student of Llanilltyd, Paul Aurelian, or Pol, who set up his first monastery on Ushant; then another in Lampaul in Ploudalmexeau, and then another on the Isle of Baty. Pol became bishop of Léon and hence the town is now known as St Pol-de-Léon, which was a prominent monastic settlement developing into one of the most important Breton bishoprics. The cathedral which survives there was rebuilt in the 13th Century AD.

Another important religious centre founded in the 6th Century AD was Quimper, the capital of the kingdom of Cornouaille, which was founded by Corentin. Legend has it that Gradlon, the ruler of Cornouaille, had his capital at Is which was swamped by the sea. In this tragedy Gradlon lost his daughter Dahut, of which a fascinating legend has arisen making the unfortunate Dahut turn into a mermaid luring men to their doom. Corentin helped Gradlon recover from the tragedy and build a new capital at Quimper.

Other important centres sprang up. Tugdual, said to be a Cornishman, founded Trégiuer; Padern built a monastery at Vannes; Brieuc founded his community at St Brieuc and Malo converted the people of Aleth (St Servan) building his monastery not far away. The historian Gildas journeyed to Vannes, in Morbihan, and just outside he founded a monastery called St Gildas de Rhuys. His tomb is said to be just behind the high altar while nearby is the tomb of another 6th Century AD missionary – Goustan.

About the turn of the 6th Century AD a man called Francan, son of a

British chieftain called Cathow, fled to Brittany with his wife, Gwen Teirbron, and his three sons – Guethennoc, Jacut and Winwalow. Jacut founded a monastery near St Malo and is remembered at the site where a fishing village now stands called St Jacut-de-la-Mer. But it was the youngest son, Winwaloe, who became better known as Gwennole or Guénolé, who left an impression on his new country. He is said to have become a disciple of Budoc, born of Breton parents but educated in Irish monasteries, who become the bishop of Dol. About 460AD Budoc founded a monastic school on the island of Lavré in the Paimpol group of islands off Bréhat. The island is of extraordinary interest for there are still remains of an early Christian settlement which dates back to Budoc's time. There are the remains of a Gallo-Roman villa having been renovated by the Christian settlers as their church. To the east is a cemetery where sixteen skeletons have been found, all buried head to west feet to east, a tradition of early Christian burials. Close by are the remains of eight round cells while the remains of other cells have been unexcavated so far.

The story of Budoc and his life in Ireland was recorded in the *Chronicle of St Brieuc* sometime before 1420AD. In this we are also told that Budoc, also known as Bothmael, was a disciple of Modez, or Maudez, whose *Life* was composed in the 11th Century AD by a cleric at Tréguier. This states that Modez founded a monastic settlement on the island which still bears his name and which is also in the Paimpol group. Having studied under Budoc, Guénolé set up his own foundation on the neighbouring island of Tibidy (House of Prayer) before making his major foundation at Landévennec. It was Landévennec which became the intellectual centre of the Celtic Church in Brittany. Guénolé's order was strict, ascetic, and highly regarded. It is thought that here a collection of canon law known as the *Collectio Hibernensis*, circulated in the Celtic Church in the 8th Century AD, was copied by the monks for circulation. When Guénolé died here he was succeeded by a Briton called Gwennant or Guenhael.

Of all the 'saints' of this period who settled in Brittany, there is no doubt that the most influential was the Welshman, Samson. He had embarked from Cornwall late in the year of 521AD with his family and followers and arrived at Mont St Michel, a granite outcrop some 250 feet high and 900 yards around. There was, according to tradition, already a monastic settlement there although the abbey can only trace its existence back to the 8th Century AD when Aubert, bishop of Avranches built an oratory there. The earliest extant building is the remnants of the Carolingian Abbey of the 10th Century AD. Samson and his followers quickly moved on to the mainland, beyond the marshland and forests around the bay of St Michel. Here he found a ruined well, built his first settlement and called it Dol. It was soon an important religious and civil centre, the leading town of the Dumnonia kingdom which was ruled by Riwal, who is also said to have governed Dumnonia in Britain.

At this time we hear of Cunomorus, the *comes* or count of Poher and Carhaix said to have governed in Cornwall in Britain as well as Brittany, who had usurped the kingdom of Dumnonia from a young chieftain named Judal (d. 580). Samson, according to his *Life* written by the anonymous Breton monk of Dol in the 7th Century AD, went to the court of the Frankish ruler Childebert seeking help to restore Judual to the kingship. Here, we must digress.

Cunomorus is said to have ruled in Brittany around 540-54AD and is regarded as a Christian who incurred the enmity of the church. In support of Judual the people rose against him and he was slain in Poher. Was Cunomorus the same man as Marcus Cunomorus of Cornwall and the Tristan and Iseult legend? In the *Life of St Pol-de-Léon*, written by Urmonek, a monk at Landévennec, we read of 'King Mark whose other name is Quonomorius'. Mark's capital lay at Castle Dore, at Carhays (in Brittany *Carhaix* was his capital), near Fowey. It is here that we get our most striking evidence of the real man for there stands a pillar stone, dated to the 6th Century AD, on which is inscribed: *Drustranus hic iacit Cunomori filius*. Drustanus in the inscription is philologically identifiable with Tristan. The wording then reads: 'Tristan lies here, the son of Cunomorus.' In the legend, Tristan is made the nephew of Mark. How much more dramatic the love affair with Iseult if, as the inscription implies, young Iseult was his step-mother? It is also interesting that Urmonek says that Paul Aurelian was chaplain to Mark before he left for Brittany. He apparently gave Mark a set of hand bells but, on setting out for Brittany, asked Mark to give him one as a memento. It is true that a 6th Century AD Celtic handbell is now preserved in the cathedral of St Pol-de-Léon and it is fun to wonder whether, on this same bell, Iseult summoned her maid Brangien.

Samson, according to his biographer, was a man of political power, especially having had a hand in the establishment of Judual as ruler of Dumnonia. From his *Life* and others we see clearly how the 'saints' were leaders of their communities. In the *Life of St Malo*, for example, we find that a disciple of Samson, Leonorus, is acting as a diplomat and lawyer on missions to the Frankish King Childebert. A story has it that Leonorus found a golden ram thrown up by moles in a field, doubtless a relic of the Roman occupation, and he demanded from the king the exact value of the ram in land and security of tenure.

Samson used other monks as emissaries. Malglorious (Maglóire), who became abbot of Dol on Samson's death but who preferred the life of a recluse and settled on the island of Sark where he founded a monastic settlement, was one such. His *Life* was writen by a monk of the abbey of St Maglóire, near Dinan, during the reign of the Breton ruler Nominoe (d. 851AD). Meén (Mervanus) was another important emissary to the ruler of Bro Erech. He originally came from what is now the Forest of Dean where his family were rulers of Archenfield. Halfway between Dol and Bro Erech lay the inhospitable forest of Brocéliande, now firmly associated with Arthurian legend, where Merlin lies forever beneath the whitehorn bush snared by the fair and faithless Vivian. On his journey, Meén put up at a village ruled by a local chieftain named Cadoun. Intrigued by the area, Meén built his first monastic settlement called Gäel there. The abbey became prosperous, its safety was afforded by its position in the forest. The district was known as Poutrocoet (the land beyond the wood) and for a while the bishops of St Malo sheltered there during the worst of the Norse raids. Meén's lifelong friend and relative, Judicael (not to be confused with Judual) the ruler of Dumnonia and descendent of Riwal, retired to the monastery to end his days as a monk. The monastery was destroyed during the Frankish invasion of 786AD but it was so valuable that Charlemagne had it rebuilt in 791AD and it was to become the great seminary of the diocese of St Malo from 1650-1792AD.

A close liaison was established between Dumnonia and Bro Erech. Bro Erech had, of course, borne the brunt of Frankish expansionism for centuries. Weroch II (577-94AD) of whom Gregory of Tours had much to say prevented the Franks penetrating into Brittany. His son Canao continued the tradition and it was under Canao that a Frankish army which tried to invade the area around Vannes was destroyed.

Inevitably, the Celtic Church in Brittany was an important mainstay of

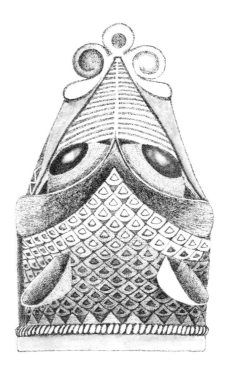

Detail from the cross of Cong. Dated to the 12th Century, this is regarded as one of the most richly worked and beautiful artefacts of the Irish Church. It is now in the National Museum of Ireland.

Breton politics. The descendants of the Frankish ruler Clovis claimed overlordship of the peninsula, recognising the Breton rulers only as *comes* or counts. However, whenever the Franks tried to assert their authority in reality they were usually driven back by the Breton armies. In 799AD Charlemagne finally succeeded in subduing Brittany for a time, having tried three separate invasions of the country. Charlemagne died in 814AD to be succeeded by Louis the Pious. In 818AD under Morvan the Bretons seized the opportunity to drive the Franks out. Louis himself led the expedition against them, bringing with him the poet Ermald le Noir (who was one of the first to claim that the British established themselves in Armorica while escaping from the Saxons). It was during this invasion that Louis came to the great monastery of Cornouaille at Landévennec and saw, to his horror, the monks with their Celtic tonsure from ear to ear and learnt about the differences in religious custom. He met the abbot, Matmonoc, and ordered him to abandon the Celtic custom and accept the Rule of St Benedict. But his conquest was temporary and soon another Breton leader, Wiomarc'h (822-25AD) was leading the Bretons once more against the Frankish rulers.

Louis the Pious led another invasion force and, after the defeat of Wiomarc'h, a personable Breton chieftain named Nominoë won the confidence of Louis and persuaded him to recognise him as 'duke' of Brittany. Nominoë was an astute political leader. He seized the opportunity of uneasy peace to consolidate Brittany, allowing it to recover from the years of armed incursion by the Franks. In 840AD Louis the Pious died. His three sons began fighting over the kingdom of the Franks which was eventually split between them. Charles the Bald took most of France; Louis took Germany east of the Rhine while Lothar took the middle kingdom stretching from Holland to the Rhone, down the Rhone and over the Alps to Rome. Twenty-seven years later Lothar's kingdom had disappeared although his name is still remembered in Lotharingia or Lorraine.

For Nominoë it was the chance he had waited for. He declared Brittany totally independent. Charles the Bald made attempts to reassert Frankish rule but they came to nothing. Nominoë defeated him at Ballon on November 22, 845AD. Charles accepted, in 846AD, Nominoë as King of Brittany. Nominoë now tried to weed out those Breton bishops who accepted Frankish jurisdiction and those who supported the Roman Order against the Celtic Church. He wrote to Pope Leo IV accusing certain bishops of simony. Leo IV replied that if there was evidence a council should meet to hear it but such a hearing should be held in Rome. Nominoë, however, held his own ecclesiastical council at Coetlea(u) of Breton priests and laymen. The bishops confessed and fled for asylum to the Frankish court. A later Pope, Nicholas I, wrote to Nominoë's successor Saloman in 862AD:

It is said that these bishops confessed the crime; but it may be believed that under the constraint of violence and fear they avowed things which they had not done, because they beheld layman and seculars united with the King against them.

Nominoë was killed in a battle with the Franks near Chartres in 851AD. His son Erispoë continued his father's work in maintaining Breton independence. He was assassinated, however, on the orders of Saloman who succeeded him. It was during the reign of Saloman (857-874AD) that the Breton Church tried to get Rome to agree to its complete independence.

In 859AD Festinius had been established as bishop of Dol and Dol was regarded by all Bretons as the seat of their primacy. Festinius wrote to Pope Nicholas I (858-867AD) asking him to confirm him in this office and give him the *pallium*: it is obvious from this that the Celtic Church of Brittany recognised the authority of Rome, if not of Tours. Nicholas replied addressing Festinius as him 'who presides over the church of St Samson' and asking him for a profession of the Catholic faith and a formal submission to Rome before a *pallium* could be granted. However, as for recognising Dol as the primacy of Brittany and Festinius as metropolitan, Nicholas was unsure. He wrote to King Saloman raising the problem of the expulsion of the pro-French bishops during the reign of Nominoë. If the Bretons felt so deeply on the question of independence they should come to Rome and discuss it. 'If you really have solid reasons in support of a Breton metropolis, let them be brought forward.'

Festinius wrote a reply asking the Pope to consult the records in which he would find that Pope Severinus had consecrated Restoald, a predecessor of Festinius at Dol, as archbishop. Festinius had his reference wrong, probably due to a copyist's error. In the *Liber Pontificalis* Pope Sergius (not Severinus) has consecrated Bertoaldus (not Restoald) *archiepiscopus Britanniae* ... this being Britain, not Brittany, and referred to the archbishopric of Canterbury during the years 692-730AD. The Pope was therefore not impressed with Festinius' arguments and made a declaration disallowing Breton ecclesiastical independence.

In spite of this, Brittany made no attempt to make an accommodation with Tours and reverted back to its former tactic of simply ignoring the metropolitan there. When Saloman was assassinated on June 25, 874AD he was regarded as a holy martyr in Brittany.

During the 9th Century, as elsewhere among the Celtic countries, Brittany was under serious attack from the Norse raids. Monasteries, convents and churches were burnt and looted. In 843AD the Norse sacked the cathedral at Nantes, putting its bishop and clergy to the sword. Such incursions lasted for nearly a century until Alan Barveck, known to the Franks as Alain Barbe-Torre (Alan Crookbeard) and who claimed descent from Riwal and other great Breton rulers, returned to the country to lead his people in their defence. He had been taken to the safety of Wales as a boy. Now, as a young man, he rallied the Bretons and in 937AD drove the Norse (Normans as they were to become known) out of Brittany and thus secured its future independence for several more centuries.

Brittany remained independent until the French finally defeated the Breton armies at Aubin du Cormier in 1488AD and Francis II was compelled to accept French overlordship. His daughter Anne tried to resume the fight but she, too, was obliged to submit and in 1491AD compelled to marry Charles VIII of France. With his death Anne tried to secure the independence of Brittany by marrying Louis XII and promising her daughter in marriage to Charles V of Austria. But after her death in 1514AD, her daughter, Claude, was betrothed to Francois I of France. Brittany could no longer avoid a unification of crowns but a treaty uniting Brittany to France in 1532AD allowed it to remain an autonomous state within the French kingdom and thus it remained until the Breton Parliament was abolished by the French Constituent Assembly after the revolution in 1790. The Bretons once more fought against the centralisation of the new French state until their leaders were beheaded in Paris in 1804AD.

As far as the Breton Church was concerned, matters began to reach a head in the 11th Century AD. Rome, still trying to reform its own observances, declared in 1127AD, that no clergy or monks should marry. All members of the church, whatever their position, were to take a vow of celibacy. The Bretons continued to observe Celtic Church practices. Juthael, bishop of Dol, was openly married while Budic, bishop of Nantes, who had obtained his episcopal dignity by simony, was married with his children holding office in the church. Budic was deposed at a Council in Rheims in 1049AD and Pope Leo IX appointed Aurard to start reforming the Breton Church. The Bretons drove Aurard out in 1054AD. Juthael was then dismissed from office but Dol persisted in its claims for independence.

As the century drew to a close the importance of Dol was clearly diminishing and more and more Breton churchmen were looking, inevitably, towards Tours. Then came a surprise. In 1076AD, Even, the bishop of Dol, was recognised by Rome and granted the *pallium* by Gregory VII who side-stepped the issue of recognising the complete independence of the Breton Church. Even's successors, John and Rolland, were also granted the *pallium* but in 1094AD Urban II once more commanded the Breton bishops to submit to Tours declaring that, after Rolland, no bishop of Dol would receive more than a Papal blessing; appointments were to be made through Tours. In spite of this pronouncement, Urban's successor, Paschal II, granted the *pallium* to Baudry, who succeeded Rolland, and who went to Rome in 1109AD to receive his symbols of office. By this time, however, only the bishoprics of St Pol-de-Léon, St Brieuc, Tréguier and St Malo supported Dol. Vannes and Quimper already accepted the authority of Tours. St Malo was to accept Tours in 1120AD and St Pol-de-Léon followed in 1128/29AD.

It was during this period that the most famous figure of the Breton Church made his appearance: Peter Abelard. The romance of Abelard and Heloise is as famous as that of the fictional lovers Romeo and Juliet and, to the romantic mind, is more tragic. Yet Abelard became one of the most profound theological logicians of his day. His tracts, letters, hymns and his personal biography, *Historia Calamitatum*, are evidence of his intellectual accomplishments. The renown he achieved as a teacher in Paris attracted students from all over Europe and laid the foundations for a university in that city. One cannot pass over the final years of the Celtic Church in Brittany without mentioning Abelard, the most famous of the abbots of St Gildas-de-Rhuys.

Abelard was born into an influential Breton family in 1079AD, in Le Pallet, near Nantes on the French border. His father, Berengar, served in the household of the Breton ruler. 'I owe my volatile temperament to my native soil and ancestry and also my natural ability for learning!' wrote Abelard in his *Historia*. He was educated in Brittany and it is thought he learnt logic under the famous scholar Roscelin at Loches. Roscelin was exiled to England in 1093AD for denying the unity of the Trinity. Abelard then went to Paris but returned to Brittany where he spent the next six years. In his late 20's he returned to Paris and became a *magister scholarum* at Notre Dame. Here, about 1117AD, he met a young girl named Heloise, the niece of a canon of the cathedral named Fulbert. They fell in love; the affair was tempestuous and entirely disapproved of by Fulbert. Heloise became pregnant and the lovers fled to Brittany where a son Astralabe was born. Returning to Paris in secret they married and tried to come to an accommodation with Fulbert. Fulbert's vindictiveness led to Heloise fleeing his house and being hidden in the convent of Argenteuil, where she had been educated. Fulbert now exacted a terrible revenge on Abelard.

> *Wild with indignation they plotted against me, and one night as I slept in an inner room in my lodgings, they bribed one of my servants to admit them and there took cruel vengeance on me of such appalling barbarity as to shock the whole world; they cut off the parts of my body whereby I had committed the wrong of which they complained.*

The shock of the castration, the horror of it, made Abelard retreat from society. He became a monk in the Abbey of St Denis in 1119AD and, at his behest, Heloise took the veil at Argenteuil. Heloise soon rose to be prioress of her order but she remained in love with Abelard. Abelard himself was persuaded by his former students, and those who wanted to study under him, to resume teaching. His theories led to his condemnation at the Council of Soisson in 1121AD. He fled to Champagne, retiring to a hermitage near Troyes, where he built an oratory called the Paraclete. Here students flocked to listen to him. From his *Historia* it seems that Abelard had developed a paranoia, believing that people were always plotting against him. It was an understandable complex in view of his experience.

In 1126AD he was invited to return to his native Brittany and become abbot of St Gildas de Rhuys which he did with the approval of 'the lord of the district'. One wonders whether this was Conon IV of Brittany or the local chieftain. Abelard was not happy. He had been too long in France. 'The country was wild and the language unknown to me, the natives were brutal and barbarous, the monks beyond control and led a dissolute life which was well known to all.'

His comments raise some points. Although Abelard was born near the French border, his family served the rulers of Brittany and his education was in Brittany where, apart from a short sojurn in Paris, he must have spent at least twenty-five years of his formative life. He could not be ignorant of the Breton language. However, Breton never achieved a 'standard' dialect and the dialects varied from district to district. It could be assumed that he was merely complaining about the differences in local dialect. As to the monks being 'beyond control' and leading 'a dissolute life', Abelard was probably complaining about their entrenchment against the Roman Order and their clinging to Celtic customs. One comment in his *Historia* is interesting: 'The monks beset me with demands for their daily needs, though there was no common allowance for me to distribute, but each one of them provided for himself, his concubine and his sons and daughters from his own purse.'

It was at St Gildas that he wrote his *Historia*, a copy of which came to the notice of Heloise. For nine years there had been no communication between them. Heloise now wrote the first of what was to become a classic correspondence by which the two of them found a path, initially through self pity, to a changed and lasting friendship. Heloise with her nuns of Argenteuil had been evicted and Abelard allowed them to establish themselves in the Paraclete. He travelled from St Gildas and met his former wife there about 1129AD. In 1131 Pope Innocent II visited Auxerre and granted Heloise a charter recognising her convent. She became famous for her learning and administrative genius as an abbess. During Pope Innocent's visit Abelard asked the Pontiff to send a papal legate to Brittany to conduct the reform of the Breton Church.

By 1136AD Abelard left Brittany and was once more teaching in Paris as a monk at Mont St Geneviève. Then in 1140AD came his famous confrontation with Bernard of Clairvaux (1090-1153AD). The clash was a *cause célèbre*; a clash between two systems of teaching – the monastic tradition and the new cathedral school of which Abelard was an innovator. Abelard was challenged to a public debate at the Council of Sens on June 3, 1140AD. Bernard had planned the scene carefully and had been lobbying the bishops on the day before the debate. Instead of an abstract theological argument, Bernard began by reading a list of what he called Abelard's heresies and demanded that he deny them, defend them or renounce them. Abelard angrily retorted that he would appeal to the Pope over the matter and left the council. In his absence Bernard swayed the council and on July 16 the Pope was persuaded to condemn him as a heretic.

Abelard had gone to Cluny, staying at the invitation of its abbot Peter the Venerable. He remained there until his death on April 21, 1142AD. Peter, writing to Heloise, paid tribute to the simplicity, piety and devotion of Abelard. He escorted the body to the Paraclete where Heloise and her nuns prepared a tomb. Peter promised Heloise to give their son Astralabe a benefice in one of the cathedrals. Heloise died on May 16, 1163AD.

While on the periphery of the Breton Church, nevertheless Abelard was a Breton and the most important Breton ecclesiastic logician it produced. He was abbot of a Breton monastery for ten years and was instrumental in getting the Pope to send a papal legate to try to implement changes in the church and bring it firmly under Rome's control.

By the end of the 12th Century AD the Breton Church had virtually accepted the Roman Order and the jurisdiction of Tours. Two years after Abelard's death in 1144AD Pope Lucius II issued a decree ordering the Bretons to submit to Tours. Strangely enough it was Bernard of Clairvaux who put forward a proposal for a compromise between Dol and Tours during the pontificate of Eugene III (1145-53AD). Finally, on June 7, 1199AD, Pope Innocent III issued a Papal Bull requiring the bishop of Dol to renounce chimerical rights and the title 'archbishop'. All Breton bishops were to be subject to Tours. Symbolically, the change came when John, who had been bishop-elect at Dol, was elected archbishop of Tours in 1201AD. At the beginning of the 13th Century AD the Celtic Church in Brittany had ceased to exist. From that time on Brittany has remained a faithful province of the Roman Church.

Detail from the Lismore Crosier, now in the National Museum, Dublin. It was found hidden in a wall cavity during building alterations to Lismore Castle in 1814, together with the 15th Century Book of Lismore (in Trinity College). Lismore monastery was founded in the 7th Century by St Carthach and it became renowned as a centre of learning. King Alfred is said to have studied here.

7
Ireland

Patrick was not the first to take Christianity to Ireland nor, by the time of his death, was Ireland a completely Christian country. It was during the following century, the 6th Century AD, that the foundations of the great monastic schools of Ireland were made, replacing the bardic schools. Within a century Ireland became the bright jewel of Christendom and was to remain so until the European Carolingian Renaissance. Until the Christian movement replaced, or was absorbed into, the druidic culture, Ireland had followed the Celtic tradition of the oral transmission of philosophy, science, history and poetry. A change in cultural attitudes was in the air just prior to the introduction of Christianity by the appearance of a native Irish alphabet called Ogham in which the first inscriptions in Irish were made. It has been argued that the Ogham inscriptions were carved in a language which was no longer spoken at the time of its use and that it was a 'religious language' used by the druids as people sometimes use Latin today for sacred reasons. It consisted of short lines drawn to or crossing a base line. There are 315 inscriptions in Ogham in Ireland and 48 in England and Wales.

Christianity brought a cultural revolution to Ireland. The Celts of Ireland, already sophisticated in their native culture, eager to extend the boundaries of their learning (a fact frequently mentioned by the ancient writers of Greece and Rome) seized on the new philosophies with a breathtaking avidity. Their monastic schools, which were probably re-dedicated bardic schools, soon became the repositories of European cultural wealth. As well as the development of their native culture in written form (Irish is acclaimed as being Europe's oldest vernacular literature) the Irish scribes and scholars were proficient in Greek, Latin and Hebrew, seeking out manuscripts in those languages and copying them for future use. Large libraries of such manuscripts were accumulated or manuscripts were re-distributed to Europe. This was done through Irish

Rock of Cashel, Caiseal Mumhan, the stone fort of Munster. For 600 years from the 4th Century AD, Cashel was the seat of the Kings of Munster. St Patrick is said to have visited here and converted the King of Munster to the New Faith. King Muirceartach Ó Bríen gave it to the church in 1101, during the Middle Ages it became the site of an archbishopric.

missionaries, as we shall see in chapter eleven, who took their new faith, with their philosophy of learning, to the pagan English and onward into Europe as far east as Kiev, north to Iceland and south to the Mediterranean.

While the period is generally known in Europe as 'The Dark Ages', for Ireland it was an age of great enlightenment and cultural achievement. Had it not been alien to the Celtic character to be militaristic, and had the Irish set out to carve themselves an empire as had the Carolingian Empire in whose cultural wake the Celtic Church foundered, one cannot help wonder how we would view the great cultural achievements of Ireland today.

It has already been remarked upon that the easy spread of Christianity through the Celtic lands, and Ireland in particular, was, I believe, due to the fact that Christianity was absorbed by the druids. There was no prolonged confrontation or conflict between the ancient religion and the new because of the similarities of the philosophies at that time. It is my contention that the majority of the early Celtic Christians were the old class of druids in a new guise. In support of this contention the earliest extant saint's *Life* refers to St Illtyd as being 'a druid by descent'. Most of the early Christian churches, monasteries and holy places appear to have a pre-Christian religious connection. The sacred druidic sites were not destroyed or shunned but utilised for the new faith. Most early Celtic churches were built in circular sites, an essential druidic concept, rather than in the Roman cruciform and rectangular patterns. Springs and wells, traditional sites of the nature philosophy of the Celts, were 'taken over', blessed and, as 'holy wells' have become an essential part of Celtic Christianity. We hear of St Kentigern rebuking the Strathclyde British for worshipping the spirit of a well, but promptly blessing the well and allowing the worship to continue in the name of Christ. The great monastic schools which arose in the 6th Century AD, so I contend, were founded on the sites of existing bardic schools which are known to have flourished long before this time. The fact that there was no conflict here, that the two philosophies simply 'merged', is witnessed by the recognition that bardic schools continued to flourish as public institutions long after the introduction of Christianity. The Synod of Drumceatt in 590AD agreed to regular lands being set apart for the endowment of bardic schools. Douglas Hyde (*A Literary History of Ireland*, 1899) says: '...representatives of the old pagan learning were allowed to continue to propagate their stories, tales, poems, and genealogies, at the price of incorporating with them a small share of Christian alloy ... But so badly has the dovetailing of the Christian and pagan parts been managed in most of the older romances, that the pieces come away quite separate in the hands of even the least skilled analyser, and the pagan substratum stands forth entirely distinct from the Christian accretion.'

One of the first of the great monastic foundations was that of Kildare (significantly the Church of the Oak) by Brigid. Brigid, we are told, was born at Faughart near Newry, Co. Down, about 455AD. Her father was Dubhtach, a druid. She became a Christian and was ordained by Moel, a bishop of Ardagh. It is recorded that she founded her first religious settlement at Drumcree, under the shadow of a high oak. Again, the references to druidic symbolism permeated the *Lives* of the early Celtic 'saints'. Brigid herself was frequently confused with Brigit the Celtic goddess of fertility and her feastday is held on the day the pre-Christian Celts kept sacred to the goddess. We are told that Brigid died at her foundation at Kildare in 525AD. Gerald of Barry (Giraldus Cambrensis) in his 12th Century AD *Itinerary* reports that a 'perpetual fire' had been kept alight there from the time of her death until that of his visit, which was another piece of druidic symbolism. Brigid is looked upon as the innovator of the first women's religious communities among the Irish. Her cult spread far beyond her native shores where she is hailed with the same titles as the Virgin Mary – Queen of Queens, Mother of the Lord – but more popularly as Mary of the Gaels.

Religious establishments for women, like Brigid's Kildare, were also numerous like Moninne's at Killeavy, near Newry, which was said to have dated to the end of the 5th Century AD; others such a Ita's at Killeady, Co. Limerick; Caireach Deargan's at Cloonburren, Co. Roscommon; Safann's at Cluain Bronaigh in Meath, followed later. Because of the Celtic social concept of equality between men and women the early foundations did not differentiate between 'convents' and 'monasteries'. Most early foundations were 'mixed houses' in which monks and nuns lived and worked as equals.

The first Irish foundation that seems to reflect the strict rule of Martin of Tours was made on Inish Mór, the largest of the Aran Islands. This was made by Enda, who is said to have been a pupil at Ninian's Candida Casa. The island was given to Enda by Angus the ruler of Munster for the specific purpose of a monastic foundation. Enda died at Killeany about 530AD but his foundation had already become 'the capital of Ireland of the saints'. Enda's famous school was soon eclipsed by the monastery of Finnian of Clonard. Finnian, who is regarded as the most outstanding of the Irish Christian leaders after Patrick, founded his monastery about the year of Enda's death. He is on record as having accompanied Cadoc back to Wales as his disciple and studied under him before returning to Ireland. His monastic school was famous for its ascetism and scholarship and the place where the 'Twelve Apostles of Ireland' were taught. Finnian is said to have died of the Yellow Plague about 549AD.

He is not to be confused with another Finnian – Finnian of Maghbhile (Moville, near Newtownards). This Finnian was a student of Ninian's Candida Casa but had to leave Strathclyde hurriedly after an unfortunate affair with a Pictish girl. He went to Rome, was ordained, and then returned to his native Ulster, making his foundation there in 540AD. This, too, became a famous teaching centre.

Another great monastic centre was established in the north about the same time. A former warrior named Comgall, born about 517AD, set up a teaching monastery at Bangor, Co. Down. Both Bangor in Ireland and Bangor in Wales derive from the same Celtic word *banchory* – the place of monks. There is a place called Banchory in Aberdeenshire. Comgall was to go to Scotland for a time, founding another monastic settlement on the island of Tiree. The famous manuscript, the *Bangor Antiphonary*, written at Bangor less than a century after Comgall's death in 603AD, contains a long hymn in his praise. Bangor remained one of the principal religious centres in Ireland until it was destroyed by a Danish raid in 823AD.

Some of the most famous monastic foundations made their appearance at this time. Cainneach, a Derry man who died about 600AD, and who worked with Colmcille in Scotland, founded Aghaboe, in Ossory, about 577AD. Cainneach, perhaps more widely known as Kenneth, worked in the Western Isles of Scotland. The famed beauty spot of Glendalough had its monastic settlement formed by Kevin, who died there about 618AD. The round tower at Glendalough is one of two examples of protective buildings built during the Danish invasions in the 10th Century AD. The other being MacCarthy's tower at Clonmacnoise. The monks being warned of a raid would climb into the towers pulling up the ladders behind them. Jarlath's monastery at Tuam, Buite's at Monasterboice and Fionnbarr at Cork were also established at this time. Fionnbar's name is also associated with David of Wales and it is said that he accompanied him to Jerusalem. At the same time Lismore was founded by a Kerryman named Cathach. He was a hermit before he founded a monastic school at Rathan in Offaly, drawing up his rule in verse – a copy of which is still extant. He was turned out of Rathan by the local clan in 635AD and re-established himself at Lismore, which became one of the most famous of all the early monastic schools.

But the most famous group of 6th Century AD church leaders and teachers were the twelve pupils of Finnian of Clonard, called the 'Twelve Apostles of Ireland'. It became a habit of the Celtic Christian teachers of 'saints' to select twelve young men and women as apostles in imitation of Jesus. The selection met with Celtic approval because a similar system, the selection of disciples, had existed under the druidic aegis. These twelve were Ciaran of Clonmacnoise; Ciaran of Saigher; Brendan of Birr (called 'the Prophet'); Brendan of Clonfert ('the Voyager'); Columba of Tir-na-glas, or Terryglass; Mobhi of Glasnevin; Rodan of Lothra; Sennanus of Iniscarthy; Ninnidh of Loch Erne; Lasserian of Devenish, Loch Erne; Cainnech of Kilkenny and, the most famous of them all, Colmcille, sometimes called Columba.

Brendan the Voyager, who founded Clonfert between his fabulous voyages, is famous as an explorer of the Western Isles of Scotland and claimed to have discovered strange lands beyond the Atlantic. Some modern scholars hail him as having discovered America eight centuries before Christopher Columbus. Columba of Terryglas, not to be confused with Colmcille, established his school on an island south-west of Loch Derg, between Galway and Clare, which became so famous that seven ships crowded with students for the school are recorded as arriving in the mouth of the Shannon at one time. Columba died about 552AD. One of his successors was Caimin whom Ussher calls St Caiminus and reports having seen part of his Psalter still extant which had 'a collation of the Hebrew text placed on the upper part of each page, and with brief *scholia* added on the exterior margin'. This confirms that Hebrew was studied as well as Greek and Latin in Irish monastic schools.

Clonmacnoise became another famous foundation made by Ciaran who died there of the Yellow Plague, the same plague which killed his master Finnian, in the same year of 549AD. Ciaran was thirty-three years old. Some of the most distinguished scholars of Ireland, and indeed Europe, were educated at Clonmacnoise. Alcuin, who became bishop of Tours, studied there and asked the emperor Charles to donate money to the monastery to which he sent with a gift of olive oil addressed to 'his blessed master and pious father Colgan'. Colgan, who was chief professor there in Alcuin's day, wrote a book in Irish *The Besom of Devotion*, which appears to have been lost, although a litany of his remains. Tighernach, the famous 11th Century AD annalist, was a student there as was O'Malone, reputed author of *Chronicon Scotorum*. The *Annals of Clonmacnoise* is one of the books which now comprises the *Annals of the Four Masters*, though an entirely different work also entitled the *Annals of Clonmacnoise* was translated into English by Macgeoghegan in 1627 but the original has vanished. The celebrated *Leabhar na h-Eidhre*, Book of the Dun Cow, was compiled at Clonmacnoise in 1100AD.

Of all Finnian of Clonard's pupils, indeed, of all the Irish 'saints' of the 6th Century AD, one man stands out head and shoulders among them. The most enigmatic of the Celtic Church Fathers was Colmcille or Columba. Indeed, so influential was he, that the Celtic Church has often been called the Columban Church. He is said to have been born at Garten, Co. Donegal, on December 7, 521AD. His father was Fedhlimidh, a chieftain of the Cenél Conaill or O'Donnell clan, and grandson of Conaill Gulban, son of Niall Naighiallach (Niall of the Nine Hostages) High King of Ireland from 379-405AD. His mother was called Sihne. It was said that the family were already Christian and gave him the names of Colm (dove) and Crimthain (wolf).

At the age of nineteen he went to Moville, Co. Down, and became a deacon of Finnian of Moville's church. Under Gemman, a famous bard of

Sarcophagus in Cormac's Chapel, Cashel. Once said to have been that of King Cormac Mac Carthy, who built the chapel about 1128-1138; the cathedral, which now dwarfs the chapel, was not erected until thirty years later by King Dónal Mór Ó Bríen.

Leinster, he studied literature and music. Then he went to Finnian of Clonard's monastery on the Boyne headwaters where Finnian, spotting his talents, chose him as one of his 'Twelve Apostles of Ireland'. He devoted himself entirely to his mission and soon won the name Colmcille – Colm of the Cell or Hermitage. In 546AD he built his first church and monastic settlement at Derry, overlooking the sea. It was called Daire Calgaich, the Oak Wood of Calgaich. Yet again the sacred druidic oak is associated with the site. Between 546AD and 562AD he founded many churches and monastic sites, usually in areas in which the druids had associations, such as Dair Maugh, the Oak Plain, or Durrow, on the borders of Co. Wexford.

In 561AD he went to stay with Finnian of Moville and there met Comgall. Now Finnian of Moville, while a student at Ninian's Candida Casa, had copied a book which was entitled *The Gospel of St Martin*. Colmcille coveted this book and each night, unknown to Finnian, he slunk down to the library and worked at copying it. Finnian discovered him one night. When it came to books he was a miser. He was furious. The matter of copyright, perhaps the first copyright case ever, was placed before the High King, Diarmid, as chief judge of the country. Diarmid made his pronouncement. 'To every cow belongs her calf, and to every book her son-book.' Therefore Colmcille's copy was the property of Finnian of Moville. There was an argument and Colmcille was imprisoned. He escaped and fled to Ulster where his Celtic temper got the better of him. He raised his clan, being related to their chieftain, and led them personally against the army of the High King. Diarmid was defeated at Cúl Dreimhe (Cooldrevny) near Sligo.

The High King now summoned the leading churchmen of Ireland and a council was held at Teltown, Co. Meath, at which Colmcille was excommunicated for causing civil war and shedding blood. Brendan of Birr, not to be confused with Brendan the Voyager, took the task of championing Colmcille's cause and argued for a reversal of the sentence. He was successful and Colmcille was reinstated on the provision that he accept penance. It was Colmcille's fellow pupil, Lasserian of Devenish, on Loch Erne, who informed him of that penance. He was to exile himself from Ireland, to go to north Britain, the land of Alba, where, in recent generations, Irishmen had established a kingdom called Dal Riada among the pagan Picts who inhabited the land. Colmcille was heartbroken. He wrote:

Were the tribute of all Alba mine
From its centre to its border,
I would prefer the site of one house
in the middle of fair Derry ...
The reason why I love Derry is
For its quietness, for its purity,
Crowded full of heaven's angels
Is every leaf of the oaks of Derry.
My Derry, my little oak grove,
My dwelling, and my little cell,
Oh, eternal God in heaven above!
Woe be to him who violates it.

So Colmcille, at the age of forty-two years, left from the shores of Loch Foyle with his followers on their journey to Alba.

My foot in my sweet little coracle,
My sad heart still bleeding,
Large is the tear of my soft grey eye
When I look back upon Ireland.

Colmcille's exile was but the start of a new exciting phase for the Celtic Church but that story properly belongs to Scotland.

The only complete site of a Celtic monastery in Ireland which was not rebuilt in later times is that of Skellig Michael, one of the three Skelligs (*Na Sceallaga* – the rocks) which stand eight miles west of Bolus Head in the Atlantic. A great many of the early Celtic ecclesiastical buildings were built of wood, either in wattle work or rough hewn timber and planks. The Gaulish Celts, on the other hand, frequently used stone. The difference in technique is underlined when Maelmaedoc Ó Morgair (St Malachy) wanted to build a church in stone at Bangor. There was a protest. 'Why have you thought good to introduce this novelty into our region? We are Irish not Gauls.' Being of wood, they eventually perished or were rebuilt in Norman times. Skellig Michael, however, is a stone structure.

The monastery is perched on one of the highest points of the island, nestling on a terraced slope of rock behind dry stone walls which rise from the brow of a five hundred feet precipice. There are six beehive cells and two oratories serviced by two wells. The monks also built a garden on this remote windswept place in which earth was gathered and enclosed by stone walls for protection. There is a small cemetery there and the remains of stone crosses. This monastery is said to date from the 6th Century AD. Its remoteness and difficult siting did not prevent it being plundered during the Norse raids of the 9th Century AD. In the 12th Century AD the monks decided to move to an easier site on the mainland at Bolus Head which they called Ballinskelligs. There they remained until the Dissolution during the Reformation. Skellig Michael itself became a place for pilgrimage – the pilgrims visiting the holy places of the monastery and then passing through a narrow fissure called the Needle's Eye to shin up a rock 10 feet long by 2 feet wide, jutting out seven hundred feet above sea level to kiss the end of it as the last station of the pilgrimage.

Many of the churches in Ireland can still be dated back to foundations in the 6th and 7th Centuries AD but very few remain without having been completely rebuilt. Among the few that are visibly of the Celtic period in origin are Inishmurray, off Streedagh Point, Co. Sligo; Inishgora, off Mullet Peninsula, Co. Mayo; Ardoilen, south of Inishboffin and Oilen Senaig, at the entrance to Tralee Bay. It is interesting to note that the church of St Ciaran, at Duleek, Co. Meath, according to tradition, was the first church to be built of stone and hence the name Duleek, a corruption of the Irish *Daim-liac* or 'house of stone'. The numerous abbeys, priories and friaries throughout the country fell into ruin during the period of the Reformation and the expropriation of church property. The monks were driven out, many went into hiding. Afterwards, some returned to their ruined buildings and continued to the 17th Century AD but very few survived the depredations of the Cromwellian period. The round towers, built during the 9th and 10th Centuries AD to afford protection from Norse raids, have survived at a few places – such as Glendalough, Clonmacnoise, Kilcooly and Quinn.

Of the oratories, built of rough hewn stone without mortar, that survive there is one at Skellig Michael, another at Valencia, Co. Kerry, and the earliest surviving one, that of Gallarus, near Ballyferriter, in Co. Kerry. This is said to date back to the 8th Century AD. Its age is considerably more than a thousand years old. It is complete and built with dry stone arranged to slope slightly downwards and outwards to throw off the rain. It is the best example of the corbel pattern of building exemplified in the *clochans* but here applied to a larger and more sophisticated building. Behind the oratory is a cross inscribed pillar to 'Colum Mac Dinet'.

The monasteries became powerful political influences in the land. One scribe, writing about 800AD, commented:

Little places, taken,
First by twos and threes,
Are like Rome reborn –
Peopled sanctuaries.

The great law system of Ireland was codified for the first time and the oral tradition of the lawgivers was now written. Tradition says this was first done during Patrick's time; certainly, it could not have taken place too long after his death. The laws are known as the Brehon Laws, from the Irish *breitheamh* – a judge.

Not only Christian literature was studied but classical Greek and Latin authors found their way into the monastic libraries. Copying these manuscripts formed an important part of the monastic occupation. Colmcille was a scribe and scholar *par excellence* and it has been argued that he and Baithin, who succeeded him as abbot at Iona, laid the foundations of Celtic scribal art which, with its later illuminated flourishes, formed one of the glories of the Celtic Church. Of the surviving manuscripts, only a handful date back to the 6th Century AD. One of these is a *Cathach*, a fragmented copy of psalms which is traditionally regarded as the work of Colmcille himself – the very one which led to his exile. This is now in the Royal Irish Academy. Trinity College possesses a 7th Century AD copy of the Four Gospels which is said to have been written at Bobbio while Columbanus was alive.

It was the Irish monks who were innovators of the 'pocket book'. Liturgical works and eligious tracts, carried abroad by Irish missionaries, had to be small enough to allow them to be carried in a leather *pera* or satchel. The *Antiphonary of Bangor*, for example, measures 9ins by 7ins while the Stowe *Missal* is only 5½ins by 4½ins. The monks loved their books, indeed, all the Celts had a special veneration for them. Thankfully for posterity, they would frequently doodle in the margins of their manuscripts. Priscian's *Institutio de arte grammatica*, which had been kept in St Gall's monastery, carried a hasty notation in Irish by its transcriber Mael-Patrice: 'Alas! my hand!' Later there is another moan: 'O my breast, Holy Virgin!' and after a few folios, a thankful note: 'It is time for dinner!' In the *Book of Fenagh* the transcriber exclaims: 'I am sad, without food today' and later 'A blessing on the soul of Fergus! Amen. I am very cold.' There is a cynical note later on: 'Love remains as long as property remains.' Another scribe complained: 'Let no reader blame this writing for my arm is cramped through excess of labour.' Another unknown scribe says: 'I will stop now for my hand is weary, and more weary is myself.' On one Irish manuscript in the British Museum is a stain which the scribe has ringed in ink with the note – 'Blood from the finger of Melaghlin.' They were all too human, these ancient transcribers.

Sometimes they would sit back from their work and reflect. In the margin of the *Leabhar Breac*, a collection of homilies and sermons dating from the second half of the 11th Century AD, there is a note: 'Wondrous is the robin there singing to us, and our cat has escaped from us.' Another monk launches into a poem in the margin of a copy of *Instituto de art grammatica*:

> *A hedge of trees surrounds me,*
> *A blackbird's lay sings to me;*
> *Above my lined booklet*
> *The trilling birds chant to me.*
> *In a grey mantle from the top of bushes*
> *The cuckoo sings:*
> *Verily—may the Lord shield me!—*
> *Well do I write under the greenwood.*

The most famous and the first extant poem written in Irish was one written by a scribe from Kildare about 800AD. It is a poem of eight stanzas set down in a book in which the author has attempted to note pieces of grammar, geography, glosses, animal lore and quotations in faulty Greek from Virgil and from Horace. The manuscript was preserved in the Benedictine monastery of St Paul in Carinthia, Austria. The poet compares his actions with those of his white cat named Pangur. I quote three of the stanzas from Robin Flower's famous translation.

> *I and Pangur Ban my cat*
> *'Tis a like task we are at;*
> *Hunting mice is his delight,*
> *Hunting words I sit all night.*
>
> *So in peace our tasks we ply,*
> *Pangur Ban, my cat, and I.*
> *In our arts we find our bliss,*
> *I have mine and he has his.*
>
> *Practice every day has made*
> *Pangur perfect in his trade.*
> *I get wisdom day and night*
> *Turning darkness into light.*

These scribes addressed their books fondly, like personal friends. 'This is sad, o little book,' wrote one. 'A day will come in truth when someone over your page will say "The hand that wrote it is no more".' Another writes at the end: 'Goodbye little book.'

The period saw not only great literary activity in the native language but also a new wave of poetry in Latin. One of the earliest of the Irish Latin verses is that attributed to Secundus in praise of Patrick. At Bangor, during the abbacy of Crónán (circa 680-691AD), a hymn was composed 'in memory of our abbots' praising "The good rule of Bangor, right and divine, strict, holy and careful – the best rules, just and wonderful".

Benchuir bone regula,
   recta atque diuina,
stricta, sancta, sedula,
   summa, iusta ac mira.

Colum moccu Cluasaif of Cork composed a hymn during the Yellow Plague of 664AD which actually mixed Latin and Irish.

Regem regum roganus
   in nostris sermonibus,
anacht Noe a luchtlach
   diluui temporibus.

Ruri anacht tri maccu
   a surnn tened co rrodai
ronn-ain amail ron-anacht
   Dauid de manu Golai.

We beseech in both our languages the King of Kings, who protected Noah and his crew in the days of the flood; the High King who protected the three children from the fiery furnace with its red heat; may He protect us as He protected David from the hand of Goliath.'

One of the most fascinating poets of the 8th Century AD was Blathmac, son of Cú Bretann son of Congus, who came from Fir Ros, present-day Monaghan. Blathmac's father was a chieftain who took part in the Battle of Allen in 722AD and who is recorded as having died in 740AD. Blathmac's brother Donn Bó, who died in 759AD, won fame in Irish saga. Blathmac's surviving poetry is pre-occupied with the Virgin Mary. Mary was certainly accorded an important place in the early Celtic Church. In Blathmac's day supposed relics – a portion of garment made by her for Jesus and a lock of her hair – were venerated in Ireland.

Come to me, loving Mary,
that I may keen with you your very dear one;
alas the going to the cross of your Son
who was a great jewel, a beautiful champion.

That with you I may beat my two hands
for your Son being in captivity;
your womb has conceived Jesus
it has not marred your virginity.

Blathmac's vision is essential Irish. He looks upon the Christian story from an Irish cultural standpoint. The Jews he thought guilty of *fingal* or kin

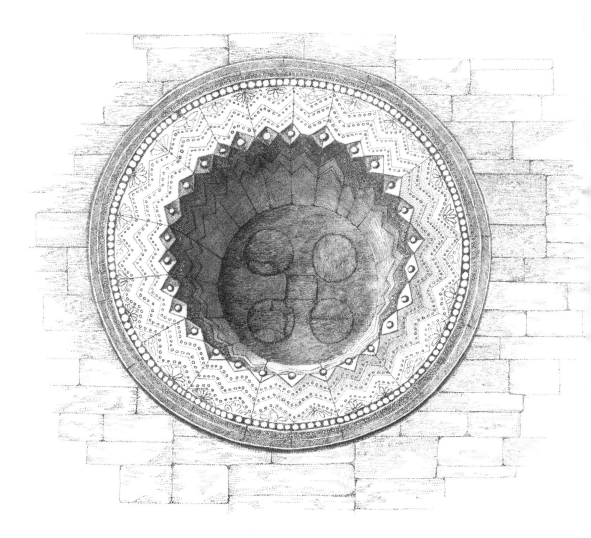

A 12th Century window of the church in Freshford, Co. Kilkenny.

slaying; when Christ was offered wine on the cross to deaden his pain, Blathmac equates this to the *deoch séto* where a host, waiting impatiently for the departure of a guest, produces a drink and pointedly defines it as 'one for the road'. As Blathmac says: 'They offered him a drink for the road in eagerness for his speedy death.'

Contemporary with Blathmac was one Cú Chuimne, a monk of Iona who died in 747AD. He had to do penance for some sin and in that spirit composed a Latin hymn in honour of Mary in which he gives evidence of the widespread cult of the Virgin among the Celts.

> Cantermus in omni die
>   concinentas uarie
> conclamantes Deo dignum
>   hymnun sanctae Mariae.

Maria de tribu Iuda
  sumni mater Domini,
opportunam dedit curam
  aegrotanti homini ...

Let us sing each day, chanting together in varied harmonies,
declaiming to God a worthy hymn for holy Mary.

Mary of the tribe of Juda, moether of the mighty Lord,
has provided a timely cure for sick humanity.

Angus the Culdee, writing circa 800AD, also mentions the prominent place Mary had and in the monastery of Tallaght it is recorded that the Magnificat, Mary's Hymn, was sung daily.

From 795AD the comfortable shelter of the monasteries in Ireland was shaken by the incursion of the fierce Danish raids. Churches, monasteries and colleges were burnt again and again only to be rebuilt and reburnt. Invaluable books and manuscripts were destroyed and gold and silver plate was carried off in quantity. Clonmacnoise was plundered and burnt on no less than ten occasions. Turgeius, leader of one bunch of ravaging Danes, set up his wife Ota as a priestess to deliver oracles from the High Altar. Cork was burnt four times betwen 822-840AD. The monastery was eventually rebuilt in the 12th Century AD by the Cormac Mac Carthy the king of Munster who also built the celebrated Cormac's chapel at Cashel. The Danish raids had a significant effect on Irish attitudes. A 9th Century AD monk wrote thankfully in the margin of his book:

The bitter wind is high tonight,
It lifts the white locks of the sea.
In such wild storms no fright
Of savage Vikings troubles me.

It was during this troubled period that Ireland produced some of her finest scholars. One of the greatest of these was Cormac mac Culinan, bishop of Cashel. To him is owed the valuable compilation known as *Cormac's Glossary* which is by far the oldest attempt at a comparative vernacular dictionary made in any language. Cormac appears to have had a knowledge of Latin, Greek, Hebrew and Danish as well as his native tongue. According to the *Annals of the Four Masters* he was killed in battle in 908AD.

Flann mac Lonáin, Cormac's contemporary, was hailed as the 'Virgil of the Irish' and eight of his poems have survived. He was from Connacht and one of his poems was an eulogy for Cormac. The *Four Masters* quotes his lament on the death of the king Aedh Finnliath who died in 877AD.

Long is the wintry night,
With fierce gusts of wind,
Under pressing grief we have to encounter it,
Since the red-haired king of the noble house no longer lives.

Nothing seemed to defeat or dismay the ravaging Danes and their fellow Norsemen and so when a defeat occurred it was literally something to sing about. One such defeat was celebrated in verse by the Irish monk Sedulius Scottus between 850-70AD. He begins his Horatian chant:

Dume florentem meritis coronam
quae necas hostes, iuuenum caterua:
namque Normannus cecidit rebellis
    praeda cruenta . . .

O take the laurel crown that you have earned by slaughter of the foe, young band of heroes; for the rebel Norseman has fallen, a bloody prey.

The Danes eventually settled in 'city states' in Limerick, Cork, Wexford, Waterford and Dublin. They became Christianised and ceased to be a threat to the monasteries and churches. Their attempt at the conquest of Ireland was firmly halted when the High King, Brían Boroimhe (Brian Boru), smashed their power at the Battle of Clontarf on Good Friday, April 23, 1014AD. The Danes remained semi-independent but owing allegiance to the High King, and soon merged themselves culturally into the Irish nation.

The attempts to urge Ireland to reform its Celtic Church practices began with Laurentis, Augustine's successor as archbishop of Canterbury. He sent a letter to the Irish bishops in 604AD exhorting them to conform with Rome and preserve the unity of the universal church. There were some among the Irish clergy, especially in the south east of the country, who favoured the adoption of the Roman Order. Cummian, abbot of Durrow, writing to Seghine, abbot of Iona, about 623/4AD, says there was a body of Irish clergy in the south-east who wanted full conformity with Rome. In 628AD Pope Honorious appealed to the Irish to accept Rome's ruling on such matters and, in reply, the pro Roman party celebrated the Roman Easter that year. In 630AD a council was held at Mag Lena (Tullamore) which decided that in future Easter would be celebrated as ordained by Rome. At that time the Celtic and Roman dates differed by as much as a full month.

The decision at Mag Lena had, apparently, been made by a minority pushing their views through. Fintan Mac Tulcháin, abbot of Taghmor, protested at the decision. A new council was held at Mag Ailbe, at the foot of Slieve Margy, north of Carlow. Here Fintan, described as 'chief and foremost of all those who defended the old Easter' clashed with Lasnian, abbot of Leighlin, who represented the 'new order which had lately come

from Rome'. Fintan and the Celtic Church prevailed but Fintan died in 636AD and in 640AD the Pope-Elect, John, wrote to Tomianus mac Ronáin, abbot and archbishop of Armagh, to Colandans, abbot and bishop of Clones, and to Cronán, bishop of Nendrum, explaining the principles of Rome's Easter computation, urging them to accept it and also asking them to crush Pelagianism which was so popular among the Celts. The pro-Romans became victorious in the south-east soon afterwards and by 716AD the north of Ireland was celebrating the Roman Easter. But many other old Celtic customs took centuries more to change.

The Celtic Church, therefore, did not pass away in the wake of the Anglo-Norman invasion but had already started to change long before that date. Indeed, it was the church that prepared the way for the invasion and subsequent feudalisation of Ireland. By the 11th Century AD many church leaders were increasingly dismayed by the lack of a strong centralist, political state in Ireland. In England, after the Norman invasion, they saw the emergence of a strong autocrat, and a new church emerging from the stagnant Anglo-Saxon Church – a new church being part of, and controlled by, the state with strict adherence to Rome. This church was governed by a Norman archbishop, Lanfranc, who was an ecclesiastical imperialist. In 1072AD he claimed that his primacy of Canterbury included Ireland as well as the entire island of Britain.

The trouble began when the Norse kingdom of Dublin, which had been allowed to appoint its own bishops since 1040AD, preferred to recognise Lanfranc's Roman Order. The Norse of the other 'city states' agreed with it. Dunan, the first Norse bishop of Dublin, died in 1074AD. His successor was Gille-Pádraig who had been educated in England as a monk under Wulfstan, bishop of Worcester. He was a poet as well as a prelate. He went to Canterbury for consecration. When he returned he bore letters from Lanfranc to Turlough O'Brien '*Rex magnificus Hiberniae*' which lectured the High King on the evils and irregularities of the Celtic Church in Ireland. Lanfranc's admirer, Queen Margaret of Scotland, was already

The Gallarus Oratory on the Dingle Peninsula, east of Ballyferriter. This is the best example of the corbal pattern of building exemplified in clocháns (early beehive huts) but here applied to a more sophisticated rectangular building. It is said to date from about the 6th or 7th Centuries. Its dry stone masonry construction with the stones arranged outwards presents a completely dry interior even after 1,400 years.

working hard to bring the Celtic Church in Scotland under Canterbury's sway. Gille-Pádraig was to be killed in a shipwreck when making another visit to England in 1084AD. Lanfranc died in 1089AD but was succeeded by Anselm who continued to maintain Canterbury's claim over Ireland.

In 1096AD the Norse of Waterford chose their first bishop named Maelisa Ó hAinmire (Malchus) and he, too, went to Canterbury for consecration. Limerick followed in 1107AD, appointing Gille-Easpuig who had been a fellow student of Anselm at Rouen. The result of these appointments was that a pro-Roman party developed among the Irish bishops, not only pro-Roman but pro-Canterbury. So well did these bishops propagandise their attitude towards the native church that Rome, in spite of the great contribution to Christianity made by Ireland, could speak of the '*vitorum enormitates*' of the Irish and, in the words of Pope Alexander III call them '*gens illa barbara inculta et divinae legis ignara*'.

The most zealous of the new reformers was Maelmaedoc Ó Morgair (St Malachy), born in Armagh in 1095AD and appointed archbishop there in 1129AD. He painted the Celtic Church in very black terms to his friend Bernard, abbot of Clairvaux. When Bernard came to write his *Life* of Ó Morgair he recorded:

> *He discovered it was not to men but to beasts he had been sent; in all the barbarians which he had yet encountered, he had never met such a people so profligate in their morals, so uncouth in their ceremonies, so impious in their faith, so barbarous in laws, so rebellious in discipline, so filthy in life. Christians in name but Pagans in reality.*

One cannot help wonder if Bernard is being ironic when he asks how 'so saintly and lovable a man (as Maelmaedoc) could come out of such a race'. Indeed, Maelmaedoc was coloured by his experiences. As abbot of Bangor, Co. Down, and bishop of Connor, he had been driven out by his enraged flocks in 1127AD. What angered them is not recorded. Having been appointed archbishop of Armagh he was still unable to take possession of his see because he was violently opposed by the local clans and chieftains. He finally did manage to take control and set about his reforms of the Celtic Order. He now led a strong lobby for reform, backed by Cellach and Gille Maic Liac, both of whom were successive bishops of Connor; Gille-Easpuig of Limerick; Lorcan of Dublin; Flaithbertach Ó Broicháin of Derry and Maelisa Ó hAinmire of Waterford.

In 1110AD a council was summoned at Rathbreasail, the first of the synods for national reform, at which the High King, Murchertach Ó Bríen, was in attendance. An ecclesiastical division of the country was suggested in which there were to be thirteen dioceses to the north subject to Armagh, and twelve in the south subject to Cashel (made into an archbishopric in 1101AD when Murchertach had given the Rock of Cashel to the church for its see). Armagh was to be supreme over the whole Irish Church. The claims of Canterbury were therefore rejected.

In 1139AD, when Maelmaedoc was on a visit to Rome, Pope Innocent II appointed him Papal Legate for Ireland. On his outward and return journeys Maelmaedoc stayed with Bernard at Clairvaux. In 1142AD he founded the abbey of Mellifont in Louth as the first Cistercian house in Ireland. He spent most of his time reforming the customs of the Celtic Church. He set out on another journey to Rome in 1148AD but was taken ill when staying with Bernard and died in the arms of the abbot of Clairvaux.

Four years after his death Pope Eugenius III sent Cardinal John Paparo as *legatus a latere* to Ireland where he attended the greatest synod yet of the Irish Church at Kells in March, 1152AD. The gathering was 'for the task of setting forth and purifying the Catholic faith'. The Cardinal brought four *pallia* from the Pope – as well as the archbishoprics of Armagh and Cashel, those of Tuam and Dublin were also created. The country was divided into thirty-six dioceses.

A few yars later, Maelmaedoc's great abbey at Mellifont was consecrated (1157AD) by Archbishop Gelasius in the presence of the new Papal Legate Christian Ó Conairce of Lismore. He was the brother on Maelisa Ó hAinmire and had become the principal figure in the reform movement on Maelmaedoc's death. By 1200AD Mellifont was able to boast no less than twenty-five daughter houses.

Another great council was held at 'the Hill of Mac Taidhg' in 1158AD when Gelasius and 25 bishops passed new regulations for the church. On the eve of the Anglo-Norman invasion, in 1167AD, an imposing council met at Athboy under the chairmanship of the High King Rory O'Connor, which attempted to make Armagh an educational centre. But the reforms had come too late.

Maelmaedoc's propaganda against the Irish and their ecclesiastical institutions had been effective in Rome and the advice of the pro-Roman bishops had been taken into account when Pope Adrian IV issued his Bull Laudabiliter in 1154-5AD giving Papal blessing to Henry II of England to invade Ireland and 'enlarge the bounds of the Church, to teach the truth of Christian faith to the ignorant and rude, and to extirpate the roots of vice from the field of the Lord'. In return Henry agreed to pay an annual sum to the Papal coffers. The fact that Adrian was an Englishman has been overemphasised by some Irish historians. Pope Alexander III was quick to confirm Adrian's Bull. The Irish Hierarchy accepted the Papal decree which is underlined by the fact that they were quick to acclaim the jurisdiction of England after the invasion. The Anglo-Norman invasion proper began in 1169AD and in October, 1171AD, Henry II landed to receive the lordship of Ireland. That month a *Curia Regis* met at Lismore at which council the Irish bishops agreed that the laws of England were accepted by them.

During the winter of 1171-2AD the Irish bishops convened a council at Cashel under the chairmanship of Christian Ó Conairce, the Papal Legate. Several decrees were passed and submitted to Henry II for confirmation. As well as various changes in custom to bring the Irish Church in line with Roman observances – on marriage, baptism and the mass – attacks were made on the Irish social system, and an attempt was made to bring it into line with feudalism. One decree directed that tithes should be paid to the church in corn, cattle and other produce; another freed all church property from the jurisdiction of the clan assemblies, making it absolute private property; another decree freed the church from having to contribute to the welfare of the community by giving refection, lodging or gifts of food to the clan needy; yet another placed the clergy above the law, excusing them from paying fines if found guilty of any breach of the Brehon system, even making them exempt from the crime of homicide. Within a few years the bishops and abbots had become feudal potentates under the English crown. But their gain was short term. They had connived at the conquest of their country to gain power but they now found that it was the conquerors who demanded the power. As early as 1216AD King John was directing that no Irishman be elected to the bishoprics and no Irishman should be appointed to the chapter of a cathedral church in case he elected an Irish bishop.

With Rome and England aligned against it, the Celtic Church in Ireland quickly vanished.

From the Book of Kells

8
Isle of Man

Little is known of the Isle of Man before the 4th Century AD. The Romans knew of its existence and called it Mona but gave a similar designation to Anglesey. Today there is a scholastic debate as to whether the island is called after Manannán Mac Lir, the Celtic ocean god. The Manx are the smallest of the Celtic nationalities, the language being a branch of Goidelic Celtic. It was only in the last century that the decline of the language proceeded with rapidity. In 1901 the Census revealed that there were 4,419 native speakers. By 1958 only a dozen elderly people spoke the language as their tongue and the last native speaker died during the mid-1970s. By that time, however, as in all the Celtic countries, a strong language revivalist movement had developed.

Scholars tend towards the theory that the early Manx were British Celtic in speech and that during the 3rd and 4th Centuries AD, Goidelic settlers from Ireland settled on the island. In support of this, one of the five Manx Ogham inscriptions is usually cited. This is the stone from Knoc y Donee in Andreas which reads:

Abicatos maqi Rocatus in Ogham and in Latin *Ammencati filius Rocati hic iacit.*

These names are obviously the Irish *Imchadh* and *Rochadh* but R.H. Kinvig points out that the form in which they are recorded is British. The four other Ogham inscriptions on Man are Goidelic. The Gaelic, or Goidelic, language brought from Ireland was, at first, common to Ireland, Man and Scotland. The divergence into the language now recognised as Manx consolidated itself about the 13th to 15th Centuries.

It is impossible to say exactly when Christianity was introduced and by whom; it is most likely to have reached the island through the Irish

Ellan Vannin, or the Isle of Man, said to be named after the Celtic ocean god Manannan Mac Lir. Christianity came with Irish monks to the island in the 6th Century and soon its monastery of Maughold rose into prominence. By the 11th Century Celtic Christianity had been mainly absorbed by Rome.

settlers. Certainly many place names, dedications of churches and holy wells, are associated with Irish saints of the 6th Century AD. There is a strong cult of Patrick on the island. Two upright pillar stones bearing crosses in Marown are designated 'St Patrick's Chair'. Seven *keeills* (*keeill*, an early chapel site, from the Irish word *cill*) and various wells bear his name. There are, of course, numerous traditions, folk tales and legends, stating that Patrick visited the island. However, there is absolutely no literary evidence for him, nor indeed any other Irish saint, visiting the island. But not only is it possible that early Irish missionaries came to the island, it is highly probable.

One legend that seems to be given credence by J. MacQueen is that Ninian of Candida Casa brought Christianity to the island. Certainly St Trinian's in Marown is a corruption of Ninian and it is recorded that the Abbey of Whithorn (Candida Casa) held lands in this area for many years. Marown itself is a corruption of Ronan to whom its church was dedicated. Other Irish 'saints' can be identified from Kirk Bride (Brigid); Arbory (Cairbre); Santam (Sanctan); Braddan (Brendan); Ochan (Conchan) and so forth. German is from Germanus of Auxerre. The parish church of Arbory is dedicated to Colmcille and a fair day is called *La Columb Killey*—Colmcille's Day—still held in the parish, having been revived in recent times.

The island was definitely under the influence of the Irish and Scottish branches of the Celtic Church for there seems little evidence of British Celtic influence.

The early churches, the *keeills*, were built of wood and wattle. One early structure at Ballachrink, Marown, measures 10 feet by 6 feet inside. The *keeills*, of course, were not made for congregational worship but as retreats for the monks or priests. Preaching was conducted out of doors and baptism was at a *chibbyr* or holy well ... re-dedicated from pre-Christian pagan sites for the purpose. There are some two hundred *keeill* sites on the island with all districts being represented except for the more inaccessible areas among the higher mountain lands and marsh areas.

By the 7th Century AD we find one monastery rising into pre-eminence on the island—Maughold. According to the legends of the Catholic Church, Maughold (Macaldus in Latin) was a brigand who was converted by Patrick and became a fervent Christian. He became bishop of the Manx after Romulus and Conindrus, of whom nothing is known. The monastic community founded by him was certainly flourishing in the 7th Century AD. The monastery was a small cluster of *keeills* in which students and priests gathered. From the site of Maughold's monastery comes Irneit's Cross Slab, the earliest cross slab found on the island and dating to the second half of the 7th Century AD. It records the name of Irniet, who seems to have been the abbot of the monastery, adding 'in the name of Christ, a figure of the Cross of Christ'. Another intriguing cross (found in 1948) commemorates the action of one Brandhui who 'diverted the water to this place' – '*huc aqua(m) dirivavit*'. The cross is dated to 820AD and is a unique memorial to the labours of the monk who managed to provide the monastery with running water.

Unfortunately, if records were kept, and there is no reason to suppose they were not if we judge the literary output among the other Celtic peoples, there are no literary remains of the early Manx scribes and scholars. They were probably all destroyed by the ravages of the Norse who were to eventually conquer the island. The Christian memorials which do remain are the stone crosses, of which sixty-five have been discovered, twenty-five of them from the Maughold area. One of the earliest of these crosses is dated to 650AD from Ballamanagh, Lezayre. But perhaps the most famous of the crosses is the *Crux Guriat*.

The *Crux Guriat* is dated to the early 9th Century AD and stands seven feet high by three feet wide. It commemorates a Welsh prince named Gwriad who is believed to have taken refuge in the island in 825AD. This formerly stood at a *keeill* near Port y Vullen, one mile from Maughold. It is a Celtic cross with five heavy bosses. According to tradition, Gwriad's son was Merfyn who appears in Welsh annals as *Merfyn o dir Manaw*, Merfyn from the land of Man. He returned to Wales to found the ruling dynasty of Gwynedd. Merfyn's son was Rhodri the Great who united the kingdoms of Wales under his rule.

Another unique cross is known as the Calf of Man Crucifixion, found in 1773AD when the ruins of a Celtic chapel were being demolished on Calf Island. It is less than three feet high and displays a Celtic interpretation of the crucifixion in which Christ appears alive, head erect, fully and elaborately robed as an eastern Mediterranean figure. This differs significantly from the usual Roman representation and it is dated at least as early as the 6th Century AD. A similar rendition of the crucifixion appears on the faded page of the Lindisfarne Gospels which Celtic monks worked in the 7th Century AD. The first complete Celtic version of the scene which survives is a bronze plaque from Athlone dated from the 8th Century AD.

In spite of the lack of written records it is clear from the remains that the Manx of this time were very much an active part of the Celtic Christian world. Then the 9th Century AD saw a setback for Christianity on the island. The Norse had appeared in the Irish Sea in the latter part of the 8th Century AD. The earliest record of one of their raids is recorded in the *Annals of Ulster* for the year 798AD and speaks of 'the burning of Inish Patrick by the heathen, and plunder taken from the districts and the shrine of Dochonna was broken into by them, and great devastations on their part between Ireland and Scotland'. It was once thought that 'Inish Patrick' was the Manx 'St Patrick's Isle' but scholars now identify it with 'St Patrick's Isle' in the Skerries off the Dublin coast.

From the Book of Kells

101

The island soon fell under Norse rule and Man and the Hebridean islands were claimed by the kings of Norway. In reality they were at the mercy of any powerful Viking chief who could occupy them. Thus the island might be ruled one year by a Norseman from Dublin, the next by a chieftain from the Orkneys, or another by a man making the island as his base. Under Norse rule the island became 'The Kingdom of Man and the Isles' encompassing many of the thirty-two Hebridean islands. It was not until 1079AD when Godred Covan became ruler of Man that it became a settled, self-governing political state.

With the conquest of the Norse, Celtic Christianity was checked for a time. But in the middle of the 10th Century AD there was a marked revival of Christianity with the Norse not only accepting the religion but becoming absorbed into the Celtic way of life. An example of this absorption can be seen in the later stone crosses written in Norse but commemorating islanders with Celtic names such as Mael Bridge, and Druian, son of Dugald. And intermarriage can clearly be seen by inscriptions such as the one erected by Thorleif for his son Fiac!

At first the Celtic Order was adopted but under Godred Covan the links with the old ways were broken. Godred ruled for sixteen years during which we find the first pro Roman bishop of the island, Roolwer, which seems to be a Manx corruption of the Norse name *Hrólfr*. There were no more native bishops after this date.

The outlook of Manx Christianity was completely changed by Olaf (1113-53AD) who was the youngest son of Godred Covan. He had been raised at the court of Henry I of England. On becoming king of Man he set about the reorganisation of the church along the lines adopted in England, introducing the parish system. In 1134AD he invited the monks of Furness (Lancashire) to establish a religious house on the island in place of the old Celtic monastery at Maughold. Furness was then a Savignian order but in 1147AD they changed to the Cistercian Rule, stressing the importance of manual work in agriculture and animal husbandry. A group of Furness monks arrived on the island in 1134AD and established themselves at Rushen Abbey which now replaced Maughold as the important Manx centre of learning. The *Chronicle of Man and the Isles* was written there and a number of Norse kings were buried in the abbey, rulers such as Olaf II, Reginald II and Magnus, the last king of Man. From now on the Roman form of all rituals and administration was adopted in spite of the protestations of some conservative Celtic monks who argued for the retention of the old Celtic ways as late as 1203AD.

Having invited the monks of Furness to establish a new religious house, Olaf further gave them the right of electing the island's bishop. The new diocese carried the title *Ecclesia Insularum* and sometimes *Ecclesia Sodorensis*. This was the Latin form of the Norse *Sudrejoy* or *Sudreys* meaning 'southern islands'. The *Nordreys* were the Shetlands and

Orkneys. Political connections between Man and the Hebrides ceased after 1266AD but the ecclesiastical link persisted until the 15th Century AD when the Pope finally established the Western Islands of Scotland as a separate bishopric based on Iona. The ecclesiastical term 'Sodor and Man', still used of the Anglican bishopric, was adopted in the 17th Century AD in ignorance of the meaning of the term 'Sodorensis'. The bishopric of Man, from 1152AD to the 15th CenturyAD, was actually under the control of the Archbishop of Trondhjem in Norway. Then, as the Norse ceased their claim on the island, it was passed to York and, in 1542AD, an act confirmed it as part of the English province of York.

Olaf's ecclesiastical changes were great but, after reigning forty years, he was murdered by his nephews. His son Godred II (1153-87AD) dealt sternly with his father's assassins and continued the religious reorganisation. Finally, Simon, bishop of the island from 1227-1247AD, completed the changes, becoming the best known of the Manx bishops. He began to build St German's on Peel Island as the cathedral church of Man in 1230AD. It was a spot of special sanctity and one of the churches on the site was dedicated to St Patrick. Its lowest courses are definitely Celtic and seem to date back to the 6th Century AD. Simon built his bishop's palace nearby at Kirk Michael.

While it is not part of this study to deal with later Christianity in the Celtic lands, it is interesting to see that when Magnus, the last independent king of Man died in 1266AD, Alexander III of Scotland tried to annex the island to his kingdom. A Manx uprising was suppressed. Then in 1290AD Edward I claimed the island for England. Balliol won it back for Scotland but the English took the island yet again. Robert Bruce recovered it for Scotland in 1313AD and stayed at the Abbey of Rushen. In 1346 the English once more took possession by force. During this period of uncertain political rule the Catholic Church increased its power on the island. The abbot of Rushen owned vast areas of farmlands and the Bishop of Man wielded power like a feudal baron with his own court, judges and a prison on Peel Island. The Manx Church passed its own laws. No written civil laws on the island date before 1422AD but the earliest ecclesiastical laws date to 1229AD.

Edward I tried to counter this power by expelling Bishop Mark for 'excesses' but the Pope, in retaliation for this civil interference, placed the island under interdict for three years – a dreadful punishment for devout Catholics in which no church services take place, except baptism and last rites. When Bishop Mark returned he had further revenge by imposing a new tax of one penny on every household with a fireplace, a tax which continued for some centuries. From 1348AD any bishop of Man had to go to Rome to be consecrated by the Pope in person. And it was during the episcopacy of Bishop Russell, ordained by the Pope in 1348AD, that Franciscans were invited to the island to establish a house at Arbory.

The English were now on the island to stay and Henry VII gave the lordship of Man to Sir John Stanley, afterwards the Earl of Derby, for helping him defeat Richard III at Bosworth. The lordship was taken over by Elizabeth I in 1594AD but James I restored it to the Derby family in 1612AD. In 1726 the lordship passed to James Murray, Duke of Atholl. The family sold it to the English government for £70,000 after 1764AD but from 1774AD the 3rd Duke of Atholl was appointed Governor General. Eventually Man received a domestic self government in 1866AD and while a crown dependency it is, under international law, not part of the United Kingdom.

With the Reformation and break with Rome, the Act of 1539AD suppressing the religious houses was enacted in the island. Rushen Abbey, the convent at Douglas and at Arbory were seized and their communities disbanded. The islands remained Catholic, the slowness of the Manx Reformation being due to the staunch Catholicism of the 3rd Earl of Derby (1521-72AD) and the Manx language. Previously religious works had been in Latin; their availability in England had no effect on the people who did not speak English. In 1625AD a *Book of Common Prayer* was written in Manx but not made available. It was not until 1748AD that a version of St Matthew's Gospel was produced under the supervision of Bishop Wilson. Finally, due to the work of Bishop Mark Hildesley (1755-72AD) the *Gospels* and *Acts* were published in 1761; *Epistles* and *Revelations* in 1767 and the *Old Testament* and *Apocrypha* in two volumes in 1770. A *Book of Common Prayer* was issued in 1765AD. The task of translating was divided between the parish clergymen with the work being revised by Philip Moore and John Kelly. Once, when Kelly was bringing the manuscript to Whitehaven for printing, his ship was wrecked and he only saved the precious papers by holding them out of the water, above his head for five hours.

During the late 18th Century AD the island fell under the spell of the Wesley brothers and during the 19th Century AD Anglicanism and Methodism existed in a comfortable union. It was not unknown that Manx families would attend the Anglican service in the morning and the Wesleyan chapel in the evening. The Manx cannot be said to have made a significant contribution to the Celtic Church but, nevertheless, they were an integral and active part of it.

Detail from a finely carved stone.

9
Scotland

It is generally accepted that Ninian, with his monastic foundation at Whithorn, first spread Christianity in North Britain, the area now known as Scotland. Legend has it, however, that a century before Ninian began his mission to the Strathclyde British and the Picts, a man called Regulus, a native of Patras (modern Patraí, in Greece), arrived in Scotland bearing the relics of St Andrew, the martyred brother of Peter and one of the Twelve Apostles of Christ. Andrew is said to have been crucified on a *crux decussata*, an 'X' shaped cross, about 60-70AD. Regulus is known in Scotland as St Rule and is not to be confused with another Regulus, known as St Rieul, who was first bishop of Senlis in Gaul. Regulus is said to have established a monastery at Kinrymond to house the relics and this became known as St Andrew's. However, Jerome records that the relics of St Andrew were taken from Patras to Constantinople by command of Constantius II in 357AD. They were then transferred to Amalfi, in Italy, in 1208AD and, in the 15th Century AD, went to Rome. In September, 1964, Pope Paul VI returned the skull of the saint to Patraí as a gesture of goodwill between the Catholic and Orthodox Churches. Whether there is substance in the Scottish legend of St Andrew's relics, the first surviving record of which is to be found in the *Breviary of Aberdeen*, prepared under the supervision of William Elphinstone, bishop of Aberdeen, in 1504AD, the saint has now become the patron saint of Scotland.

Ninian's main work was in the kingdom of Strathclyde or Strath-Clóta, the British Celtic kingdom whose capital was at Alcluyd which the Gaelic-speaking people called 'fortress of the Britons', Dùn Breatann or Dumbarton. One of the most important Christian teachers to come out

Iona (I-shona, the isle of saints). According to ancient records, on 12 May 563, Colmcille (St Columba) and his followers landed here, having been exiled from Ireland, to found what has become the most evocative Celtic monastic settlement of all. Iona became one of the great centres of the Celtic Church and its influence did not decline until the 11th Century.

of Strathclyde in the period immediately prior to the arrival of Colmcille from Ireland was Kentigern, also known by the nickname of Mungo. Kentigern is *Cuno-tigern* meaning 'hound lord' from which the diminutive Mungo or 'my hound' is logical. The first surviving *Life* of Kentigern was written by Jocelin of Furness, a Welshman or Cumbrian educated in Co. Down in Ireland. We are told that Kentigern was born in the Strathclyde area about 518AD and studied under Fergus of Cannoch. In 550AD he became bishop of the Strathclyde kingdom and his name appears in the records as attending a Council in Paris in 565AD.

He moved south, to the area of modern Wales, and stayed at Menevia where he was friendly with David. Whether he had already met David at Candida Casa is not certain. However, he formed a friendship with him and was given permission to build a monastic settlement at Llanelwy in North Wales. The monastery was re-named after Kentigern's young relative Asaph, who became its abbot when Kentigern decided to return to Strathclyde. Kentigern had learnt that the Angles had sacked Candida Casa, burning almost all of its precious library of books. In 573AD Roderick, the ruler of Strathclyde, repulsed the invaders and fortified his kingdom against them. It was he who actually asked Kentigern to return and help in the work of reconstruction. Kentigern returned and decided to establish his see in Glasgow – 'the dear, green place'. It was here that he met the enigmatic Colmcille and where he died on January 13, 600AD.

In 563AD, Colmcille, at the age of forty-two, arrived in Argyll with, we are told, a following of twenty bishops, forty priests, thirty deacons and fifty students. He was to become a profound influence on the Christian movement among the kingdoms of North Britain. The area then consisted of the British Celtic kingdoms of Cumbria, south of the Roman wall, and Strathclyde; the recently established Irish kingdom of Dal Riada and the kingdoms of the Goidelic Picts – the Cruithne-tuath.

Colmcille was apparently a kinsman of Conall, the sixth ruler of the Dal Riadans, whose settlement was on the Argyll seaboard – Airer Ghàidheal the coast of the Gaels. It had been settled by Cairbre Riada, son of Conaire II of Munster, and his clans, who had been driven there by famine. The Irish were then designated as *Scotti* or Scots and were, eventually, to give the unified country its name. According to the *Annals of Tighernach* Conall gave Colmcille a small island off the south-west of Mull for a site for a monastic foundation. The island was eventually to be known as the 'Isle of Saints' or I-Shona – Iona. During and after Colmcille's time it was simply referred to as 'the island' or 'Hy'. But other sources say that a missionary named Oran had already formed a Christian community on the island which had been there for thirteen years before Colmcille's arrival and when he landed there he found a college of seven bishops, two of whom came down to the shore to dissuade him from landing.

It is not revealed what happened to Oran and his followers; whether they moved on or accepted Colmcille as their new leader. We are told that Colmcille landed at Port à Churiach, the Bay of the Coracle, and named a nearby point as *Carn cul ri Erin* – the rock of the back turned to Ireland. Tradition has it that he composed a poem here and an Irish manuscript was discovered in the Burgundian library of Brussels marked '*Columkille fecit*' which W. F. Skene translated.

Delightful would it be to me to be in Uchd Ailium
  On the pinnacle of a rock,
That I might often see
  The face of the ocean;
That I might see its heaving waves
  Over the wide sea,
When they chant music to the Father
  Upon the world's course;
That I might see its level sparkling shroud,
  It would be no cause of sorrow,
That I might hear the song of the wonderful birds,
  Sense of happiness;
That I might hear the thunder of crowding waves
  Upon the rocks;
That I might hear the sound by the side of the church
  Of the surrounding sea;
That I might see its noble flocks
  Over the watery ocean,
That I might see the sea monsters,
  The greatest of all wonders;
That I might see its ebb and flood
  In their career;
That my mystical name might be, I say,
  Cul ri Erin;
That contrition might come upon my heart
  Upon looking at her;
That I might bewail my evils all,
  Though it were difficult to compute them;
That I might bless this land
  Which conserves all,
Heaven with its countless bright orders,
  Land, strand and flood,
That I might be good for my soul;

At times kneeling to Beloved Heaven,
  At times at psalm singing,
At times contemplating the King of Heaven,

Holy the Chief,
At times at work without compulsion,
That would be delightful.
At times plucking duilisc from the rocks,
At times fishing,
At times giving food to the poor,
At times in a carcair *(solitary cell),*
The best advice in the presence of God
To me has been vouchsafed;
The King whose servant I am will not let
Anything deceive me.

For two years Colmcille and his followers stayed on the island building their churches and cells, although of the buildings erected by him and his followers no traces remain save one or two individual stones. Then Colmcille decided on his first missionary journey into the interior of the country. Only the Picts, although visited by Ninian, were still pagans and in 565AD decided to see Brude, the ruler of the Cruithne-tuath. With him he took Comgall and Cainneach because it is reported that they were Irish Picts. At first Brude and his chief druid, Broichan, greeted Colmcille without enthusiasm but the Pictish ruler was eventually converted and this was an important victory for Colmcille, who now became a powerful political figure in the land.

In 574AD, the year Kentigern returned to Strathclyde, Conall of Dal Riada died and Colmcille, flexing his political power, succeeded in having Aidan appointed as his successor. The first recorded 'coronation ceremony' in the British Isles took place that year when Colmcille installed Aidan on the sacred *Lia Fail* (Stone of Destiny) which is now kept in Westminster Abbey. About this time Colmcille met Kentigern and it seems that Iona was beginning to be regarded as replacing the half destroyed Candida Casa as the centre of northern Christianity. Many workers flocked there such as Moluag, who spread the faith in Mull, Lewis and Skye yet who appears to have had clashes of temperament with Colmcille. And there was Donnan, a Strathclyde Briton, trained at Candida Casa, who worked on Eigg and who was slain there in 618AD with fifty-two of his followers during a Norse raid.

The year 574AD was also the year that Aedh, son of Ainmire, High King of Ireland, summoned a convention at Drumceatt, near Roc, in Derry. Colmcille was allowed to return from his exile to attend. Also in attendance was the bard Dall Forgaill who wrote *Amhra Choluin Cille* (The Praises of Colmcille). At this council Colmcille won three objectives worthy of note: he had the political independence of Dal Riada recognised by the Irish. It was no longer a province of Ireland under the jurisdiction of the High King. He won the exemption from military service of women.

Lastly he succeeded in preserving the institution of the bards against a proposed suppression of their order as being 'pagan' by his fellow ecclesiastics. The same council approved the setting aside of land for the subsistence of bardic schools. It was during this visit to his beloved Derry that Colmcille is said to have written a poem which is regarded as his masterpiece. It opens:

Horror of night when none can work,
Wailing of men and flooding tears,
Opening the books by conscience write,
Rising of hearts with guilty tears

Kings early glory fleeteth fast,
And for a moment is its stay,
God hath all might, and at a nod,
The giants fall beneath his sway.

Mark the power of God supreme,
Hath held aloft earth's giant ball,
And fixed the encircling deep,
His mighty hand supporting all.

The Monymusk Reliquary or Brechennoch. This most famous portable reliquary, or 'house shaped shrine', is 105 mm across with gilt and silver ornamentation on wood, and is dated to the 7th or 8th Century. Legend has it that it contained the relics of St Columba, which were transferred from Iona to Dunkeld.

In 579AD Colmcille and his former disciple Comgall quarrelled about a church at Ross Tarathair, near Coleraine, which resulted in a physical clash between the members of Colmcille's clan and Comgall's Dal Araidhe. It is not known who was victorious but the battle of Rathain (Coleraine) is on record. In 585AD Colmcille paid another visit to Ireland to Durrow and Ciaran's monastery at Clonmacnoise. Two years later it seems that Colmcille had a connection with another battle fought in Ireland. Baodan, son of Finneadh, the High King, was slain by Cuimin, son of Colman Mac Diarmada, at *Leim-an-erich* (Limerick) in violation of a sanctuary given by Colmcille. Baodan's kinsman, Aedh, led his clan to battle against Colman Mac Diarmada at Cuilfedha (Kilfeather).

By the time of Colmcille's death in 597AD, significantly the year in which Augustine arrived to preach to the Anglo-Saxons, Iona had become the most important Celtic monastic institution in the north. Churches had been founded on many parts of the mainland as well as daughter houses. Cormac, a disciple of Colmcille, is recorded as having sailed north spreading the faith not only in the Hebrides but in the Faroes and Iceland, while Machar was designated to work among the Picts and is remembered in the dedication of the old cathedral of Aberdeen. Machar was said to be the son of Fiachana, an Irish chieftain, who accompanied Colmcille's first mission to Brude. Legend has it that Machar went to Rome and was appointed bishop to the Picts by Gregory the Great. On his return journey he took ill in Tours and died.

Colmcille himself died on Iona on Saturday, January 9, 597AD, and was succeeded by Baithin, sometimes called Baethe, who was abbot of Iona from 597-600AD. Tradition has it that the relics of Colmcille were placed in the Monymusk Reliquary which, when borne by its keeper into battle, was held to bring victory providing the cause was just. The famous Reliquary appears to have been borne by the Scots at the battle of Bannockburn. However, records state that Colmcille's relics were taken permanently to Ireland in 831AD.

The first *Life of Colmcille* was set down by Cummian, the 7th abbot of Iona (657-669AD). He was the son of Eruan Mac Fiach, of Colmcille's clan the Conall Gulban of Tyrconnell. The most famous *Life* was that written by Adamnán, the 9th abbot of Iona (679-704AD) a century after Colmcille's death. Adamnán became famous in his own right. He was born at Drumhome, in south west Donegal, about 624AD, the son of Ronan, a descendant of Sedne, an uncle of Colmcille. Adamnán, as well as his *Life* of Colmcille also wrote a tract *De Locus Sanctis* which was an account of Bishop Arculf's pilgrimage to the Holy Land. He is also said to have written a Life of Patrick, an Irish history, and a tract of mathematics as well as poetry. He was one of the great scholastic abbots of Iona.

Having become abbot in 657AD he is recorded as visiting Aldfrith of Northumbria to plead the cause of some Irish captives in the year 686AD.

The captives were apparently carried off from Meath by a kinsman of Aldfrith during the previous year. In 688AD he visited Aldfrith again and established a friendship with the Northumbrian ruler. In 692AD he went to Ireland and is recorded as attending a Council at Tara in 701AD. He returned to Iona and died there on September 23, 704AD and was succeeded as abbot by Conamhail (704-710AD).

The most important aspect of Adamnán's career was his conversion to the Roman Order. Significantly, after his second visit to Aldfrith in 688AD, he succeeded in getting the Strathclyde British to adopt the Roman liturgy and computation of Easter. Cuthbert of Lindisfarne is known to have been a friend of his and this influence also had a lot to do with his rejection of the Celtic Order. The monks of Iona flatly refused to obey the ruling of their abbot and so, too, did the other churchmen of Scotland. Only Sedulius of Strathclyde converted to Rome. The name Sedulius corresponds to the Irish Siaduil, or Shiel. He is recorded as being *Brittaniae Episcopus de genre Scotorum* – bishop of the British in Scotland. This form of address could only mean that Sedulius was bishop over Strathclyde and/or the Cumbrians. He is noted as attending a council in Rome in 721AD called by Pope Gregory II (715-731AD) to condemn the iconoclast Byzantine emperor Leo III, who had been hailed as emperor by his troops in 717AD. Among the other signatories of this council, which decreed that no Italian need pay Leo III allegiance, was *Fergustus, Episcopus Scotiae Pictus* – Fergus, bishop of the Picts whose see was in Caithness.

In 710AD Nechtan, the Pictish ruler, sent a letter to Ceolfrid, abbot of Jarrow, requesting him to send a letter setting out Rome's basis for the celebration of Easter and the arguments against the Celtic Order. He also requested, in anticipation, that Ceolfrid send him an architect to build a Roman style church. In 717AD Nechtan declared his full support for the Roman Order and, according to the *Annals of Tighernach*, expelled the monks of Iona from his kingdom when they refused to change to the Roman liturgy. It was in 729AD that the majority of monks at Iona are recorded as having accepted the Roman Order but it was only the start of an internal conflict at the monastery; between 729-772AD there were two conflicting schools at the monastery but the Roman Order was finally accepted.

No sooner were the internal struggles resolved than external problems presented themselves in the shape of the Vikings. As early as Easter Day, 618AD, Donnan was said to have been celebrating the Offering on Eigg when Norsemen raided the island and killed him and his congregation. It was an indication of things to come. In 722AD Maol Rubha, a former abbot of Bangor, Co. Down, was killed when Norsemen sacked his monastery at Apor Crosán, Applecross, in Ross. Maol Rubha had founded the monastery in 673AD, two years after he had decided to leave Ireland. There was now no holding back the Norse. In 794AD most of the

Cross slab from Riskbuie, Colonsay, Scotland.

islands were laid waste. In 795AD Iona itself was sacked. In 802AD the monastery was completely burnt to the ground. In 806AD sixty-eight monks were slaughtered in another Norse raid, traditionally called Martyrs' Bay. Cellach, the 19th abbot, decided to remove the community temporarily to Kells, in Ireland, in 814AD. It is said that the great *Book of Kells* was started at Iona and finished by the monks of Iona at their new home from which it took its name. Some of the monks returned to Iona, building a new monastery of stone and on a better and more protected site where the Abbey Church now stands. But the Norse returned yet again. In 825AD they burst into the monastery and slew Blathmac, the acting superior, along with many of the monks. During this period, Colmcille's relics were taken several times to Ireland for safety and, it seems, remained there after 831AD.

Great political changes were taking place among the kingdoms of north Britain. Kenneth Mac Alpin of Dal Riada united it with the Pictish kingdom of Cruithne-tuath in 843AD, placing the capital at Sgáin (Scone). The Strathclyde British did not come under the suzerainty of Scone until the reign of Constantine MacBeth (900-942AD); Cumbria became part of Scotland during the reign of Malcolm I (943-954AD) while the northern part of Bernicia was annexed in 1018AD by Malcolm I. At this time Scotland reached its greatest territorial expansion. Only Cumbria was lost to Scotland by English annexation in the late 11th Century AD.

In 843AD, with the capital of the unified Dal Riada and kingdom of the Picts — called Alba — at Scone, Kenneth Mac Alpin also decided that the primacy of Scotland should be nearer the capital. The place chosen was Dún Chailleann, the fortress of the Caledonians, or Dunkeld. The site had been visited by Colmcille and, under his auspices, a church and monastic community had been built. The famous *Lia Fail,* the coronation stone, was brought to Scone. Thereafter all the kings of Scotland were crowned on it until Edward I (1272-1307AD) looted it during his invasion and removed it to England. Every English monarch, in imitation of the Scots, has been crowned on its since.

But it seems that nowhere was safe from the Norse for even Dunkeld was sacked by them in 904AD. The primacy then passed to Abernethy and finally, in 908AD, passed to St Andrews. Constantine III and Bishop Cellach of St Andrews met at *Colle Credulitatius* (The Hill of Credulity) near the royal capital and 'pledged themselves to the laws and discipline of the Faith and the right of the churches and of the Gospels'. St Andrews was not recognised as an archbishopric by the Roman Church until 1472AD.

Iona continued to be a powerful religious centre and all the lawful kings of Scotland continued to be buried there. The first break in this tradition came with Malcolm Canmore who overthrew Macbeth. It is MacBeth who has come down to us as an usurper in the person of Shakespeare's character 'Macbeth' but it was MacBeth who ruled Scotland wisely and well for seventeen years before Malcolm Canmore had him slain and seized power contrary to the Celtic laws of succession, thus becoming the usurper himself. The break in burial custom is therefore significant.

By 870AD the Western Islands had been subdued by the Norse and became part of the territory ruled by the powerful jarls, or earls, of the Orkneys. The ravages of the Norsemen destroyed many books and works of art in the Celtic monastic settlements. Lives of such early missionaries as Colmcille, Comgall, Moluag, Columbanus, Gall and others were only preserved by Celtic monasteries on the mainland of Europe.

During the 9th Century AD there emerged another important church leader who has remained a shadowy figure. This was Serf or Servanus who is said to have studied for thirteen years at Alexandria before arriving in Scotland to build his monastery on an island in Loch Leven. According to Angus the Culdee, writing about the same time, Serf's father was Proc, King of Canaan in Egypt, while his mother was Alma, daughter of the ruler of the Picts. Another Irish source says his father was Obeyh, king of Canaan, and his mother was Alpia, an Arabian princess. Serf apparently arrived in 843AD in Fife, and Dergard, the last king of the Picts 'gave the island of Loch Leven to God the Omnipotent and to Servanus and the Cele Dé hermits dwelling there and who are serving, and shall serve, God in the island'. The Cele Dé, or Culdees as they have become popularly known, were a monastic Celtic movement which sought to revive the purity and austerity of the early Celtic monasticism. It is said that the movement was formed by Mael Ruain, founder of the monastery of Tallacht (d. 792AD). The name means Servant of God. MacBeth and his wife Gruoch are on record as confirming this deed of gift to the Cele Dé.

Of this period, from the ravages of the Norse and the equally savage ravages of the Scottish Reformation in later years, there survives only one great Scottish religious book – *The Book of Deer*. This was written by the monks of the monastery of Deer, Aberdeenshire, in the 9th Century AD. It is now kept in the Library of Cambridge University. It is most important for its glosses, the first evidence of the emergence of the Scottish Gaelic language as opposed to Old Irish. Its historical notations tell how Colmcille and his disciple Drostan arrived in the area on their way to see Brude, the king of the Picts. The book goes on 'and it was he that gave them that town in freedom for ever from mormaer and toisech'. (Mormaer means High Steward. Toisech means Chief). Colmcille delegated Drostan to found a monastic community there.

The *Book of Deer* is written all in one uniform hand in an Irish style. It consists of parts of the gospels of Matthew, Mark and Luke and the entire gospel of John, a fragment of Office for the Visitation of the Sick and the important glosses and notes in the Scottish Gaelic language. It is colourfully ornamented in typical Celtic style. The glosses belong mainly to the 11th or 12th Centuries AD and as well as the story of the foundation of the monastery by Colmcille and Drostan there are entries dealing with grants of land to the monastery by local chieftains. They provide a fascinating glimpse of Celtic Scotland. The final entry in the book is a charter in Latin from David I verifying earlier inscriptions 'as it is written in their Book and as they pleaded at Banff and swore at Aberdeen'. At the end of the book comes the Apostles Creed followed by a colophon in Scottish Gaelic: 'Be it on the conscience of every one in whom shall be grace, the booklet with splendour, that he give a blessing on the soul of the wretch who wrote it'. This is Scotland's oldest book and the only piece of pre-11th Century AD Scottish Gaelic which survives.

After the turbulent 9th Century AD, Iona once more became a place of refuge. In 980AD Anlaf, king of the Danish kingdom of Dublin, came to spend his last days there in penance as a monk. He followed a tradition established by Niall Frassach, High King of Ireland, and Artgal, king of Connacht, who two centuries earlier had relinquished their kingdoms for monastic life on Iona. The fact that a Danish king had become a monk on the island did not protect it, however, from Viking raids. In 986AD they descended once more on the island and slaughtered the abbot with fifteen of his monks. In 1097AD King Magnus Barelegs of Norway came to the island, not as a conqueror, but to pay homage to Colmcille there.

While the monks of Iona had accepted the Roman Order in the late 8th Century AD, it was not until the 11th Century AD that it can be said that the Celtic Church in Scotland was merged completely into Roman orthodoxy. While there was an acceptance of the Eastern calculation, and the authority of Rome as the centre of Western Christendom, the Celtic Church in Scotland still clung to its cultural outlook. The organisation was still monastic, there were no parishes nor dioceses, and each clan had its own priest and bishops. The church did not own property but was allotted land by the clan to hold in accordance with Celtic law.

It was with the fall of MacBeth (1040-57AD) that the Celtic Church in Scotland also fell. This is not to say that, with the concepts of private property and primogeniture being brought back from missionaries returning from England and Europe, the ideas of land tenure were not changing. By the beginning of the 11th Century AD the concepts of feudalisation and private property were being introduced into Scotland; the titles of landholders, once temporary, were hardening into permanent ownership, and in parts of the country, particularly on the southern borders with England, the old communal clan ownership became, in many cases, little more than a superior jurisdiction, the exercise of which was rarely invoked.

Most people are only familiar with the story of MacBeth as he features in William Shakespeare's superb drama which owes much to the circumstances surrounding the accession of James VI and I to the throne of England; the MacBeth of history is vastly different from the 'Macbeth' of fiction. MacBeth, Mormaer of the northern province of Moray, grandson of Malcolm III (1005-34AD) became High King of Scotland in August, 1040AD. His cousin Duncan Mac Crinan, High King from 1034-40AD, was an arrogant and despotic young man whose territorial ambitions had caused him to embark on wars against England and the Jarl of the Orkneys. He suffered four defeats in battle in rapid succession. In Celtic law, it must be remembered, the office of High King, like all rulers from petty chieftain to the highest office of all, was elective, rather like the president of a modern day democratic republic. If he did not promote the welfare of his people he could be, and was, deposed under the law. The early chroniclers all agree that Duncan was not a popular ruler but avaricious and incompetent.

Leading the Scottish dissidents, MacBeth made common cause with Thorfinn Sigurdsson, Jarl of the Orkneys, whose territory Duncan invaded. Thorfinn was MacBeth's cousin. A battle was fought in which Duncan was slain. MacBeth went to Scone and was elected High King by the assembled clan chieftains and churchmen. He ruled Scotland well for seventeen years and at no time during his reign was Scotland engaged in external warfare. Only Duncan's father, Crinan, the abbot of Dunkeld, tried to avenge his son by organising an uprising against MacBeth in 1045AD. This was quickly suppressed and so secure and popular was MacBeth that in 1050AD he was able to go on a pilgrimage to Rome – something few other European monarchs could do without fear of being deposed in their absence.

However, Duncan's eldest son Maol Colm (Malcolm) was growing to manhood at the English court and was imbued with the idea of primogeniture and feudal rights. His father had been king of Scotland therefore, it followed in English eyes, he had the right to succeed him. It was on the basis of this alien concept and not the law system of Scotland that Malcolm persuaded the English to supply him with an army to overthrow MacBeth. Even so, it took him several years for the Scottish people fought valiantly against this outside aggression. When MacBeth was finally slain in 1057AD it was not Malcolm whom the Scots hailed as their next High King but Lulach. It took Malcolm a further six months to have Lulach assassinated before he imposed his will on the Scottish people and introduced the hereditary system and feudal concepts.

It was from this time onwards that Celtic Scotland went into decline for Malcolm was English in education and upbringing. He had also married Margaret, sister of Edgar the Atheling, claimant of the English throne since William of Normandy had overthrown Harold. It was Margaret, sanctified by a grateful church, who was to be the instrument of Scotland's final change to Roman orthodoxy. Margaret, like her brother, had been born in Hungary of a German mother and had only gone to England in

1057AD. The popular myth that she introduced *English* to the Scottish court is demonstrably untrue. In fact, her brother was rejected for consideration as a claimant for the English throne because he did not speak the language having lived in exile since his birth. However, Margaret was deeply religious and a fierce adherent of Rome. Her whole influence, and she was by all accounts a very strong willed woman, was directed towards imposing Anglo-Norman manners and institutions on Scotland and displacing the native Celtic outlook.

Margaret protested against the use of Gaelic in the churches of Scotland where mass was celebrated 'with I know not what barbaric rites'. She instigated a debate on the state of the church in Scotland and requested Lanfranc of Canterbury to send three Benedictine monks to argue matters with the Scottish clergy. The result of this debate caused the Scottish church to become completely Romanised. Marriage was no longer tolerated among the priesthood, although, ironically, Malcolms' father was the son of a priest – Crinan, abbot of Dunkeld. Fothudáin, or Fothad, the bishop of St Andrews, died in 1093AD, and seems to have been the last native Celtic primate. Margaret's own confessor, Turgot, became bishop there in 1107AD. It was he who wrote a *Life* of Margaret in which this formidable woman seems to possess more of the qualities of Shakespeare's Lady Macbeth than ever did Gruoch, MacBeth's wife. So great was her influence over Malcolm that he is reported to have solemnly kissed the books she read and stolen them from her chamber while she slept, returning them rebound in gold and jewels. He allowed her a totally free hand in the reorganisation of the church and court.

Malcolm and Margaret actually visited Iona and it was on Margaret's orders that the monastery was rebuilt – 'it had fallen into ruin in the storms of war and lapses of ages, but the faithful queen rebuilt and restored it, and gave the monks an endowment for the performance of the Lord's work' (*Ordericus Vitalis*).

After the death of Malcolm in 1093AD there were many years of struggle between the English and Scottish factions in Scotland – between the Anglicised sons of Malcolm and Margaret and those who still adhered to the Celtic ways. The latter were represented by Donal Ban, Malcolm's brother, who had been raised in the Hebrides. He was elected High King and set about restoring the Celtic Order. Malcolm's children, again with English military help, deposed him and the momentary respite from Anglicisation was over. It was Margaret's son David I who finally abolished the Celtic liturgy, organised regular dioceses administered by bishops and parish priests and replaced the Celtic monks by Benedictines and Augustinians. The Cele Dé still existed, hermits leading a life of prayer and contemplation in cells and caves scattered across the country. Mention is still made of their isolated existence as late as the 14th Century AD.

The Cele Dé were still on Iona in 1164AD but about 1200AD 'the family of Hy' were ousted by Reginald, Lord of the Isles, who established a community of Benedictines, monks and nuns, in their place. In 1188AD Pope Clement III declared that the Scottish Church should be independent of England and Canterbury, for Canterbury was still arguing that it had spiritual authority over all the kingdoms in the British Isles. Nine bishops were appointed. In 1203AD Pope Clement took Iona under his own protection. It was in 1498AD, when Scotland asked the Pope to form a new bishopric for the Western Isles of Scotland, that Rome recognised the separation of the Isle of Man from ecclesiastic incorporation with the islands. In 1500AD Iona was designated as the see of the Western Isles and its abbey became a cathedral church. Within sixty years, however, the Reformation had started and the Scottish Church became Protestant. The following year the monks were expelled from Iona and in 1574AD the nuns were also expelled.

The Reformation became the biggest blow to the old Celtic culture of Scotland. It has been described as one of the earliest achievements of English foreign policy. Whatever lay behind the attitudes of the Reformation, there arose in Scotland an anti-Gaelic government dedicated to the total extirpation of the language and its culture. The new Protestant leaders saw Gaelic as an obstacle to the spread of their ideas and so created institutions described as 'English schools for rooting out the Irish language and other pious usages'. It was essential to alienate Scottish Gaelic from the people and thus a language which had been properly called 'Scottish' was now called 'Irish' or 'Erse' while the English spoken in Scotland was now called 'Scots' and later 'Lallans' or 'Lowlands'. Thus the myth of Highlander and Lowlander took root and while these educational institutions are still regarded as progressive by some, they were merely instruments of a sustained policy of cultural genocide.

The Reformation can be blamed for the lack of old literature in Scottish Gaelic. Libraries full of Gaelic works appear to have been destroyed by the anti-Gaelic administrators of the country. All that is now left is the *Book of Deer* with its Gaelic notations, one 11th Century AD poem, and then a surprising gap before we find the Islay Charter of 1408AD. The charter not only demonstrates a sophisticated literary language, the obvious product of a long tradition of writing, but also proves that Gaelic was being used as an administrative language. The *Book of the Dean of Lismore*, compiled between 1512-1526AD, is the most important surviving manuscript in that it contains an anthology of Gaelic poetry. Bishop John Carswell's *Form na h-Ordaigh*, a prayer book, is the first known printed work in the language, being published in 1567AD. It was not until 1690AD that the entire Bible was published in Gaelic. The destruction of Scotland's national language was almost complete but, pathetic though the remnants are, they are evidence of a wealth of literature and records

Detail of three clerics, from a 9th Century cross slab, Invergowrie, Angus, Scotland.

in Gaelic which the Reformation destroyed. Scotland is, perhaps, the saddest of the modern Celtic nationalities because, as a result of the genocidal abuses there, a proportion of its population deny their Celtic heritage.

10
England

When the Angles and Saxons pushed into Britain they were pagans, worshippers of the Germanic gods Woden, Thunor, Freya, Tyr and others. It is an irony that Bede, in criticising the British Celts, levels the charge at them that they made no attempt to convert the Angles and Saxons to Christianity. From a Celtic viewpoint it would have been similar to an attempt to convert the Nazis to Judaism. However, Rome became aware of the pagan Anglo-Saxons and during the pontificate of Benedict I (574-8AD) it was decided to send a mission led by Gregory, a monk from the monastery of St Andrews, on the Coelian Hill, in Rome. Gregory was recalled to Rome before even setting foot among them. When Gregory himself became Pope in 590AD he was still keen to extend Rome's ecclesiastical rule among the pagans.

In 597AD, the year of Colmcille's death at Iona, a former prior of St Andrews in Rome, Augustine, arrived with forty monks on a mission from Pope Gregory. They landed in Kent. The king of Kent was Aethelberht who had married Bertha, a daughter of Childebert, the king of the Franks. The Franks were Arian Christians and Bertha retained her religion when she went to live among the pagans, taking with her, her own chaplain Luidhard, bishop of Senlis. A former Celtic church dedicated to Martin of Tours, situated in Canterbury, was once more allowed for Christian worship. This was the situation when Augustine arrived and he was soon successful in converting Aethelberht, the groundwork presumably having been done by Bertha. Augustine established himself at Canterbury and spent several years preaching among the Anglo-Saxons with some success. He established a monastery dedicated to SS Peter and Paul and afterwards called St Augustine's. He was consecrated archbishop of the English at Arles. In 601AD a further mission was sent by Pope Gregory to help him; among the new arrivals was Mellitus, appointed bishop to the East Saxons in London, where Aethelberht had a church built for him dedicated to St Paul; Justus was appointed bishop in Rochester and Paulinus was to preach to the northern kingdoms.

Lindisfarne. The remaining buildings were erected by the Normans on the site of the original Celtic monastery, which had been founded in the 7th Century by monks from Iona. The Celtic structures were destroyed in a Viking raid in the late 8th Century.

Having consolidated his base among the Anglo-Saxons, Augustine now made moves to meet the Celtic bishops, arranging a meeting on the borders of Wessex, probably at Aust, opposite Chepstow, on the Severn. Augustine's message to the British Celts was a simple one: he had been sent by the Pope with jurisdiction over the whole island of Britain and they must now conform to Rome and accept his see of Canterbury as their spiritual centre. He urged the British to preserve the unity of the Church of Rome and join with him in preaching the faith to the English. The Celtic bishops requested another meeting, replying that they could not abandon their customs *without consent of their people*; an interesting phrase supporting the continued adherence to the Celtic law system. A second and more representative conference was arranged.

This second conference was attended by seven prominent British Celtic bishops with a retinue of monks and priests from various Celtic monastic centres, notably Bangor. Bede refers to the abbot of Bangor as 'Dinool'. Bangor was founded by Dunawd Fawr who, according to the *Annales Cambriae*, died in 584AD. He had three sons—Deiniol, Cynwul and Gwarthan. Cynwul and Gwarthan founded Bangor Iscoed, by Dee, in Flint, while Deiniol became abbot of Bangor, thus the 'Dinool' of Bede. According to tradition Dunawd Fawr had been a chieftain among the Strathclyde British. His brother, Sawye Benuchil, died a monk at Bangor. The family were related to Kentigern, and Sawye Benuchil's son, Asaph, took over from Kentigern as abbot at Llanelwy, which was later renamed St Asaph's. Alas, we know nothing of the other leaders at this council which was of great importance for the Celtic Church. It was at this council that Augustine lost the Celtic Church for Rome for another five hundred years.

Augustine, as a Roman, appears as a haughty and aristocratic man who undoubtedly considered himself superior to the 'barbarians' he was confronting. When the Celtic bishops approached he did not even bother to rise to greet them but remained seated and launched into a tirade accusing them of acting contrary to Church teachings, failing to keep Easter at the prescribed time and not administering baptism according to Roman rite. Lastly, they had failed in their duty as Christians by not converting the Anglo-Saxons to the faith. They should now submit to his authority and conform to Roman orthodoxy.

The Celts immediately resented the haughty bearing of Augustine and saw in him the chief representative of their enemies, the anglo-Saxons. They wisely saw the dangers of placing themselves under ecclesiastical tutelage from Canterbury in the midst of their struggle against Anglo-Saxon domination. They observed that if Augustine had not the manners to rise to greet them as fellow bishops, how much more would he hold them in contempt if they then agreed to subject themselves to him?

Augustine, obviously not used to being addressed in this fashion or having his word questioned, seems to have lost his temper and blustered that if they would not accept his jurisdiction peacefully then they would be met by war and suffer vengeance at the hands of the Anglo-Saxons. It was the last thing to say to the Celts had he wished to win them over. The threat probably confirmed their opinion of Augustine and the council ended abruptly.

Bede, the main source for this conference, who was pro-Augustine, turned Augustine's threat into a prophecy by pointing to the defeat of the Celts at Chester in 616AD by Ethelfrith of Northumbria. More than one thousand monks from the monastery of Bangor were slaughtered by Ethelfrith's men after they had assembled near the battlefield to pray for a Celtic victory, after the old druidic tradition. Among those slain was Deiniol. Bede, to appease his Christian conscience, excuses the deed by putting these words into Ethelfrith's mouth: 'If they cry to their God against us, and load us with imprecations, then, though unarmed, they fight against us.'

A few months after his conference with the British Celts, Augustine died and his successor was Laurentius. Like Augustine, Laurentius was concerned with bringing the Celts into line with Rome. He is on record as writing a letter of complaint to the Irish about the differences between them. In 610AD Dagan, the bishop of Inverdaoile, Wexford, visited Canterbury, authorised by the Irish bishops to discuss with Laurentius the differences between the churches. Dagan was one of the leading Irish churchmen of his day; he had visited Rome, taking the monastic Rule of St Molua to Gregory (d. 604AD) for his approval. Dagan, if we read between the lines, was obviously upset by Laurentius' superior attitude, lost his temper during the discussions and walked out, even refusing Laurentius' hospitality. Laurentius was furious and wrote to the Irish bishops to complain about Dagan's behaviour. Bede quotes his letter.

To our most dear Brothers, the lord bishops and abbots throughout all Ireland; Laurentius, Mellitus and Justus, servants of God. When the Apostolic See, according to universal custom which it has followed elsewhere throughout the world, sent us to these western parts to preach to pagan nations, we came to this island, which is called Britain, without possessing any previous knowledge of its inhabitants. We held the Britons and Irish in great esteem for sanctity, believing that they followed the custom of the universal church; but after becoming acquainted with the Britons we supposed that the Irish should be more observant. We have been informed, however, by Bishop Dagan, coming into this aforesaid island, and by the Abbot Columbanus in Gaul, that the Irish in no way differ from the Britons in the observance; for Bishop Dagan coming to us, not only refused to eat with us, but even to take his repast in the same house where we entertained.

In 617AD, however, the work of the Roman missionaries among the Anglo-Saxons was almost undone. Aethelberht of Kent had died and his son Eadbald became king and resumed pagan worship. Mellitus was driven out of London as a new zeal for the worship of Woden flared up. Mellitus and Justus actually fled the country but Laurentius remained and succeeded in re-converting Eadbald back to Christianity. In the north, too, Paulinus, was having a hard time. Ethelfrith, the conqueror of Chester in 616AD, had come to the throne by usurping the position of a young boy Edwin, son of Aelle of Deira, who, by the Anglo-Saxon law of primogeniture, was said to be rightful king. Edwin was brought up by a British chieftain who was slain at Chester. Edwin had been too young to get support against Ethelfrith who became king of Bernicia and overlord of Deira (they were not to unite into the kingdom of Northumbria until 655AD). But a year after the battle of Chester, in 617AD, Edwin succeeded in toppling Ethelfrith and becoming king. Ethelburga, the sister of Eadbald of Kent, went north to marry him and Paulinus accompanied her as her chaplain. Honorius I recognised Paulinus as the first bishop of York.

Ethelfrith's sons, Eanfrith and Oswald, sought refuge in Iona and were greatly influenced by the Christian monks there. Through his wife Ethelburga and the efforts of Paulinus, Edwin of Northumbria now accepted Roman Christianity. However, in October, 633AD, the great pagan king of Mercia, Penda, who had joined forces with a British ruler, Cadwallon, slew Edin at Hatfield. Paulinus was forced to flee, taking Ethelburga and her children back to Kent for safety. Northumbria reverted to pagan worship. Paulinus took over as bishop of Rochester and died there on October 10, 644AD.

In the meantime Eanfrith, having returned from exile in Iona, seized power in Bernicia only to be slain by a relative of Edwin called Osric. Then in 634/5AD Eanfrith's brother, Oswald, made himself king of Bernicia and overlord of Deira, generously allowing Osric to continue as sub-king of Deira. Oswald defeated Cadwallon at a battle at Heavenfield, near Hexham, and thus secured the borders of his domain. Oswald had been born in 604AD and educated at Iona. It was therefore natural for him to write to Abbot Seghine of Iona and ask him to send missionaries from the monastery to convert his kingdom to Christianity.

Abbot Seghine sent a monk named Colman in 635AD. Colman, however, withdrew in despair after a short while saying that the mission was too difficult. Another monk was sent in his stead. This was Aidan, an Irishman trained at St Senanus monastery at Iniscattery on the Shannon. He was already a prominent churchman, named as fifth bishop of Clogher in the *Annals of Ulster*. He was made welcome at Oswald's court at Bamburgh. Aidan decided to form his first monastic community on a small island off the Northumbrian coast, connected to it at low tide by a causeway. It was called Lindisfarne. Bede says that Aidan accepted money and gifts from the English lords so that they could be used to obtain the release of slaves, many of whom he then educated to become priests. Aidan is said to have chosen twelve English disciples, after the Celtic fashion, to follow him. His gifts as a teacher were attested to by Bede. Thanks to his efforts, Irish manned monasteries rose at Lastingham, Tynemouth, Whitby, Barrow, Coldingham and Hartlepool by 651AD.

Aidan was not fluent in English, says Bede, but 'it was a pleasing sight to see the king himself interpreting God's word to his thanes and chief men, for he had learned the Irish tongue during his long exile'. Bede, while criticising Aidan for his Celticism, added:

> Yet this I approve in him, that in the celebration of his Easter, the object which he had now in all he said, did, or preached, was the same as ours, that is the redemption of Mankind, through the passion, resurrection and ascension into heaven of the man Jesus Christ, who is the mediator betwixt God and Man.

Among the Anglo-Saxon disciples whom he chose were women, reflecting the equality of place they held in Celtic society, although such equality must have been looked upon with astonishment by the Northumbrians. Among them was Oswald's half-sister, Ebba, who founded the convent at Coldingham, near Berwick, about 640AD. Her niece Elfleda, who eventually became abbess at Whitby, also became a disciple. But the most famous of Aidan's female disciples was Hilda, a grand niece of Edwin of Northumbria. She had been born in 614AD and, it seems, christened by Paulinus when she was thirteen years old. In 649AD Aidan persuaded her to establish a 'double monastery' at Hartlepool. Monks and nuns lived in the same community. The monastery that she established was called Streonaeshalc at Whitby, where she ruled as abbess. Among her disciples was Beverley, who became bishop of Hexham and ordained Bede as a priest there in 703AD. More famous was Caedmon, a herdsman at the monastery, who is now acclaimed as the first English religious poet. Hilda, at whose monastery the famous debate on the merits of the Celtic Church and Roman Church was held, was a staunch supporter of the Celtic Order. She died at Whitby on November 17, 680AD.

Oswald the king had now married Cyneburga, daughter of Cynegils, the first Christian king of Wessex. But the reign which had begun so promisingly lasted only eight years. Penda, king of Mercia, the greatest of the pagan Anglo-Saxon monarchs, moved against Northumbria once more. Oswald was slain at a battle at Maserfelth (perhaps Oswestry). His death deeply affected Aidan but the Celtic Christians were still made welcome in Northumbria by Oswald's successor and cousin, Oswin. He became king in November, 643AD. Bede says he was handsome and courteous 'and among his other qualities of virtue and moderation the greatest was humbleness'. Oswin was murdered by another cousin, Oswy

Corbel from the church of St Mary and St David, Kilpeck, Herefordshire, showing a dog and a rabbit.

(Oswiu) at Gilling in 651AD and was venerated as a martyr. Aidan survived his royal patron a fortnight and died, apparently of grief, and was buried on Lindisfarne.

To succeed Aidan, Finan, who had accompanied Aidan from Iona, was chosen. He, too, was an Irishman, not to be confused with another of the same name who was founder and abbot of Cluain Ednech, East Meath (d. 603AD). Finan was very active during his ten years as bishop of Lindisfarne. He began to send missionaries to the other English kingdoms and succeeded in converting Peada the son of the obstinately anti-Christian Penda of Mercia. At the same time when Finan became religious leader in Northumbria, Oswy, who had murdered Oswin, became king and did penance for his deed, thereafter becoming a strong and, comparatively, just ruler. Oswy allowed Oswin's son, Aethelwald, to rule in Deira as sub king until 655AD. It was this year when Oswy united Deira and Bernica into the Northumbrian kingdom. He ruled it until 671AD. It was the same year when Penda of Mercia, making a final attempt to extend his boundaries, met the Northumbrians at Winwaed Field and was slain. Oswy's daughter had married Peada, Penda's son, who had been king of the Middle Angles, and so Oswy allowed Peada to become king of Mercia.

In 661AD Finan died to be succeeded by another Irishman named Colman. He, too, had been a monk at Iona. There are many Colmans in the lists of early Irish 'saints'; about most of them nothing is known. There is a story which illustrates the fact in the *Vita of St Carthage*. Once when a party of Irish monks were working by a stream, the one in charge cried: 'Colman, get into the water!' and twelve Colmans jumped in. Colman of Lindisfarne, however, has come down in history as the bishop under whose jurisdiction the famous Synod, or Council, of Whitby was held which is generally assumed to be the council which ended Celtic ecclesiastical influence in England.

The paradox was that the Celts had been criticised by Rome for not converting the English. Now that they were successfully proselytising them, Rome was worried. Oswy had married Eanfled, daughter of Edwin of Kent, who followed Roman orthodoxy. Oswy's son Alchfrith became an outspoken supporter of the Roman Order. At the Northumbrian court there grew together a small group of pro-Roman clerics. Romanus, Eanfled's confessor, was supported by James, who had been a deacon under Paulinus. Agilbert, bishop of Wessex, was pro-Roman even though he had been trained in Irish monasteries. And there was Tuda, an Irishman, consecrated bishop in Ireland, who now supported the Roman Order. But the pro-Romans found their greatest champion in Wilfred. He had been born in Northumbria in 634AD and educated at Lindisfarne. He had left the monastery to travel abroad, spending some years at Lyons and in Rome, where he studied ecclesiastical law with his friend Benet Biscop, another Northumbrian who established Benedictine houses at Wearmouth and Jarrow after the fall of the Celtic Order. Benet Biscop made five journeys to Rome and brought back a fuller knowledge of the Roman chant and ceremonial, plus many books and holy images. He is accredited with being the first to build churches of stone with glass windows instead of the simple wooden structures built by the Celtic monks. He died on January 12, 690AD.

Wilfred, on his return to Northumbria, was convinced that the Roman Order was the correct one. He and his fellow pro-Romans were a powerful lobby at Oswy's court. Finally, Oswy decided that a special council should be convened, over which he would preside, at which representatives of the Celtic and Roman Orders should state their cases. He would then make a final decision on the merits of the case put. The conference was held at Whitby in 664AD. The main debate took place between Colman and Wilfred and the main point of contention centered around the computation of Easter, although the other points of custom were also discussed. The debate finally arrived at the key question ... did Rome have greater authority than Iona or elsewhere in Christendom?

It was, of course, accepted without question that Peter had died at Rome and Wilfred was not backward in producing the quotation from the Gospel of Matthew, 16 v. 17: '. . . thou art Peter, and upon this rock I will build my church; and the gates of hell shall not prevail against it. And I will give unto thee the keys of the kingdom of heaven . . .' Peter had gone to Rome, Wilfred pointed out, and it was there that the church was founded. All members of the Christian movement must therefore look to Rome as the centre of that movement.

Oswy turned to Colman and asked him if he agreed that Jesus had said these words to Peter. Colman agreed. Oswy pressed him to see if Colman could claim any similar authority for Colmcille, whose authority Colman had quoted during the debates, especially as to the computation of Easter. Colman shook his head. 'You are then both agreed in this, that the keys of heaven were given to Peter by our Lord?' pressed Oswy of both men. Both agreed. Then Oswy delivered his decision.

> 'I say to you both that this is the doorkeeper of heaven, whom I do not choose to gainsay and that I will not oppose him, but as far as I know and am able, I desire in all things to obey his rulings, lest when I reach the doors of the celestial kingdom, there be no one to open them for me, if I am the adversary of him who carries the keys. In all my life I will neither do or approve anything or any person that may be contrary to him.'

The decision made, Colman felt he could not continue as bishop of Lindisfarne with honour. He resigned his office and departed for Iona, taking with him the majority of Celtic monks and some thirty Anglo-Saxons who adhered to the Celtic Order. From Iona, Colman and his followers went to the isle of Inishboffin off the Connacht coast (which was to become a penal settlement for all Catholic priests during the Cromwellian period). The Anglo-Saxons eventually moved to the mainland to found a monastic settlement at Mayo whose first abbot was a Northumbrian named Gerald. Before leaving Northumbria, Colman had requested that Oswy appoint Eata, a Northumbrian disciple of his, as bishop at Lindisfarne. This Oswy did.

Popular history claims that this was the end of Celtic Christian influence in England. It was not. Many Celtic monks and priests continued to work among the English after Colman and his followers had departed and many Anglo-Saxons continued to go to Ireland for their education. Bede records that during this time there were in Ireland 'many nobles as well as common sort of English race, who in the time of the bishops Finan and Colman, had left their native island and departed thither to either read sacred writings or to learn more strictly. And certain of them forthwith bound themselves faithfully to the monastical life, while others wandering rather about the cells of such as taught gladly, gave good heed to reading; all of whom the Irish entertained cheerfully, and were forward to give them daily sustenance free, also books for reading and teaching without payment.'

The famous *Gospels of Lindisfarne*, dating from this period, reveal traits of the Irish scribal school. A colophon names one of its makers as Bishop Eadfrith, who ruled at Lindisfarne from 689 to 721AD and to whom Bede dedicated his *Life of St Cuthbert*. Its artwork and scriptic style are definitely Celtic. Stone crosses appearing at this time also show the use of Celtic motifs. One of the most famous is the Ruthwell Cross, standing over seventeen feet high. The arrangement of the figures is Celtic rather than Roman. Another cross in Bewcastle, in Cumbria, is of interest here because it is thought to commemorate Oswy's part at Whitby.

Celtic influence has also been seen in early English literature. The famous Anglo-Saxon saga of *Beowulf* was written in Northumbria and kept for a time at Lindisfarne. C. W. von Sydow in his *Beowulfskalden och nordisk tradition* (Arsbok, 1923) believes that the *Beowulf* poet either studied at an Irish school or was well acquainted with Irish sagas. This was supported by Gerald Murphy in his work *Duanaire Finn* (Dublin, 1953). It is argued that the saga of the *Táin Bó Fraích* provided a model for *Beowulf* because of nine extremely close similarities. It has also been argued that King Aldfrith of Northumbria, educated in Ireland and the author of poetry in Irish, might have been 'the begetter of *Beowulf*'.

Just after the council of Whitby the Irish pro-Roman Tuda died of the Yellow Plague which had appeared again in the spring of 664AD. Earconberht of Kent had died from it on July 14, followed by the archbishop of Canterbury. It was not until 668AD that a new archbishop arrived from Rome. He was a Greek – Theodore of Tarsus. With his eastern approach he appeared to feel a sympathy for the Celtic trained

churchmen. He endeavoured to bring the two sides together and a
Council at Hertford in 673AD drew up ten rules designed to merge the
two different schools of thought.

Wilfred, flushed from his victory at Whitby, had claimed the monastery
of Ripon and then the bishopric of York but the Celtic Order had
prevented him taking over. On Theodore's arrival he was allowed to take
over the see of York but, in 678AD, Theodore decided to divide York into
two bishoprics. Wilfred appealed to Rome; the case was decided in his
favour but when Wilfred arrived back from Rome, Oswy's successor,
Egfrid of Northumbria, had him imprisoned. Wilfred fled to Sussex where
for a time he immersed himself in the conversion of the South Saxons.

Under Theodore, now accepted as primate of all the English kingdoms,
the last Irish bishop of Lindisfarne was appointed. This was Cuthbert, who
is said to have been born at Kells and originally named Mo-Uallog (My
Proud One). He was supposed to have descended from Muirchertach Mac
Ercae Maic Eogain, High King of Ireland circa 507-536AD. He made his

Corbel from the church of
St Mary and St David,
Kilpeck, Herefordshire,
showing Sheela-na-gig, the
Celtic deity representing
both creation and
destruction.

127

way to Scotland and then to Northumbria where he decided to join the monastic community at Melrose (*Moel Ros* – The Bare Promontory). In 661AD he had been sent with other monks to Ripon. When Boisil, abbot of Melrose, died of the Yellow Plague, Cuthbert became his successor. In 683AD Theodore of Canterbury held a council at Twyford, on the Alne, and Cuthbert was elected bishop of Lindisfarne. He died on the Isle of Farne on March 20, 687AD.

The 'Golden Age' of Celtic learning in Northumbria began to reach its end. In May, 685AD, Aldfrith, a son of Oswy, became king. Oswy had re-married an Irish woman and his son Aldfrith had been born at Druffield, north Humberside. When a youth, he was sent for safety to Ireland and educated at the Irish monastic schools. He remained in exile *ob studium literarum exulabat* until he was a young man, living at Lisgoole, on the west bank of Lough Erne. He composed poetry in Irish and the authorship of three separate compositions has been ascribed to him. Irish annalists hailed him as 'the wondrous sage, Adamnán's pupil'. One of his poems praises the land of his exile.

> *I found in Armagh the Splendid,*
> *Meekness, wisdom, circumspection,*
> *Fasting in obedience to the Son of God,*
> *Noble, prosperous sages.*
>
> *I found in each great church,*
> *Whether inland, on shore or island,*
> *Learning, wisdom, devotion to God,*
> *Holy welcome protection.*
>
> *I found in the country of Tirconnell,*
> *Brave, victorious heroes,*
> *Fierce men, with fair complexion,*
> *The high stars of Ireland.*

Aldfrith, as has already been remarked, might have had a hand in the authorship of *Beowulf*. His reign can be described as the last of the age which saw Irish influence in Northumbria. Fifty years later the Vikings were raiding the coast, making their first appearance in 787AD. The books, art and learning of the Celts were almost extinguished. Lindisfarne itself was destroyed in a Norse raid in 793AD.

Celtic Christian influence had not been confined to the Northumbrian English. Celtic missionaries made their presence felt throughout all the Anglo-Saxon kingdoms. During the time of Bishop Finan, the Middle Angles were ruled by Peada, son of Penda of Mercia. The land of Middle Angles was situated between the Trent and Bedford. Peada married a daughter of Oswy of Northumbria and converted to Christianity. He asked his father-in-law if missionaries from Lindisfarne could be sent to preach to his people. Finan sent an Irish monk named Diuma with Northumbrians – Cedd, Adda and Bethin – in 653AD. Diuma soon left his companions to carry on the work and moved into Mercia. In 655AD Penda was killed and Peada, who succeeded him as ruler of Mercia, asked that Diuma be appointed bishop of the kingdom. In 659AD another Irishman, Cellach, succeeded Diuma. Cellach soon returned to Iona and thence back to Ireland. In turn he was succeeded by an Englishman named Trumhere and then by another Irishman named Jeruman, who was bishop of Mercia until 669AD when he was succeeded by Chad, the famous brother of Cedd, Chad was trained by Aidan and received some of his education in Ireland. He fixed his episcopal see at Lichfield where he died on March 2, 672AD.

Celtic influence swept south. In 653AD Sigebert of the East Saxons, (Essex) paid a visit to the Northumbrian court and was converted to Christianity, being baptised by Finan. He, too, asked for missionaries to work among his people. Cedd, the founder of the abbey at Lastingham, was made bishop of the territory and worked for ten years among the East Saxons, building a monastery at Bradwell-on-Sea, at the mouth of the Blackwater, and another at Tilbury. When Cedd was attending the council at Whitby, Sigebert was assassinated. Cedd, who had supported Colman in the debate, disheartened, retired to Lastingham where he died of the Yellow Plague. Some thirty-four priests whom he had ordained in Essex made a pilgrimage to the monastery and vowed to end their days at the shrine of their teacher. This, however, left Essex once more under pagan influence and Eata of Lindisfarne sent the Irishman Jaruman to reclaim it to the Christian fold.

At the same time the kingdom of the East Angles (East Anglia) was ruled by another Sigebert who had been brought up in Gaul and had become a Christian under the guidance of the Irish missionary, Columbanus. Sigebert returned to East Anglia in 631AD with a Burgundian bishop named Felix, who had been approved of by Honorius of Canterbury. Felix established his see at Dunwich, established a school and is remembered in the place name of Felixstowe. He died in Dunwich in 648AD. At the same time that Felix was engaged in converting the East Angles, there arrived a group of Irish missionaries led by Fursa, sometimes called Fursey. He arrived in 633AD with his brothers Foillan and Ultan and some other followers among whom were Gobban and Dicuil. Fursa is said to have been born in Ireland about 575AD, educated in the monastery of Medan on the isle of Insequin in Lough Corrib on which the ruins known as Killursa (Cill Fursa) stand.

Sigebert welcomed him and gave him some land at Cnobbersburgh (Burghcastle) in modern Suffolk, where he erected a monastery which, for twelve years, was the centre of his mission. Sigebert was impressed with Fursa and renounced his kingship to join his order as a monk, allowing a relative named Egric to succeed him. In 636AD Penda of Mercia, the ever greedy, land-hungry pagan, attacked East Anglia. The people demanded that Sigebert come out of the monastery to lead them in battle. Both Sigebert and Egric were killed but Penda was driven off. Anna became king and, fortunately, he was an ardent Christian.

However, in 645AD, Fursa put the monastery into the hands of his brother Foillan and went to live with Ultan in a hermitage in some desolate spot. Soon after he embarked for Gaul and it was not long before his brothers Foillan and Ultan followed him.

Dicuil, one of Fursa's companions, left East Anglia about 645AD to spread the faith further south. He took the first Christian mission into the land of the South Saxons (Sussex) which was one of the oldest Saxon settlements on the strip of land cut off from the rest of the country by the Andredsweald, a thick, hilly wood. Dicuil established a monastery at Bosham, near Chichester, and succeeded in converting the king of the South Saxons to Christianity, thus paving the way for Wilfred who, thirty years later, established his mission at Selsey. It is now Wilfred, rather than Dicuil, who is regarded as the apostle of Sussex.

Birinus, a Roman, was sent to England by Pope Honorius I to convert the 'inner parts' of England. The great kingdom of the West Saxons (Wessex) was still heathen and he decided to work amongst them. He succeeded in converting their ruler Cynegils about 635AD and was allowed to establish his see at the Wessex capital of Dorchester. He died in 650AD having laid the foundations for the bishoprics of Winchester, Salisbury and Wells. Cynegils died in 643AD, his daughter married Oswy of Northumbria, and his son Cenwalh ruled until 645AD when the ever warring Penda of Mercia drove him out. Cenwalh returned to rule in 648AD and died about 672-75AD. During his reign Birinus was succeeded by Agilbert, a Frank, who, according to Bede 'had then lived a long time in Ireland'. Agilbert, although trained in the Celtic Order, was a pro-Roman and attended the debate at Whitby in support of Wilfred.

Agilbert was visited in Dorchester by a former Irish colleague named Moeldubh (Mailduff) who decided to settle among the West Saxons. He built his cell near Ingelborne and pupils flocked to him from all over the country because of his fame for wisdom and learning. The place was called Mailduff's Burgh, eventually corrupted into Malmesbury and it is from William of Malmesbury we hear the story of its foundation. The most illustrious of Moeldubh's pupils was Aldhelm, who succeeded him as abbot of Malmesbury in 675AD. Aldhelm visited Rome at the request of Pope Sergius I and in 705AD King Ine of Wessex appointed him first bishop of Sherborne. During his episcopacy he became famous for his letter to Geraint of Dumnonia rebuking the Celts for their adherence to the Celtic Order. He died in 709AD.

While the Anglo-Saxons were eager, or so it seems, to learn from the

Celts, particularly from the Irish, the old racial antagonisms which they felt towards the Celtic world soon overshadowed the cultural wealth the Celts were passing on to them. In 810AD at the Council of Celchyth (Chelsea) it was decreed that no one of the Irish nation should be permitted to exercise any religious authority in England. And yet there is a footnote here for when Alfred the Great (849-899AD) became eager for literacy and learning it was to the Celts he turned for guidance. In 886AD he asked Asser, bishop and abbot of St David's to come to his court as his teacher and adviser. Under Asser's guidance, Alfred attempted to revive monasticism, the principal support of the Celtic Church; he codified the laws and it has been suggested that many progressive elements were taken from the Celtic law systems. Alfred rewarded Asser by making him bishop of Sherborne as well as abbot of lesser religious institutions. Asser became the biographer of this best known of the Anglo-Saxon kings.

The Celtic influence in converting the Anglo-Saxon kingdoms to Christianity cannot be underestimated although the subject tends to receive sparse mention. To the Irish, in particular, English Christendom owes an immeasurable debt; a debt later repaid with blood and conquest and the near destruction of the Irish nation.

Detail from the 7th Century tooled leatherwork cover of the Stonyhurst Gospel.

131

11
Europe

The establishment of Celtic monasteries and churches across the mainland of Europe from the 6th Century AD was the enthusiastic work of Irish monks and missionaries rather than the British Celts. There is little evidence that the British preached to other than their own people. The biggest movement of the British to mainland Europe was their settlement among their fellow Celts of Brittany. But we must not overlook the establishment of another British settlement at the mouth of the Rhine which became known as Brittenburg, town of the Britons. This was apparently Christianised in the time of Magnus Maximus. At the same time as the great exodus into Armorica, or Brittany, many other British Celtic tribes moved further southward to the Iberian peninsula. Here, under their priests and monks, they settled and gave the name Galicia to the new country. Galicia, it has been argued, has the same etymological root as Galatia and is thought to derive from the word *gallu* – strong. Orosius in the 5th Century AD speaks of the Celts in Galicia but wrongly ascribes their origins as being Irish.

The Council of Lugo, held by King Thiudemir, in 567AD, records a division of his realm into two provinces, each with its own bishop. It specifies that nine dioceses belonged to the bishop of Galicia, adding: 'To the See of Bretona belongs the churches which are among the Britons, together with the monastery of Maximus and the churches which are in Asturia.' The monastery was, in fact, that of Santa Maria de Bretona at Pastoriza, near Mondonedo.

In 572AD the bishop of Bretona emerges into history as Mahiloc (Mailoc) who signed the *acta* of the 2nd Council of Braga. The British Celts are represented at the 4th Council of Toledo in 633AD when they formally accepted Roman Orthodoxy. They also attended the 7th (646AD) and 8th (653AD) Councils of Toledo and the 3rd (675AD) Council of Braga. The See of Bretona existed until at least 830AD when it was ravaged by the Moors; perhaps it existed as late as the Council of Oviedo in 900AD. It was finally merged with the See of Oviedo and Mondonedo but the name still occurs in lists dating from 962AD. The place is still called Bretona as late as 1156AD in a *Privilegium* of Alphonso VII. The monastery of Santa Maria de Bretona was the centre of this Celtic diocese, extending its jurisdiction to all the Celts in the area. The *Life of St Fructuosus of Braga*, who died in about 655AD, and is not to be confused with his namesake who was martyred at Tarragona in 259AD, is believed to have been written just after his death. The Galician Church as described in this early *Life* is certainly Celtic in practice rather than Roman. The Celtic Church in Galicia was no longer recognisable as such by the early 8th Century AD. There is now little evidence of this Celtic settlement. Language and customs quickly merged. Today Galician and Portuguese derive from the same Hispanic dialect current in north west Spain in the Middle Ages. It crystallised into Portuguese which has been encouraged to be distinct from Spanish from the 16th Century AD while Galician, now in a Castilian Spanish speaking orbit, is fast disappearing.

It was the Irish, however, who were to be the *peregrinati pro Christo*. From the 6th Century AD they travelled as far east as Kiev and as far north as Iceland spreading the faith. Early sources state that it was Colmcille's disciple Cormac who sailed to the Faroes and then on to Iceland. The Irish geographer Dicuil, trained at Iona, writing his *De Mensura orbis terrae* about 835AD, also declares that Irish monks had established themselves on the Faroes. He is more specific about the Irish monastic settlement in Iceland, giving the date of 795AD, nearly seventy years before the Scandinavian discovery. Dicuil's testimony is borne out by Icelandic sources such as the *Islendígabók* and the *Landnámobók*.

Notwithstanding Colmcille, regarded as the 'First Exile', it was a namesake Columbanus who became the pioneer of the Irish religious mission in Europe. He was said to have been born in Leinster in 540AD and studied for six years under Sennanus (Senell) at Cluain Inis on Lough Erne. He then joined Comgall's monastic settlement at Bangor, Co. Down, and was ordained in 572AD. At the age of 50 he left for a mission to Gaul, then a divided and ravaged country, taking with him a small group of followers. Arriving in the territory now known as Burgundy he founded monastic settlements at Annegray, Luxeuil and Fontaines.

Luxeuil was his most famous foundation and a great many leading churchmen of the next generation received their training there. It was regarded as the most outstanding mother house of European monasticism. Its monks worked as far east as Bavaria. When the Celtic Church went into its decline, the monks of Luxeuil adopted the Rule of Benedict and survived until the French Revolution. Today the monastery buildings are still used as a seminary and the former abbey church possesses relics of St Columbanus which were brought from Bobbio in 1923. It also houses relics of Columbanus' famous disciple, St Gall, brought in 1950 from the Swiss city named after him. It was in 1950 that the Papal Nuncio to France, later to become Pope John XXIII blessed a statue of Columbanus at Luxeuil in a ceremony attended by the Irish President, Eamon de Valera.

It was Annegray, however, which was Columbanus' first monastic foundation and excavations on the site have revealed foundations and tombs dating back to the 7th Century AD. The site of Fontaines is nearby. Columbanus' Celtic monasticism and his celebration of Easter in accordance with the Celtic Church brought him into conflict with the pro-Roman bishops of Gaul. In 602AD they demanded that he appear before a Council at Châlons to explain himself. Columbanus firmly believed that the Celtic Order was right and that Rome was wrong; so firmly did he hold his views that he wrote to Pope Gregory (590-604AD) asking him to pronounce against the Roman Easter, saying that the learned men of Ireland thought Victorius' computations were deserving of laughter and pity. He claimed that the Celtic Church followed the computation of Anatolius of Laodicea which had been 'praised by St Jerome' but which scholars now believe was a computation concocted in Britain only fifty years before Columbanus was born. Three points in Columbanus' letter are important: he admitted that the Bishop of Rome and the Celts were united in the same movement; that he desired the Pope's *authority* to observe the Celtic Easter and, finally, that it lay with the Pope to decide what was acceptable to the Christian Movement. There is no evidence that the Pope replied. Laurentius, Augustine's successor as archbishop of Canterbury, had followed the conflict carefully for, in his letter to the Irish bishops, following Dagan's visit in 610AD, he mentions: 'We have been informed, however, by Bishop Dagan, coming into the aforesaid island, and by the Abbot Columbanus in Gaul, that the Irish in no way differ from the Britons in the observance ...'

In 610AD Columbanus was in trouble again, this time seriously. He incurred the enmity of the Frankish Queen Brunhild, widow of Sigebert, by rebuking her grandson Thierry II of Burgundy for his loose living. He and all Irish-born monks at Luxeuil were ordered to leave the country and, we are told, were taken by military escort and put on a ship for Ireland. A storm drove them back to land and, evading the authorities, Columbanus and his followers set out across Gaul eventually reaching Bregenz on Lake Constance in modern Germany.

Columbanus was now a prominent figure in European Christianity. He had busied himself not only with ecclesiastical matters but with politics and had emerged as a poet as well. It is strange to find such an ascetic, as he undoubtedly was, delighting in making parodies of ancient Greek and

Latin writers such as his poem to Fidolius based on an Ode by Horace which was an invective against avarice. It begins:

Accipe, quaeso,
nunc bipedali
condita uersu
carminulorum
minera parua;

Receive, I pray
now in two foot
verses measured,
of little songs
my tiny gifts;

For perhaps
it seems a novelty,
this scheme of verse
as you read it.
But yet that
famous poet
of the Grecians
by name Sappho
used to write
a lovely song.

His most quoted Latin verse is usually called 'The Boat Song' which is a poetic exhortation to his followers to persevere and was probably written on his journey to Lake Constance.

En siluis caesa fluctu meata acta carina
bicornis hreni et pelagus perlabitur uncta.
Heia ulri! nostrum reboans echo sonet heia!

See, cut in woods, through flood of twin horned Rhine
passed the keel, and greased slips over seas—
  Heave men! And let resounding echo sound our heave!

The wind raise blasts, wild rain-storms wreak their spite
but ready strength of men subdues it all—
  Heave men! And let resounding echo sound our heave!

Clouds melt away and the harsh tempest stills,
effort tames all, great toil is conqueror—
  Heave men! And let resounding echo sound our heave!

Endure and keep yourselves for happy things:
ye suffered worse, and these too God shall end—
  Heave men! And let resounding echo sound our heave!

Detail from a 9th Century cross slab at Nigg, Ross-shire, Scotland.

135

Thus acts the foul fiend; wearing out the heart
and with temptation shaking inmost parts—
  Ye men, remember Christ with mind still sounding heave!

Stand firm in soul and spurn the foul fiend's tricks
and seek defence in virtue's armoury—
  Ye men, remember Christ with mind still sounding heave!

Firm faith will conquer all and blessed zeal
and the old fiend yielding breaks at last his darts—
  Ye men, remember Christ with mind still sounding heave!

Supreme of virtues, King and fount of things,
He promises in strife, gives prizes in victory—
  Ye men, remember Christ with mind still sounding heave!

Columbanus had planned to establish a monastery at Bregenz but his antagonist Thierry had won a victory at Tolbiac in 612AD which extended his authority to the area and made it necessary for Columbanus to move on. However, one of his companions named Gall, who had been trained at Bangor, Co. Down, decided he would remain in the wild territory south of Lake Constance. Columbanus was furious and the two argued. Gall stayed and eventually founded a monastery around which a town grew and took its name from the monk – St Gall in Switzerland. Gall died in 640AD. His monastery, although not exclusively an Irish house, was certainly a centre to which many Irishmen came. One of the most notable was Moengal who became abbot there about 850AD. In 925AD, threatened by the Huns, the monks fled temporarily to Reichenau where there was another Irish settlement. They returned and the monastery existed until its suppression in 1797. It accumulated a priceless collection of manuscripts written by Irish scribes, many of which are still preserved today; works such as an 8th/9th Century AD *Gospel* which has equal illumination to the more famous *Book of Kells*, as well as a 9th Century AD *Priscian* grammar containing delightful lyric verses in Irish in the margins.

Leaving Gall behind him, Columbanus continued over the Alps and settled in Lombardy, establishing his monastic settlement at Bobbio in 612AD. He died there on November 3, 615AD. On his death bed he sent his *cambutta* or pastoral staff to Gall as a token that the quarrel between them was ended. The staff was long preserved at St Gall but disappeared in medieval times, although the churches in Kempten and Füssen claim to have portions of it still. Bobbio eventually adopted the Benedictine Rule and existed until its suppression in 1803. The former abbey church contains the white marble tomb of Columbanus; villages bear his name on both sides of the Alps and thirty-four Italian parishes claim him as their patron saint. The library at Bobbio, once celebrated for its wealth of early

Irish manuscripts, was eventually scattered to libraries in Florence, Vienna, Paris, Milan, Turin and the Vatican.

During the 7th Century AD countless Irish monks followed the example of Columbanus and flooded into Europe. The monasteries of Faremoutiers (627AD), Jouarre (630AD) and Rebais (636AD), all in the Brie, owe their origins to disciples of Columbanus. Rebais became a favourite stopping place for Irish pilgrims on the road to Rome. About 630AD two Irish monks named Fiachra (Fiacre) and Kilian arrived in Meaux. Kilian settled down at Aubigny where he is still venerated while Fiachra led a hermit's life at Breuil, outside Meaux. He then established a hostel for pilgrims and on his death, about 670AD, the place took his name, eventually becoming the famous School of St Fiacre in medieval times. The monastery was destroyed during the French Revolution but St Fiacre remains as the French patron saint of gardeners.

About the time another Irishman, Toimene, known by his Latin designation, Tomianus, became bishop of Angoulême. He signed the *acta* of the Council of Bordeaux (663-675AD) and helped reconstruct a monastery at Mazerolles, appointing another Irishman, Ronan, as its abbot. Angoulême had another Irish bishop in later years, Ailill, a pupil of the famous Irish philosopher Eriugena. He was appointed in 860AD. Another Irish trained monk Alcuin became bishop of Martin's famous see at Tours in 796AD and presided over its rise as one of the great scholastic centres of the Carolingian empire. Irish clerics and scholars frequented it, especially during the 9th Century AD. Various manuscripts are still preserved from this period such as the *Gospel of St Martin*, the *Gospel of Marmoutier* and the *Gospel of St Gatien*, all showing strong Irish affinities in script and ornamentation.

After a period as bishop among the East Saxons, Fursa crossed to Gaul. In 646AD he established a monastery at Lagny-en-Brie, on the banks of the Marne, near Paris. He began building a church at Péronne. He died at Mezerolles and a disciple named Erchinoald brought his body to Péronne. Around his shrine a new *monasterium Scottorum*, (Irish monastery) grew up, whose first abbot was Fursa's brother Foillan. Foillan had followed his brother to Gaul with his other brother Ultan, who became the second abbot of the monastery. Péronne remained under Irish control until its destruction by the Norse in 880AD. In Irish annals the town was called Cathair Fhursa, Fursa's Town, while other chronicles refer to it as Peronna Scottum – Irish Péronne. It was one of the earliest centres of St Patrick's cult in Europe. On the site of the destroyed Irish monastery there arose a collegiate church of 'St Furcy' which was destroyed during the French Revolution. Fursa's original monastic settlement at Lagny was taken over at his death by a fellow Irishman named Aemilian. Fursa, whom Bede said was 'renowned for his works and outstanding in goodness', became patron saint of Picardy.

Fursa's brother Foillan (also known as Faolan) was a friend of Gertrude of Nivelles. Her mother Itta, on the death of her husband, founded a monastery at Nivelles and appointed Gertrude as its abbess. She was only a teenager but she managed the settlement with her mother's help. She became friendly with Foillan who left Péronne to form a monastery for Irishmen near to her foundation at Fosses, in modern Belgium. In 655AD, while returning from a visit to Gertrude at Nivelles, Foillan was attacked and killed by robbers in the forest of Seneffe. Gertrude was heartbroken and, in the same year, she resigned as abbess, being only thirty years old, and died not long afterwards. Every seventh year, on September 25, the relics of Foillan are borne in solemn procession around the territory which once formed his monastic settlement. It is now one of the great folk festivals in the Belgian calendar. Nearby a church is dedicated to St Brigid and the cult of Brigid can also be found in many other parts of Belgium, including Liège and Amay where an annual pilgrimage is held in her honour on the first Sunday of May.

Another Irish missionary venerated in Belgium was Livinius of Ghent. He is said to have been martyred to pagan tribes near Hauthen in 660AD. Little else is known about him. Another Irish 'saint' who found her way to Belgium in the 7th Century AD is Dymphna of Geel who has been identified with Damhnait of Slieve Beagh, and whose name is still enshrined in the place name of Tydavnet (Tigh Damhnata) in Co. Monaghan. Tradition has it that Dymphna was the daughter of a pagan Irish ruler who fled to Geel because she wanted to devote herself to a Christian life. Her father followed her there and slew her with his own hand.

Irish missionaries had reached as far as Würzburg in Germany during the 7th Century AD. Kilian, who had settled for a time at Aubigny, said to be a native of Mullagh, Co. Cavan, converted Gozbert, the king of Würzburg, Gozbert was married to his brother's widow, Geilana, a proscribed marriage under Christian rule. Kilian persuaded Gozbert to separate from her. In revenge Geilana had Kilian murdered together with two fellow Irish missionaries, Colman and Totnan, on July 6, 689AD. Burchard, the first bishop of Würzburg, had their relics placed in his cathedral in 752AD and they are now enshrined in the crypt of Neumünster, erected, according to tradition on the site of the murder.

Würzburg was to become a prominent centre for Irish missionaries. Clemens Scottus, who succeeded the Irish-educated Alcuin as master of the Palace School of Charlemagne, died there during the 9th Century AD. The famous Irish chronicler Muirchertach mac Robertaig, known as Marianus Scottus, was ordained a priest here in 1059AD. David Scottus became master of the Würzburg cathedral school during the reign of Emperor Henry V. The permanent Irish community was recognised in the 12th Century AD as the Würzburg Schottenkloster which became an Irish

Benedictine monastery, and remained in Irish hands until 1497. By that time the real meaning of the word Scot had been forgotten. Clerics from Scotland claimed that the monastery was, by name, a Scottish one and demanded the expulsion of the Irish. With equal ignorance, the Pope agreed and a Scottish community moved in and remained there until 1803. The church there is still called the Schottenkirche. A similar Scottenkirche existed at Ratisbon, an Irish foundation, in 1515AD and here again the singularly ignorant and unjust claims of Scottish Benedictines were upheld and the Irish community removed. Scottish monks occupied Ratisbon until 1893. Würzburg University still retains many manuscripts brought by the Irish monks of which the most celebrated is the 8th Century AD *Codex of St Paul's Epistles* with its notes in Irish providing the earliest corpus of written Irish to survive from the period. The name Kilian is to be found everywhere in the city, including the Kilianfest, Würzburg's annual festival.

During the 8th Century AD the Irish missionaries continued to stream into Europe. One of the most notable of this period was Dungal, many of whose writings have survived including letters to the Emperor Charlemagne and some Latin poems. He made a notable contribution to the Carolingian Renaissance. He appears to have settled at St Denis, beside Paris' Le Bourget aerodrome, about 784AD and was still living there in 827AD. Some scholars have attempted to identify him with Dungal, appointed supervisor of education at Pavia in Lombardy by Lothar. However, the contribution of Dungal of St Denis, as well as countless other Irish scholars, to the Carolingian Renaissance was immense. Aix-La-Chapelle (Aachen) was the Carolingian capital and it was to this spot that many Irish scholars came. The *Gesta Caroli Magni* mentions two Irishmen who were the first to arrive—one of them was Dungal and the other was Clemens Scottus who wrote *Ars Grammatica* (dedicated to Lothar) about 809-812AD. When Alcuin left his post as master of Charlemagne's palace school, Clemens succeeded him. Among the other Irish scholars at the court at this time was Alcuin's friend, the poet Joseph; Tomás, a teacher and composer of puzzles; Cruinnmaol, the author of a tract on prosody; and Dicuil from Iona, who wrote the first and best geographical work of the new empire—*De Mensura orbis terrae* in 825AD.

In 744AD an Irishman named Abel became archbishop of Rheims. He was appointed on the advice of an Englishman—Boniface of Crediton—who ironically won the title of 'hammer of the Celtic Church'. Boniface, who had been christened Wynfrith, was born in Crediton in Wessex about 675AD. In 718AD, having won renown as a teacher, he left to preach to the Germans, visited Rome three times and was made a bishop with his see at Mainz. In 732AD Pope Gregory III appointed him archbishop. He urged the Frankish King Pippin the Short to reform his church and suppress any trace of the Celtic Order being brought in by

Irish missionaries. In 755AD, in Dokkum, modern Holland, he was slain by heathen tribesmen. Abel must have been an adherent of the Roman Order for Boniface to have recommended him. At the time of his appointment he was a monk in the monastery of Lobbes, in Hainault. He did not last in Rheims long because Melo, his deposed predecessor returned and threw him out and Abel returned to Lobbes to be its abbot. In the following century, however, Rheims became the headquarters of a group of Irish scholars and the unusual style of Latin poetry composed there seems to have been influenced by Irish metrics. Dunchad (Donatus), who once taught in the monastery of San Remi, became the second Irishman to be appointed archbishop of Rheims.

The Englishman Boniface won his reputation as 'hammer of the Celtic Church' not only for his reforms with Pippin the Short but for his feud with the Irish monk named Fearghal, known as Virgilius. Fearghal had been placed in charge of St Peter's monastery at Salzburg by Odilo, ruler of Bavaria, in 742AD. He ruled his diocese according to the customs of the Celtic Church remaining only as an abbot and having any sacraments which demanded episcopal orders conferred by a fellow Irishman Dubhdachrich (sometimes Latinised as Dobdagrecus). Dubhdachrich was bishop of Chiemsee. Fearghal only accepted an episcopacy in 767AD at the Pope's insistence. He died on November 27, 784AD. Fearghal was a source of annoyance to Boniface who regarded Bavaria as his personal ecclesiastical territory. Boniface accused Fearghal of sowing hatred between himself and Odilo of Bavaria. Fearghal survived this but not long afterwards attained some fame with his cosmographical writings. Boniface promptly seized upon them as the subject for complaint to Pope Zachary. The Pope saw nothing wrong with them and supported Fearghal. But Boniface had another try, presumably with another tract by Fearghal, pointing out the implications of some cosmological speculations which it is reported Zachary found shocking. However, whatever Fearghal's ideas were, he was appointed ecclesiastical administrator of Salzburg in 767AD and was eventually canonised by Pope Gregory IX in 1233AD.

In the same area, at Wilparting, the church contains the relics of two other 8th Century AD Irish missionaries – Anian and Marin – who worked in the region. Their bodies are entombed in the centre of the church before the high altar; their skulls are enshrined in the sanctuary which also contains an early Irish ecclesiastical bell. Yet another Irishman, Permin, who died about 754AD, having founded the monastery of Reichenaeu on an island in Lake Constance made it into one of the richest continental libraries containing one of the biggest sources of early Irish material. The monastery was suppressed in 1757AD and its books were scattered throughout various libraries in Europe. Nearby the town of Constance (Konstanz) boasted a Schottenkloster which, in the 12th Century AD, became an Irish Benedictine house. At Gottschalk the abbot Remigius became the centre of a controversy on predestination, the abbot seemingly holding Pelagian views. It may be significant that Remigius was a pupil of Donchad, archbishop of Rheims.

So many Irishmen had arrived in Europe and obtained important positions that in 870AD Heiric, the bishop of Auxerre, could claim: 'Almost all Ireland, despising the sea, is migrating to our shores with a herd of philosophers.' This 'herd' produced the most considerable philosopher in the Western world between Augustine of Hippo and Thomas Aquinas. He has come down to us as Eriugena, which, like the name Scotus at this time, simply means Irishman. He is also referred to as Johannes Scotus but, under this name, is often confused with John Duns Scotus (1266-1308AD). Eriugena as we shall call him, was an idealist, a poet, mystic as well as philosopher. He seems to have begun his writing career around 850AD and his last known writing was in 875AD. Some fourteen works of his have been identified to date.

Attempts to guess the date of his birth vary between 800AD and 828AD. What is certain is that he appears at the court of Charles the Bald in the early 840's AD at the time Charles was deciding to create a culture worthy of his conquests and thus instigated the Carolingian Renaissance. Of the scholars who contributed to this great renaissance of learning, listed by Cappuyns, there were a quarter with obvious Irish names.

The first certain echo of Eriugena's existence comes in 851-2AD when Pardulus, bishop of Laon, speaks of him writing at the king's court. Heiric of Auxerre refers to him as being a distinguished philosopher before that date. There are other tributes to his fame in a letter from Pope Nicholas I to Charles the Bald. Eriugena was, in fact, the only scholar at Charles' court who was able to translate the Greek of the pseudo-Dionysius thanks to his training in the Irish monastic schools. Charles sent the translation to Pope Anastasius and his librarian is on record as being filled with astonishment at the high standard of scholarship.

Eriugena's first major work seems to be a refutation of the philosophy of predestination in 850AD entitled *De Praedestinatione* which caused some embarrassment for it was seen as a pro-Pelagian tract. The next work to be identified was a commentary on the work of Martianus Capella. His greatest work was undoubtedly his *De divisione naturae* – On the Division of Nature. In this work Eriugena rises from being just a philosopher to poetical heights. His teaching was difficult to comprehend and was therefore ignored for three hundred years after his death when it gave rise to a controversy. The basic idea was that nothing could be predicted of God in human terms, not even existence! We have an idea which seems to echo the Zen of the druids. Eriugena wrote:

God exists; no, He does not exist. He is superior to the mere existence with which He Himself endows all His Creatures. He rules the universe which

141

He created and pervades the whole of it with His Own being while adhering to no part of it. His Nature is of the highest kind, far removed from all else, since He is Himself the simple Essence underlying everything: He is the end and the beginning of all things which have existence; He is good and beautiful, being the very shape of beauty in all forms.

Again there is an echo of druidic teaching; all things have a soul and man is but a tiny fragment of a world soul. Eriugena undoubtedly derived much of his pantheism from the mass of Irish thought and produced a system which resembles neo-Platonism. He saw reality as a movement within infinite repose, expressing things in terms of evolution to emphasise movement or in terms of continuum to draw attention to repose. He concentrated on a picture of man as part of the harmony of creation – again an echo of druidic philosophy. There seems no trace of Eriugena after 875AD and it is assumed that he died shortly thereafter.

The great contemporary of Eriugena was Sedulius Scottus, Siadhuil or Shiel the Irishman. Sedulius is thought to have been a Leinsterman. He, with two fellow Irishmen, arrived in Gaul at Christmas, 845AD, and presented themselves to Hartgar, the bishop of Liège, asking for employment. Hartgar gave them a house with some land where sheep could be grazed and became the patron of the Irish monks. Sedulius soon launched forth in praise of him.

Then, Hartgar, powerful prelate, raise the weak,
Cherish the learned Irish with gentle heart,
So blessed in heaven's high temples may you walk,
Celestial Jerusalem and enduring Zion.

Soon the group of three Irishmen were joined by others. In one affectionate poem Sedulius names four Irish companions – Fergus, Marcus,. Blandus and Beuchell – as 'four charioteers of the Lord, lights of the Irish race'. The house in Liège became a miniature Celtic monastic settlement, with Sedulius as its head. Many of his colleagues actually autographed the manuscripts of his poems – Fearghus, Dubthach, Cathasach, Suadbar, Comhglan and others. Liège was becoming one of the important bishoprics and Hartgar was winning a reputation as a powerful potentate with a fine establishment. Indeed, so rich was Hartgar's house compared with the little Irish monastery that Sedulius felt obliged to make a poetical protest.

Our dwelling shudders in a cloak of black;
When daylight comes she promptly sends it back,
Grows ever blacker and assumes a guise
Not fit, I say, for scholars or the wise
Such as love splendour and the gifts of light,
But more for moles and owls and things of night.

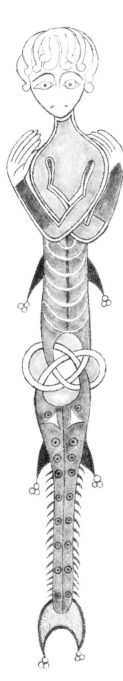

From the Book of Kells

> *Oh, Hartgar! All such that cannot see*
> *Gather together and bring them here to me –*
> *For this dark house a fitting use we'll find.*
> *We christen it: 'Asylum for the Blind'.*

Suitably rehoused, Sedulius gave himself over to pursuing his poetic career but not for him the harsh asceticism of the Cele Dé.

> *The crops are green and fields are all in flower,*
> *Budding the vine – the year now has its hour,*
> *Gay-painted songbirds fill the air with glee,*
> *There's smile on land and sky and laughs the sea.*

> *Of mirth-provoking sap, I, too, have need,*
> *Some beer, or Bacchus' gift or perhaps some mead;*
> *And then there's meat, produce of earth and sky,*
> *And I have none, but ask the reason why.*

> *Now Muse, I write and sing, am Orpheus reborn,*
> *But too have needs, the ox that treads the corn;*
> *Your champion I, with wisdom's arms I fight:*
> *Off Muse to the bishop, acquaint him with my plight.*

As early as 851AD some of his verses were being embroidered in silk by the emperor Lothar's wife, Ermingarde. Apart from his few works directed to his Irish colleagues, his poetry was aimed at the Frankish world and written in Latin rather than Irish. Sedulius liked to live near to the top of society, was an urban character, witty and fond of conversation. He liked a joke and left us with a poem which mocks at his faults. His poems were in the Celtic bardic style; when Hartgar died he wrote a typical Celtic elegy and was also ready with a panegyric in praise of Hartgar's successor, Bishop Franco (854-901AD). The University of Leyden (Holland) contains four letters written by Irish pilgrims en route to Rome to Bishop Franco, who seemed to take over from Hartgar as a patron of the Irish monks.

However, to imply that Sedulius was simply a pleasure-loving poet is to do him injustice. He was an outstanding Greek and Latin scholar. He wrote commentaries on the works of Eutyches and Priscian, a commentary on the *Gospel of Matthew* and another on the *Epistles of Paul*. His most important ecclesiastical work was *De Rectoribus Christianis*, On Christian Rulers, a treatise on the duties of kingship, written for Lothar II, son of Lothar I. It deals with the problems of the relationship between state and church and is regarded as an important contribution to the development of political thought in the Middle Ages. The work is in prose but every section is reiterated in verse, a form of writing which was becoming increasingly popular in his native Ireland. Of the eighty of his poems which have survived, most of them are scattered in various European libraries. One remnant is a Greek Psalter in his own hand. Sedulius' epitaph could be one of his own poems.

Auto lega vel scribo, doceo scrutorve sophiam:
  obsecro celsithronum nocte dieque meum.
Vescor, poto libens, rithmizans invoco Musas,
  dormisco stertens: oro Deum vigilans.
Conscia mens scelereum deflet peccamina vitae;
  parcite vos misero, Christe Maria, viro.

I read, write, I teach or wonder what is truth,
  I call upon my God by night and day.
I eat and freely drink, I make my rhymes,
  And snoring sleep, or vigil keep and pray.
And very aware of all my faults I am:
  Ah, Christ and Mary, have mercy on your man.

The middle of the 9th Century AD saw another increase in Irish monasteries and hospices, this time outside the borders of the Frankish kingdom. They became scattered widely throughout the Germanic dominions. In 883AD Charles the Fat gave the villa of Rotis to an Irish monk named Eusebius who maintained it as a hospice for Irish pilgrims en route to Rome. In the next century St Michael's abbey in Thierache and an abbey at Waulsort, near Dinant, in the Ardennes, were established by groups of Irish pilgrims. Cadroe, the Irish abbot of Waulsort, was summoned to Metz by Bishop Adalbero I (929-62AD) and asked to reform the abbey there in 953AD. He was succeeded in his task by another Irishman, Forannan. Under Adalbero II (984-1005AD) Fingen, abbot of St Clement in Metz, was appointed abbot of St Symphorien, which was given a charter by Pope John XVII and from the Emperor Otto III laying down the rule that only Irish monks should be received at the monastery. Fingen ended his career at the monastery of St Vannes in Verdun where, it is recorded, 'only seven Irish monks (were) under his abbacy'. He died there in 1005AD. Cologne boasted a considerable Irish colony at this time and in 975AD the archbishop Eberger assigned the monastery of St Martin to the Irish in perpetuity. Marianus Scottus, who lived here from 1056-58AD, records the names of all the abbots from 975AD to 1061AD and all were Irish. Another monastery in Cologne, St. Pantaleon, was granted to the Irish in 1042AD.

In the dying years of the Celtic Church a new wave of asceticism gripped the Irish monks — it manifested itself in a movement called the '*inclusus*'. Many Irish monks had themselves walled up in their cells. Marianus Scottus records the tragic death of one Irish *inclusus* named Paternus who was burnt to death in his cell in 1058AD having been walled up for many years. Marianus himself became an *inclusus* and was walled up in his cell at Mainz from 1069-82AD. Another Irish *inclusus* was Muircheartach who lived near Obermünster in Regensburg. Nearby at Ratisbon an Irish Benedictine monastery was founded which became the mother house for several continental Irish monasteries. Its third abbot Ciolla Crios Mac Carthaigh received considerable financial aid from his family in Ireland to build the place. It remained in Irish hands until 1515AD. The relics of Muircheartach are kept there still in the sacristy of the seminary which stands where Obermünster once stood.

Muircheartach influenced another Irishman named John, who met the *inclusus* in Bavaria. John went on a pilgrimage down the Danube to Melk where a tomb had been erected in honour of an Irish monk Colman who had been murdered at Stockerau in 1012AD while making a pilgrimage to Jerusalem. According to tradition Colman was the son of Maolsheachlainn II High King of Ireland 980-1002AD and 1014-22AD. A community of wood cuters thought Colman was a Magyar spy and he was tortured and hanged on July 16, 1012AD. His tomb became a place of Austrian pilgrimage in medieval times. Also at Melk is the tomb of another Irishman, Gothalm, who set out from Ireland in search of his friend Colman and died there in 1019AD. He, too, is widely venerated in Austria.

An Irish monastery was established at Vienna, by Gille-na-Maemh and monks from this house established a daughter house in Kiev at the end of the 12th Century AD. They had to withdraw from it in 1241AD in the face of the Mongol invasion. The Vienna community passed to the Austrian Benedictines at the beginning of the 15th Century AD. The city which grew up around the monastic settlement still recalls the original Irish monks with Scotten-Gasse and Scotten-Ring while the abbey bears the evocative title of *Abtei Unserer Lieben Frau zu den Schotten*. To the north another Irish monastery was founded at Nuremburg in 1140AD and remained in Irish hands until the 15th Century AD. Adam of Bremen, master of the cathedral school of Mecklenburg, recounts how the city of Nuremburg was converted from paganism by Bishop John of Ireland who suffered martyrdom there about 1066AD. Erfurt was another Irish monastic foundation represented at a council of the abbots of the Irish monasteries held in Regensburg in 1211AD under the presidency of the abbot of Regensburg, Crinat.

With the crusading zeal of the early Celtic Church it is obvious that the Irish missionaries would not be daunted by moving into Italy itself. Columbanus was not the first Irishman to establish himself there. In 560AD there is a reference to Fridian becoming bishop of Lucca having led a hermit's life on Monte Pisano for some time. He died on March 18, 588AD, and was buried at the church that bears his name. In 782AD his relics were removed and are now kept in a glass coffin beneath the high altar. Another Irishman Sillan, or Silanus, is said to have become bishop here at the turn of the 12th Century AD and his relics are preserved at the convent of La Secca.

The Irish established four monasteries in Italy: Columbanus' Bobbio; Fridian's Lucca, St Martin's in Mensola and the Holy Trinity of the Scots in Rome itself. A hospice at Piacenza was established by Donatus in 850AD and a hospice in Vercelli and one in Pavia.

Fiesole, inland from Lucca, preserves the memory of Donatus, the Irishman who became bishop here in 829AD and whose remains repose in the cathedral. Of Donatus' literary activity, three specimens have survived: a metrical *Credo*; an epitaph and a description of Ireland in verse, elegiac and based on the model of Virgil's praise of Italy. The poem begins:

The noblest share of earth is the far western world
Whose name is written Ireland in the ancient books;
Rich in goods, in silver, jewels, cloth and gold,
Benign to the body, in air and mellow soil.

There no poison harms, no serpent glides in the grass,
No frogs harshly sing loud complaint in the lake.
Worthy are the Irish to dwell in this their land,
A race of men renown in war; in peace, renowned in faith.

Also venerated at Fiesole is Andrew, said to be born of an Irish chieftain's family in the early years of the 9th Century AD, who followed Donatus as his disciple and died shortly after him.

The Irish establishments in Italy caused the widespread veneration of Irish saints throughout the country. The cults of Patrick, Brigid, and Gall are to be found in many places. Ursus is honoured in Aosta; Gunifort in Pavia; Columbanus at Bobbio; Cummian at Bobbio; Fulco at Piacenza; Emilian at Faenza; Pellegrino in Parma and Reggio; Fridian at Lucca, Sillen at Lucca; and Donatus and Andrew at Fiesole. But no Irish saint, not even Columbanus, is the object of a cult as widespread over Italy as Cathal.

Cathal was born in Ireland at Canty near Waterford, early in the 7th Century AD. He studied at Lismore and some have suggested that he taught there. About 666AD he went on a pilgrimage to the Holy Land and on his return journey he was shipwrecked off the Italian coast in the Gulf of Taranto. As the people of Taranto were without a bishop at this time it was looked upon as divine providence and he was appointed their bishop. He lived and worked there for fifteen years and, when he died, was buried in the cathedral. In 1071AD when the cathedral was being rebuilt, workmen reported the discovery of a sarcophagus containing the uncorrupted body of a man with a gold cross on his breast bearing the words 'Cataldus Rachau'. The relics were subsequently enshrined and are preserved with a medieval statue of the saint in silver in the cathedral which is dedicated to him. The Irish place name Rachau has been identified with Shanrathan (Old Rathan) an ancient monastic site in Co. Tipperary. Cathal's cult is spread not only across Italy but France and Malta. Sicily's town of San Cataldo is named after him. During World War II his name was invoked as the patron saint of Italian soldiers.

It must not be presumed that the Irish monks, who took their faith into the farthest corners of Europe, never looked back to their homeland nor felt homesick. Their feelings of exile are summed up in a remarkable 9th Century AD poem written by a poet-monk named Colman to his namesake who was just about to depart for Ireland. Helen Waddell has translated it thus:

> So, since your heart is set on those sweet fields
>   And you must leave me here,
> Swift be your going, heed not my prayers,
>   Althou the voice be dear.
> Vanquished art though by love of thine own land,
>   And who shall hinder love?
> Why should I blame thee for thy weariness,
>   And try thy heart to move?
> Since, if but Christ would give me back the past,
>   And that first strength of days,
> And this white head of mine were dark again,
>   I, too, might go your ways.
>
> All those far seas and shores that must be crossed,
>   They terrify me; yet
> Go thou, my son, swift be thy cleaving prow
>   And do not quite forget.

The Irish missionary influence continued for many centuries after the original outward missionary push of the Celtic Church. Men like Tadhg Machar of Co. Cork who died in Aosta on October 24, 1492AD, are still venerated outside their native country. Philosophers, too, continued to make their way to the courts of Europe or to the religious houses founded by Irish monks.

One of the last outstanding Celtic philosophers was the Scottish Franciscan John Duns Scotus who left his native country to become a teacher at the University of Oxford. By the 13th Century AD 'Scot' had arrived at its modern meaning, although he has been claimed for Ireland. In 1304AD he went to Paris and then spent four years at Cologne. John first shook the confidence of scholars in their own power. He recognised the distinction between matters of faith and reason. He did not believe, as did Thomas Aquinas, that such matters as the immortality of the soul or the resurrection of the body could eventually be proved by science and logic. Faith was to him a divine gift by which men could believe. A world without faith was simply a world of blind men and the revelation of faith was more convincing than the revelation of sight.

In recognising the widespread missions of the Irish monks and scholars, we have seen them penetrate as far east as Kiev and as far north as Iceland. Many scholars now toy with the theory that intrepid Irish monks could have reached as far west as the New World – America. We have previously mentioned that the Kerryman, Brendan the Voyager, who established the monastery of Clonfert, Co. Galway, about 560AD, was an intrepid explorer who voyaged through the Western Isles of Scotland, reaching their remotest outpost – St Kilda. Not long after his foundation at Clonfert it is said that he set off on a long voyage into the Atlantic where his biographer, Cummian, says 'he spent seven years on the great whale's back' – a poetic version of a voyage in a large curragh. *Betha Brenainn*, in the *Book of Lismore*, is the earliest version of the voyage, while *Vita St Brendani* in the *Codex Kilkenniensis* is substantially a translation into Latin from the Irish source. Many scholars, examining the details, have tried to identify the 'Land of Promise' to which Brendan is said to have sailed, far west in the Atlantic. Some have suggested the Canary Isles, others have suggested Greenland while a growing body say Brendan actually landed on the North American continent. A new dimension to this theory was provided in 1976 when a Harvard professor, Tim Severin, and a small group, constructed a boat, in the style of a curragh, making it of hides according to instructions in an 8th Century AD Latin-Irish text. They named it after Brendan and proceeded to sail it across the North Atlantic. They succeeded in reaching America and, astonishingly, their voyage compared to the many incidents in the voyage described in the Irish *Life*; they encountered the same landscape, animals and marine phenomena. Professor Severin has therefore proved it possible that Brendan and his monks reached America at least four centuries before the Norse claim and nine centuries before Christopher Columbus.

There is an additional note of interest to the theory of early Celtic voyages to America. As early as 1946 William B. Goodwin, in a publication entitled *The Remains of Greater Ireland in New England*, maintained that an ancient site called Mystery Hill in North Salem, New Hampshire, was the remains of a monastery erected by Cele Dé monks. In 1976 the world of Celtic scholarship was disturbed by the publication of a book by another Harvard professor, Barry Fell, entitled *America Ba*. The astonishing claim in this book was that there were several Celtic sites in America and that they were pre-Christian. Professor Fell had been a student of Celtic studies at Edinburgh University, Scotland, and as a professor at Harvard his work carries a degree of authority, especially his intriguing examination of what he sees as Gaelic loan words in the Algonquin Indian language. The work was received with an icy silence among Celtic scholars. Professor Gearóid Mac Eoin, Professor of Old and

Middle Irish at Galway, has pointed out the weakness of Professor Fell's contentions. In arguing the case for loan-words on the similarity of words in Goidelic Celtic and the Algonquin language, he has ignored the linguistic changes which have occurred in Goidelic Celtic during the last two thousand years, for Fell's contention is that contact was made between the Celts and the American Indians in the period 500BC – 1AD. Goidelic, which split into Irish, Scottish Gaelic and Manx long after this period, obviously went through cataclysmic changes. In citing the word *cuithe* (pit) as the origin for the Algonquin word *cuiche* (gorge) he demonstrates the weakness of his argument. The word *cuithe* was borrowed from the Latin *puteus*, a fact which puts it as late as the 4/5th Century AD. Therefore, no Celt in the period of the first five centuries BC could have taken the word to the Algonquin nation. Similarly, Fell assumes that the Algonquin language has also remained stagnant for two thousand years. This is simply linguistically impossible.

However, the fact remains, as Tim Severin demonstrated in his account of his expedition, *The Brendan Voyage* (1978) that there is a strong possibility that Celts did reach the New World during the early Christian period. According to Professor Gwyn Willians of Cardiff, a Welsh claim ante-dates the claim of Brendan in the voyage of Madoc. It is a field of study which is just beginning to open up before scholastic research.

Detail of a capital letter from an illuminated manuscript, Amiens, France.

Epilogue

The phenomenon of the Celtic Church was, without doubt, one of the most important cultural influences in Europe during the Dark Ages. Without the Celtic scholastic foundations, the Celtic love of literacy and their great libraries, it can be argued that an enormous amount of Europe's cultural heritage would have perished in the destructive ravages of their more warlike neighbours. It was in the Celtic monasteries that many valuable works of Hebrew, Greek and Latin were preserved in safe-keeping for posterity; it was in those same monasteries where the Celts' own significant literatures were safe-guarded. The merger of Celtic culture with Christian religion produced an entity which was unique; a fierce asceticism; a philosophical approach which would be recognised instantly by Zen masters, and an overwhelming love of learning, of knowledge and literacy.

In the 6th Century AD, the British Celtic bard Taliesin wrote: 'Christ the Word from the beginning was from the beginning our teacher, and we never lost his teaching. Christianity was in Asia a new thing, but there never was a time when the Druids of Britain held not its doctrines.' In these lines we see recognised the fact which early chapters of this work have tried to underline: – that the transition by the Celts from their pre-Christian religion to Christianity was an easy one.

It is also demonstrably arguable that the Celtic Church played an important part in the evolution of mainstream Christianity and was not simply a peripheral phenomenon. The marriage of their own social and religious teachings with Christianity from Rome played an important part in the shaping of the new religion. The first Celt to emerge on the international Christian stage was Gaulish bishop of Poitiers, Hilary (circa 315-367AD) who wrote the theological discourse *De Trinitate* expressing the concept of the Holy Trinity which is so much an accepted part of Christianity today. We have already seen that the trinity concept was an integral part of pre-Christian Celtic religion and philosophical experience. It has been argued, therefore, that this important piece of Christian philosophical doctrine was a Celtic import as it is not found in the Greek or Judaic origins of Christianity.

Philosophically, the Celtic Church provided a counter to the materialistic consciousness of the rest of Christendom. Hilary, Pelagius, Colmcille, Columbanus, Eriugena, Sedulius Scottus, were representative of a culture which looked on nature and the material world as a spiritual entity; all forms of life were holy; all forms of life were possessed of spirit. Accepting the brevity of life, its conditions, the Celtic philosophers strove not for the mastery of the world, the imposition of will or the concept of imperial continuity; the goal that was sought was an inner illumination, the growth of spiritual awareness within the external world.

Through their ancient religion, and then with the new vibrancy of Celto-Christianity, they applauded the battle of the individual against outside domination. The individual struggle was a portion of the battle against the oppression of empires; the state; between light and darkness; good and evil; spirituality and materialism; above all it was a constant exuberant celebration of the expression of Free Will.

From the outset the Celts emphasised the Free Will aspect of their Christianity in the face of the anti-Free Will concepts of the Greco-Latin philosophers. Augustine of Hippo would have had the people believe that Free Will did not exist and it was that teaching which caused the British Celt Pelagius to denounce it as an obnoxious philosophy, imperilling the entire moral law. Pelagius said that man and woman were responsible for all their deeds – good and evil. If, as Augustine claimed, they were not and everything was pre-ordained, or predestined, what was there to restrain people from giving up to the baser side of their natures? Today, every Christian would accept the philosophy of Free Will although Pelagius is still considered, officially, as a heretic.

In August, 1923, during the celebrations at Bobbio in honour of Columbanus, Pope Pius XI (*Civiltà Cattolica*) paid tribute to the work of the Celtic Church and especially to the work of the Irish monks. 'The more light is thrown on the dark places of the early Middle Ages by patient investigations of scholars,' said Pope Pius, 'the more manifest it becomes that the re-birth to Christian wisdom and civilisation in various parts of France, the Germanies, and Italy is due to the labours and the zeal of Columbanus – a striking testimony to the merits of the priesthood and more particularly to Catholic Ireland.'

Yet the heritage of Celtic Christianity as a vibrant philosophical force no longer seems to exist today, even in the countries which gave it birth. Across the world most people view Northern Ireland as a symbol of narrow religious intolerance and bigotry. The anti-Catholic rhetoric of Northern Irish Protestant leaders such as Ian Paisley rings around the world to the abashment of the ecumenical movement. It would be wrong to pass over this conflict when considering the historical influences of Celtic Christianity, for Ian Paisley is as much a descendant of the Celtic Church as Irish Catholics, Welsh Methodists and Manx Anglicans.

From the outset it should be made clear that religious intolerance as the cause of the problems of Northern Ireland is a myth; the basis of the problem is a political one but religion was developed and honed as a political weapon by unscrupulous manipulative people who fed on the fears of one or other groups for their own political ends. Before dealing with this conflict one must first look to the Scottish Reformation which gave birth to Presbyterianism.

The Reformation came late to Scotland and yet the Catholic Church there was in a more corrupt and degraded state than in other countries. The Church was rich and made richer by lavish ecclesiastical subsidies by the Pope. The Bishop of Moray had nine children to keep and daughters to provide dowries for out of Church funds; Father Adam Colquhoun of Stobo lived in splendid luxury in Drygate, Glasgow, with his mistress Mary Boyd and his two sons. Alexander Stewart, illegitimate son of James IV, was made Archbishop of St Andrews at the age of eleven. Unrest against such injustices was rife as the church wallowed in feudal splendour.

There were exceptions, men such as Bishop Dunbar of Aberdeen, who wanted reforms from within the Church, and young priests such as Father John Knox who were prepared to take 'direct action'. Knox was involved in the murder of Cardinal James Beaton, Archbishop of St Andrews. He was captured and sentenced to the galleys. On his release he went to England to serve as chaplain to Edward VI but, on the accession of Mary Tudor, he went to Geneva and came under the influence of Calvin. Eventually he returned to Scotland where his impact was formidable.

In 1560 the Scottish Parliament abolished the authority of the Pope and the celebration of the Latin Mass. John Knox was among the men who were given the task of formulating a new creed and constitution for the reformed church. Compared with the Reformation in other countries there were few martyrs in Scotland: – seven Protestants before it and only two Catholics afterwards. The majority of the clergy either joined the new church or were pensioned off. Such was the corruption and decay into which Queen Margaret's reforms had sent the Scottish Church plunging that it fell apart of its own accord. The time for bloodshed was to come later.

The new church became governed by a Kirk Session of lay elders and later by district Presbyteries possessing power to ordain ministers. New ideas took over from Knox's original liturgy. Knox – for example – had seen Holy Communion as being a central part of the reformed religion. But his ideas were abandoned in favour of a new austerity which was called Presbyterianism.

The bloody years of Mary, Queen of Scots, gave way to the equally bloody years of James VI, who became James I of England. James VI declared himself in favour of episcopacy, church government by bishops, as had happened with the Church of England. He was soon in conflict with the Presbyterians now led by Andrew Melville, who was more zealous in his views than ever Knox was. He maintained that the Presbyterian Church should be able to instruct civil magistrates and direct the affairs of the state and not *vice versa*. There thus began a fresh trend towards extreme Calvinism.

James VI was able to manipulate the new zeal as a springboard for an attempt to stamp out those clans among which the native Celtic culture and traditions persisted. His 'Letters of Fire and Sword' became notorious in which he ordered the genocide of entire clans, such as Clàn Gregor, the Macdonalds of Islay, and others. The Reformation thereby became a genocidal engine to smash Celtic culture.

At the same time, James VI tried to check Presbyterianism and dis-establish it as the national church in Scotland. In 1638 the Scottish National Council rebelled and re-established it, and Charles I sent an army into Scotland to bring his Scottish subjects to heel.

In the early 17th Century, therefore, many Presbyterian Scots seized the opportunity to go as colonists to Ireland. The opportunity had been opened up during the Tudor colonisation schemes and in 1607, following the defeat and flight of the Ulster chieftains, Tyrone and Tyrconell, 511,645 acres of land were confiscated from the Ulster clans and opened to colonisation. The majority of new colonists came from Scotland, seeking lands in which to be able to practise their new Presbyterian religion in freedom. They came from Galloway and Fife, both areas which were still Scottish-Gaelic speaking, so that – religion apart – they had few cultural differences. There was even widespread intermarriage.

However, the Anglican Church persecuted the new colonists as much as they persecuted native Catholics. Lord Strafford, Lord Deputy of Ireland led the persecution and was chosen to command Charles I's army against Scotland. The Presbyterian colonists fared no better under the Parliamentarian regime, nor Cromwell's dictatorship.

It was in 1689 that the Jacobite Parliament, sitting in Dublin, had tried to abolish all religious discrimination in Ireland by law, passing Acts XIII and XV. They declared that all religions should be equal under the law and that each priest or minister should be supported by his own congregation only, and that no tithes should be levied upon any person for the support of a church to which he did not belong. After William of Orange became victorious in Ireland, the only religion officially allowed was Anglicanism. Penal laws were enacted against Catholic and dissenting Protestant. Both Irish Catholic and the descendants of the Scots Presbyterian colonists suffered equally.

William of Orange's courts were liable to jail a Presbyterian minister for three months for delivering a sermon and a fine of £100 was made for celebrating the Lord's Supper. Presbyterians were also punished if they were discovered to have been married by a Presbyterian minister. An Act in 1704 excluded all Presbyterians from holding office in the law, army, navy, customs and excise or municipal government. In 1715 a further act made it an offence for Presbyterian ministers to teach children and this was punishable with three months in prison. Intermarriage between Presbyterians and Anglicans was declared illegal. As late as 1772 Presbyterians were punished for holding religious meetings.

Some 250,000 Protestant Ulstermen were forced to migrate to America in search of religious freedom between the years 1717 and 1776 alone. Yet such is the strength of mythology in Northern Ireland today that Presbyterians, of which Ian Paisley claims he is one, can celebrate the victories of William of Orange and Paisley, during his anti-Catholic tirades, can hail William's action at the Battle of the Boyne as ushering in a 'new era of religious freedom'! One must remember that the majority Protestant religion in Northern Ireland is Presbyterianism. How could such an amazing phenomenon be?

The descendants of the Presbyterian Ulstermen who went to America in search of religious freedom from Anglican persecution were to play a prominent part in the American War of Independence and the creed of republicanism was to find a fertile ground among them and their cousins still in Ireland. It was this new creed of republicanism which united Catholic and Presbyterian under the common name of Irishman in their bid to throw off the English imperial yoke. The administration became aware of the danger as Hugh Boulter, Anglican Archbishop of Armagh, wrote at the time: 'The worst of this is that it stands to unite Protestant and Papist and whenever that happens, goodbye to English interest in Ireland forever.'

From that time on the English administration in Ireland singled out all Protestants for special privileges and treatment in Ireland, gradually weeding away the superficial roots of Presbyterian resentment against England and playing on the fears of Catholic domination. By the end of the 19th Century political skill had sown the seeds of the sectarian divide in Northern Ireland and the Battle of the Boyne had become a symbol of the distortion of Irish history. When Ireland demanded independence, Lord Randolph Churchill, the father of Winston S. Churchill, could boast of 'playing the Orange card' and know that the English Establishment could rely on the brainwashed Presbyterians to hold the rest of Ireland in check. Such is the problem of Northern Ireland today where Christian sectarianism is only a symptom and not a cause of the problem. One can therefore see such outrageous figures as Ian Paisley as victims of the political skills of yesteryear rather than free minded protagonists in a modern world.

Throughout all the Celtic countries there have been profound changes in philosophical and religious attitudes. It is valid to ask whether any traditions have been handed down from the age of the Celtic Church.

Since the absorption by Rome, Brittany has remained devoutly Catholic and the Reformation has passed her by; the majority of Ireland also remains Catholic in addition to the significant Presbyterian minority. The 'native' population's adherence to Catholicism has been for political rather than ascetic reasons. The reforming zeal of the English Protestants was seen simply as just one more alien attack on Irish culture, thus making the Irish cling more doggedly to their 'old faith'.

In Wales a similar attitude attained and caused the eventual rejection of both Catholicism and Anglicanism and the acceptance of Nonconformity in a country where the other doctrines had been imposed at the whim of an alien government. Cornwall, left for centuries in a limbo by an uncaring clergy, also turned to the Nonconformity of Wesleyan Methodism. In Scotland the Reformation, as we have stated, came as a savage genocidal policy against native culture. Today, various forms of Protestantism, from extreme to liberal, and Catholicism, exist side by side in an uneasy way. Only on the tiny island of Man is there a comfortable tolerance between Anglicanism and Methodism.

Little remains in modern Celtic Christianity of the old spiritual nature of the Celtic Church. The period of the Celtic Church is one fascinating epoch in the history of an extraordinary civilisation which can claim three thousand years of hitherto unbroken continuity. From at least 1000 BC the Celts have been a bright thread in the tapestry of the evolution of European civilisation. Yet it is one of the great tragedies of history that Europe has repaid these people in shoddy fashion by the near destruction of their languages and culture. The remnants of Celtic civilisation have been all but absorbed into the body of the English and French nations; the ultimate badge of their culture, language, the product of the centuries of cultural development and the repository of all the wisdom, poetry, legend, history and philosophy of the people, has reached a stage where death is imminent. Today, on the edge of north west Europe, the Celts are reaching the ultimate crisis in their long history. By the end of the century it will be possible to judge if they will be erased by the very progress to which they have contributed so much, or whether they will be able to survive and carve a valid future for themselves.

At the moment Celtic civilisation is not dead since at least two-and-a-half million people speak one or other of the Celtic languages as their native tongue. But since no Celtic language has succeeded in dominating an independent territory, a political state, most speakers are perforce bilingual and bilingualism under these conditions will ultimately lead to the loss of the less important language.

Yet language apart, these descendants of the Celtic Church still cling fiercely to their various brands of Christianity. They tend to hold their doctrines with a passionate intolerance. Unlike their ancestors, many of their religious leaders make a virtue and dogma out of their intolerance.

One can see traces of a fierce paganism which would have surprised the druids who were far more liberal and less bigoted than their 20th Century Christian offspring. Yet if one should look for reasons as to why this is so, I would venture the following: by conquest, dispossession and the near destruction of their languages and culture, the Celtic communities have become severed from their traditions.

Giolla Brighde Mac Con Midhe (circa 1240-80AD) wrote:

If poetry were destroyed
so that there were no history or ancient lays
every man would die
without hearing of any ancestors except his father.

The Celtic communities have been separated from their forefathers by a deep cultural gulf, cast adrift among the accidents of translation. They have been told that their languages, culture and the values they enshrine are anachronisms in the modern world. They are therefore becoming, and, indeed have become, gawky provincials in other cultures; not knowing their past, insecure in the present and uncertain of the future. The real heritage of the Celtic Church which their ancestors evolved and stubbornly defended through the early centuries of the Christian epoch has not been passed on.

Selected Bibliography

The studies which cover the early Christian period in the Celtic countries are many and varied and an entire volume could be filled in simply listing them. The following works have been selected to give the reader not only an indication of sources for this volume but to point to future reading on the subject. It will be noted that ancient writers and the Latin Church Fathers are not listed nor are general histories essential to a background knowledge of the period.

Alexander, W. Lindsay. *Iona*, 1850.
Allcroft, A.H. *The Circle and the Cross*. 2 vols. Macmillan, London, 1927.

Barley, Maurice W. and Hanson, Richard P.C. *Christianity in Britain 300-700AD*, Leicester University Press, Leicester, 1968.
Blight, J.T. *Churches of West Cornwall*, J.H. & J. Parker, London, 1865.
  Ancient Crosses and other Antiquaries in West Cornwall, Simpkin Marshall & Co, London, 1858.
Bowen, E.G. *The Settlement of Celtic Saints in Wales*, University of Wales Press, Cardiff, 1956.
Bury, John B. *Conversion of the Kelts*, Cambridge Medieval History, vol II, 1911-32.

Carney, James. *The Problem of St Patrick*, Dublin Institute for Advanced Studies, Dublin, 1961.
  Early Irish Poetry, Mercier Press, Cork, 1965.
Chadwick, Nora K. *The Age of Saints in the Early Celtic Church*, Oxford University Press, London, 1961.
  Studies in the Early British Church, Cambridge University Press, Cambridge, 1958.

De Paor, Maire & Liam. *Early Christian Ireland*, Thames & Hudson, London, 1958.
Dood, B.E. & Heritage, T.C. *The Early Christians in Britain*, London, 1966.

Duke, John A. *The Columban Church*, Oxford University Press, Longman, London, 1932.
History of the Church of Scotland to the Reformation, Oliver & Boyd, Edinburgh, 1936.

Edmonds, Don Columba. *The Early Scottish Church*, Sands & Co, Edinburgh, 1906.
Ellis, Peter Berresford. *The Cornish Language & its Literature*, Routledge & Kegan Paul, London, 1974.
Caesar's Invasion of Britain, Orbis Publishing, London, 1978.
MacBeth: High King of Scotland 1040-50 AD, Muller, London, 1981.
Emerson, N.D. *St Columba and his Mission*, SPCK, Dublin, 1963.
Evans, Arthur Wade. *Welsh Christian Origins*, Alden Press, Oxford, 1934.
Vitae sanctorum Britanniae, University of Wales Press, Cardiff, 1944.

Fell, Barry. *America BC*, Quadrangle: New York Times Book Co, New York, 1976.
Ferguson, J. *Pelagius*, Cambridge University Press, Cambridge, 1956.

Gould, Sabine (Baring-Gould) and Fisher, John. *The Lives of the British Saints*. 4 vols. Cymrodorion Society, London 1907-12.
Gougard, Dom Louis. *Christianity in Celtic Lands*, trs. Maud Joyce, Sheed & Ward, London, 1932.
Graham, Hugh. *The Early Irish Monastic Schools*, Talbot Press, Dublin, 1923.

Hardinge, Leslie. *The Celtic Church in Britain*, London 1975.
Haslehurst, R.S.T. *The Works of Fastidius*, Society of SS Peter & Paul, Westminster, 1927.
Hayden, Mary & Moonan, George. *Short History of the Irish People*, Dublin, 1921.
Herron, James. *The Celtic Church in Ireland*, Service & Paton, London, 1898.
Hughes, Kathleen. *The Church in Early Irish Society*, Dublin, 1966.
Huyshe, Wentworth. *The Life of St Columba*, New Universal Library, London, 1906.

John, Catherine Rachel. *The Saints of Cornwall*, Lodenek/Truan, Padstow/Redruth, Cornwall, 1982.

Kinvig, R.G. *The Isle of Man*, Liverpool University Press, 1975.
Knowles, J.A. *St Brigid, Patroness of Ireland*. Browne & Nolan, Dublin, 1907.

Leatham: Diana. *They Built on Rock (the story of how the men and women of the Celtic Church carried Light to the people who dwelt in the Dark Ages)*, Celtic Arts Society, Glasgow, 1948.
Celtic Sunrise; an outline of Celtic Christianity, Hodder & Stoughton, London, 1951.
The Story of St Brigid of Ireland, Faith Press, London, 1950.
The Story of St David of Wales, Carraway, London, 1952.
Loomis, Roger. *The Grail from Celtic Myth to Christian Symbol*, University of Wales Press, Cardiff, 1963.
Loth, Joseph. *Les Noms des saints bretons*, Paris, 1910.

Mac Cana, Proinsias. *Celtic Mythology*, Hamlyn, London, 1970.
Mac Culloch, J.A. *The Religion of the Ancient Celts*, T. & T. Clarke, Edinburgh, 1911.
Mac Nally, Robert ed. *Old Ireland*, Gill & Son, Dublin, 1965.
Mac Naught, John C. *The Celtic Church and the See of St Peter*, Basil Blackwell, Oxford, 1927.
Mac Neill, Eoin. *Celtic Religion*, Catholic Truth Society, London, 1910.
Saint Patrick, Dublin, 1964.
Mac Queen, John. *St Nynia*, Oliver & Boyd, Edinburgh, 1961.
Mc Neill, F. Marian. *Iona*, Blackie, 1920 (revised ed. 1973).
Montgomery, William E. *Land Tenure in Ireland*, Dublin, 1899.
Moran, Patrick F. *Irish Saints in Great Britain*, M.H. Gill, Dublin, 1879.
Morris, John. gen. ed. *St Patrick: His Writings & Murchu's Life*, Phillimore, London, 1978.
Gildas, Phillimore, London, 1978.
Nennius, Phillimore, London, 1980.
Mould, D.C. *The Celtic Saints*, Clonmore & Reynolds, Dublin, 1956.

Newell, E.J. *A History of the Welsh Church to the Dissolution of the Monasteries*, Elhurst Stock, London, 1895.

O Donoghue, Denis. *Brendaniana (St Brendan the Voyager)*, Browne & Nolan, Dublin, 1893.
O Hanluain, Enri M.S. *The First Church Altars & Early Christian Inscriptions of Ireland*, Dublin, 1935.
O Meara, John J. *Eriugena*, Mercier Press, Cork, 1969.
O Rahilly, Thomas F. *The Two Patricks*, Dublin Institute for Advanced Studies, Dublin, 1942.

Pim, Herbert M. *A Short History of Celtic Philosophy*, Dundalk, 1920.
Power, Patrick. *Early Christian Ireland*, M.H. Gill, Dublin, 1925.

Rees, W.J. ed. *Lives of the Cambro-British Saints*, Welsh Manuscript Society, Llandovy, 1853.

Salmon, John. *The Ancient Irish Church*, Gill & Son, Dublin, 1897.
Severin, Tim. *The Brendan Voyage*, MacGraw Hill, 1978.
Sharkey, John. *Celtic Mysteries*, Thames & Hudson, London, 1975.
Simpson, W.D. *Saint Ninian and the Origin of the Christian Church in Scotland*, Oliver & Boyd, Edinburgh, 1940.
  The Celtic Church in Scotland, Aberdeen University Studies, Vol. III, 1935.
Sjoestedt, M.L. *Gods & Heroes of the Celts*, London, 1949.
Stokes, George T. *Ireland and the Celtic Church*, Hodder & Stoughton, London, 1886.

Thomas, Charles. *Britain and Ireland in Early Christian Times*, AD400-800 (reprint from *The Dark Ages* ed. David Talbot Rice, 1965), BCA, London.
Tommasini, Anselmo M. *Irish Saints in Italy*, Sands & Co, London, 1935.

Vacandard, E.A. *St Victrice*, Paris, 1909.

Warren, F.E. *The Liturgy and Ritual of the Celtic Church*, Clarendon Press, Oxford, 1881.
Williams, Hugh. *Christianity in Early Britain*, Clarendon Press, Oxford, 1912.

Zimmer, H. *The Celtic Church in Britain and Ireland* (trs. A. Meyer), David Nutt, London, 1902.
  Gaelic Pioneers of Christianity: The Work & Influence of Irish Monks and Saints in Continental Europe, (trs. Victor Collins), M.H. Gill, Dublin, 1923.

Articles

Anonymous: 'The Book of Deer', Scotland's Magazine, November, 1965.
Binchey, D.A. 'Patrick and His Biographers', Studia Hibernica, Vol. II (1962).
Chadwick, Nora K. 'The Colonization of Brittany from Celtic Britain', Proceedings of the British Academy, Vol LI, Oxford University Press, 1967.
Haverfield F. 'Early British Christianity', English Historical Review, Vol xi, 1896.
Hughes, Kathleen. 'The Celtic Church: Is this a valid concept?' Cambridge Medieval Celtic Studies, No. 1, Summer, 1981.

Jackson, Kenneth. 'Gildas and the Names of the British Princes' Cambridge Medieval Celtic Studies, No. 3, Summer, 1982.

Megaw, B.R.S. 'Who Was St Conchan?' Journal of the Manx Museum Vol vi, 1962/3.

Wilson, P.A. 'Romano British and Welsh Christianity – Continuity or Discontinuity?' Welsh History Review, No. 3, (1966-7).

Index

Index